Reading Israel, Reading America

Stanford Studies in Jewish History and Culture

Edited by David Biale and Sarah Abrevaya Stein

Reading Israel, Reading America

The Politics of Translation between Jews

Omri Asscher

Stanford University Press

Stanford, California

Stanford University Press
Stanford, California

Printed in the United States of America on acid-free, archival-quality paper

Library of Congress Cataloging-in-Publication Data

Names: Asscher, Omri, author.
Title: Reading Israel, reading America : the politics of translation between Jews / Omri Asscher.
Description: Stanford, California : Stanford University Press, 2019. | Series: Stanford studies in Jewish history and culture | Includes bibliographical references and index.
Identifiers: LCCN 2019012963 (print) | LCCN 2019017672 (ebook) | ISBN 9781503610941 (ebook) | ISBN 9781503610057 (cloth: alk. paper) | ISBN 9781503610934 (pbk.: alk. paper)
Subjects: LCSH: Translating and interpreting—Political aspects. | Israeli literature—Translations into English—History and criticism. | American literature—Translations into Hebrew—History and criticism. | American literature—Jewish authors—History and criticism. | Israeli literature—Appreciation—United States. | American literature—Appreciation—Israel. | Jews—United States—Identity. | Jews—Israel—Identity.
Classification: LCC P306.97.P65 (ebook) | LCC P306.97.P65 A84 2019 (print) | DDC 492.4/80221—dc23
LC record available at https://lccn.loc.gov/2019012963

Cover design: Anne Jordan

Contents

Acknowledgments

It is my great pleasure to thank the people without whom this book would not have come to fruition in its current form. While undertaking this project, I have benefited greatly from the knowledgeability and guidance of many teachers, some of whom stand out in particular. From the first translation workshop I attended and throughout the years of research that led to this book, Nitsa Ben-Ari has infected me with a love for and curiosity about translation and translation studies. Her frankness and kindness were a source of encouragement, her commonsensical approach a measure of balance. In his humaneness and generosity, and his soft-spoken advice, Ofer Shiff was no less a friend than a mentor; our many discussions of the intersection between homeland–diaspora relations and questions of Jewish identity were always inspiring and thought-provoking. Conversations with Hana Wirth-Nesher provided me with intriguing new perspectives on Jewish American literary culture, and heartfelt reassurance. Whether revolving around new directions in translation studies or particular methodological considerations, discussions with Rachel Weissbrod were always engaging and enlightening. From Gur Alroey and Zohar Segev, I not only learned a great deal about American Jewish history and culture but also drew inspiration with regard to their commitment to promoting these topics in Israeli academy, and expanding Israeli comprehension of American Jewish life, as a matter of social significance. Jonathan Sarna has shared with me his immense knowledge and broad understanding of Jewish history, along with genuinely warm words of encouragement. I also had the true privilege of learning from my colleagues and friends Ofir Abu, David

Barak-Gorodetsky, Yael Dekel, Noam Gil, Renana Kristal, Shaul Levin, Aviad Moreno, Hemi Sheinblat, Adi Sherzer, Dvir Tzur, and Tanya Zion-Waldoks; I am thankful to them for their thoughtful remarks and suggestions as well as their friendship, which is dear to me.

During the years of writing this book, I have been fortunate to receive generous fellowships from several institutions: the Ruderman Program for American Jewish Studies and the Herzl Institute for the Study of Zionism at the University of Haifa; the Lisa and Michael Leffell Foundation Stipend for Study of the Impact of Israel on American Jewry; the Kreitman School of Advanced Graduate Studies and the Ben-Gurion Research Institute for the Study of Israel and Zionism at the Ben-Gurion University of the Negev; and the Younes and Soraya Nazarian Center for Israel Studies at the University of California, Los Angeles. My research could not have been completed without this invaluable support.

I feel privileged to publish a book in the Stanford Studies in Jewish History and Culture series, and am grateful to the series editors, Sarah Stein and David Biale, and Stanford Press's acquisition editor Margo Irvin, for having interest and faith in this project.

My very special gratitude goes to my parents, Micha and Yael; they have provided me with a backbone of endless support, for which I am forever grateful. And last but most important, I am indebted to my beloved wife and best friend, Aya—for everything.

Reading Israel, Reading America

Introduction
Translating across the Homeland–Diaspora Divide

In Israeli author David Shahar's *His Majesty's Agent*, the Israeli narrator, a soldier in the Yom Kippur War, is instructed to accompany American Jewish author and intellectual Abie Driesel to a military post in Sinai. Driesel had been invited by the Ministry of Foreign Affairs to observe the events of the war and shine a flattering light on Israel in the United States. Shahar makes little effort to conceal that Driesel, who arrives with an extravagant entourage of adoring aides, is the mirror image of American Jewish icon Elie Wiesel. He also does little to disguise what he thinks of him: from the outset, Driesel is described in a particularly negative light, as a pompous, greedy, and self-indulgent man. Considering Wiesel's iconic status in the American Jewish community and the weighty circumstances of his visit—an existential war in Israel—Shahar's satirical tone would seem to imply a blunt attack on American Jewry as a whole. However, the American objects of this criticism never faced this critique as it was written. As a close textual comparison of the original and translated versions reveals, Wiesel-Driesel in the Hebrew source was reincarnated as an entirely different character en route to a (Jewish) American audience. In addition to changing the character's name from Abie Driesel to Jules Levi in order to mask his true identity, various manipulations in the translated version systematically subdue the attack on Wiesel. Without the knowledge of the translator or author, paragraphs and sometimes entire pages ridiculing Wiesel in the original novel were edited out.[1]

A 1971 review of Saul Bellow's novel *Herzog* by Israeli critic Alexander

Barzel suggested an explicit correlation between the establishment of the state of Israel and the fact that "Jewish men of letters around the world have begun to speak their mind, and not only as authors, but *as Jews*, with a full consciousness of their uniqueness." The review went on to assume that "the Jewish state is perhaps the 'sound box' of the Jewish writer's voice in the world, lending power to his voice."[2] Jewish American literature, according to Barzel, does not prosper on its merits alone; Israel not only inspired Bellow to use a "Jewish" voice but also amplified the literary effect of his work. Jewish creativity in the diaspora, it is implied, cannot be credited with independent achievements. The review, though gushing with admiration for the novel and its creator, ended with the following somber statement: "A sad thought pierces the heart: why don't *Sha'ul* Bellow and his peers come *home, to the nation's homeland*, to forge the conceptual weaponry and armor of the Jewish soul?"[3] The common spelling *Saul* was used throughout the rest of his review, yet here Barzel chose to Hebraize the name of the Jewish American author and underscore precisely where, in his view, the home and homeland of the Jews is—and thereby precisely where it *is not*. Clearly, according to Barzel, the Jewish American novelist ought to have belonged to the national endeavor of Israeli culture, whose setting and language provide the means for authentic Jewish creation. This statement seals the review, suggesting the impression Barzel might have sought to leave on his readers and lending it greater weight. Barzel's review, as a prism through which the Hebrew reader could discover the novel and comprehend its meaning, was vastly different from the critical lens through which American Jewish readers experienced the same novel.

The genre and language of the two texts I've described here, the country in which they were published, their role in the target audience culture—all of these differ. The ways in which the texts mediated the source works to their readers aimed for, and probably achieved, different outcomes. But these texts nonetheless offer particular instances of one broad, complex phenomenon: the politics of translation between Jews. In both cases, a literary text written in one language by a Jewish author was mediated by a Jewish cultural agent to the audience of its translation—a primarily Jewish audience. In both cases, the novel was part of an oeuvre often framed as "Jewish," or having traits that were considered "Jewish." Indeed, Hebrew literature and Jewish American literature are both linked by academic research and public discourse to the large Jewish communities in Israel and the United States, and questions regarding the history and core identity of these communities are central to the respective literary fields.[4] Therefore, the translation and mediation of literary texts for readers across these communities represent a symbolic and practical juncture between these two Jewish groups, staging a conversation of sorts, or negotiation of ideas, between two platforms of Jewish identity.

These cases may be usefully and productively seen as instances of "internal" Jewish translation, then, because the Jewish communities in Israel and America are not only the two major centers of world Jewry since the end of World War II but also the two primary sources of collective and individual Jewish identity. Both of these societies offer possible answers to the question of what it means to be Jewish in the modern era, and each has sometimes been highly critical of the other's answers when they diverge from its own. The answers and misgivings these communities offer, and the versions of Jewish identity they represent, vary to a great extent. These disparate identities represent differences in national, ethnic, and religious affiliation, social and cultural circumstances, and the challenges posed for Jews in the past and present. Their histories, too, are largely unique; the ways in which these communities have come to understand themselves, and their roles in the Jewish world, clearly differ.

One of the most intriguing, evocative arenas in which these contrasts have been expressed is the literary production of each of these cultures. Thus the movement of such literary works across the two cultures, their migration from "home turf" to foreign field, innately challenged and confronted each community with the otherness of its counterpart. The features of translation, and other mediations surrounding *belles-lettres*, could thus attest to the degree of closeness or detachment between the two groups. Moreover, they could reveal what each group has sought to find in the other, what it has chosen to reject and adopt, and how it has pursued these ends, often covertly, through literary discourse. The two aforementioned examples are cases in point, the first in relation to the absorption of Hebrew literature by American (Jewish) culture and the second to the absorption of Jewish American literature in Israel. By testifying to ideological dispositions above and below the surface of Israel–diaspora interplay, they demonstrate the hidden potential of defining such literary translation as internal Jewish exchange. They show that this definition not only is conceptually sound but also serves as a fruitful source of insight.

As scholars have increasingly recognized in recent decades, translation is not simply a "mirror," and its significance as an object of study extends well beyond its reflection of cultural and ideological sensibilities. In fact, translation plays an *active* role in the cross-cultural transfer of ideas, narratives, and symbols. The field of translation studies, a relatively young discipline, has been described as "the framework par excellence for research into the formation, transfer and change of cultural (and not just textual or linguistic) repertoires."[5] Indeed, it is hard to imagine the histories of Eastern and Western thought without the profound effect of translation on the transfer of concepts, aesthetics, and ideologies—and Jewish history is no different in this respect. This is as true for the annals of cultural intersections between Jews and non-Jews as it is for interaction among different Jewish groups.[6] All agents of literary translation, in the words of translation theorist Michaela Wolf, are "socially constructed and constructing subjects"—a description that easily applies to those involved in the movements of Jewish literature as well.[7] For this reason, the omission of any reference to the Palestinian *Nakba* in the English translation of Yoram Kaniuk's *Confessions of a Good Arab*, say, or the selective interpretation in Israeli reviews of Jewish/non-Jewish boundaries in Bernard Malamud's *The Assistant* not only reflect an ideological leaning but also participate in its perpetuation. The mediation of images and ideas, so deeply ingrained in the movement of text across cultures, has carried a significance well beyond the realm of literary style. Influential cultural agents such as translators, editors, and literary critics have participated both overtly and covertly in crafting a portrait of the "Jewishness" across the ocean for their local readers.

Divergent Historical Destinies

Processes of translation provide a unique lens for the examination of social and ideological relations between any two groups. However, I argue that the practice of translation carries a particularly profound meaning in the juncture between a diaspora and its country of origin or symbolic homeland. This holds especially true in the context of the intra-Jewish translation at the heart of this book. The divergent histories of Israeli and American Jews, and the nature of the relationship between these two centers of Jewry, transform translation into a doubly powerful research paradigm.

The reason for the particularly revealing quality of translation in the case of the relationship between these two centers of Jewry is rooted in a combination of historical factors. Broadly speaking, the most influential twentieth-century forms of Jewish collectivity in Israel and the United States sprang from a common Jewish geographical space in Eastern Europe, where a shared Jewish language was spoken. Upon migration to Jewish centers in Palestine and the United States, the common "territory" and "language" were replaced with new, distinct territories and languages, which were destined to fill a vital role in the cultivation of a new ethos and divergent cultural identities in each center. The reliance of each society on its own territory and language, along with the historical significance that these concepts would come to embody, created ideological discrepancies between the two centers. Nonetheless, these two societies never ceased to feel a sense of belonging to *Klal Yisrael*, the broader Jewish collective, and largely saw themselves as partners in a common Jewish identity. The two communities felt an affinity to one another and sought to sustain a mutual relationship (to varying degrees, depending on historical circumstances).

Translation is, inherently, a practice that crosses spatial and linguistic boundaries. Precisely by replacing the original territory and language of the text with another, translation enables, mirrors, and impacts the aforementioned cross-cultural link. In both Jewish societies, literature played an undeniable role in the cultivation of collective identity, both reflecting this identity and offering a useful key to its understanding. By crossing geolinguistic boundaries, literary translation mediated these representations of identity to audiences across the ocean, serving as a textual bridge between the two centers of world Jewry. Thus literary translation and its accompanying discourse make ideal vessels for examining the relationship between the two centers.

In the case of Israel and American Jewry, then, literary translation does more than enrich our knowledge of an intricate intercultural encounter in the twentieth century. It goes beyond offering a fresh perspective that can reveal the underlying ideologies that remain unmentioned in political or religious discourse, speeches, sermons, or legislation. In our particular context, translation *inherently* underscores the tension stemming from the simultaneous, comparative, mutual existence of the two major segments of world Jewry, Israel and the United States; it touches, by definition, on a tension intrinsic to the very being of these two centers and their ideological disparities.

Key differences between the histories of these groups help to establish a wider context for this tension. The end of the nineteenth and beginning of the twentieth century saw a far-reaching "quiet revolution" in the Jewish world: millions of Jews left their homes in vast regions of Eastern Europe, mainly the Russian Empire, with no intention of returning.[8] They uprooted their families and traveled to foreign shores, where they hoped to establish new lives. This historical shift irreversibly changed the Jewish world in modern times, repositioning it in new centers of influence. Fewer Jews may have chosen to immigrate to Palestine than traveled to America, but the scale gradually balanced out over the course of the twentieth century. Largely due to the horrific outcome of World War II, Israel and the United States became the two largest and most significant centers of the Jewish world. There was no competing with the dominance of these two collectives in Jewish life—not in terms of population size, cultural and intellectual creation, or political significance. Unlike the stories of European Jewish communities, which were all but ended by World War II and the Holocaust, or the story of Jewish life in Muslim countries, which had largely dwindled during the immigration waves of the 1950s and 1960s—and notwithstanding the vitality and importance of smaller Jewish communities in other parts of the world—the ongoing histories of these two centers reflect the broad Jewish story still being told and the major Jewish history still being written.

The relationship between these two Jewish centers has always attracted intellectual contemplation. What has been the historical significance of each center, or what should it be, in light of its counterpart? Does each constitute a conceptual or practical challenge to the validity of the other? Scores of historians, intellectuals, and rabbis in Israel and the United States have addressed these and similar questions, each in his or her own way. Different thinkers have worked to articulate the substance of a primarily ethnoreligious Jewish life in the American diaspora in light of the challenging presence of a sovereign Jewish state and to describe Israeli life against the background of the pluralistic, flourishing model of acculturated Jewish existence in America. To be sure, approaches to defining the underpinnings of identity in these two communities have varied widely. Still, many of the thinkers who have dwelled on the subject share two common premises: territory and language. Whether they endorsed or rejected the negation of exile (or diasporism), assumed a hierarchy between the two centers, or sought to equalize them, most engaged theoretically and concretely with these two concepts.[9] Even if divided on their relative significance or meaning, historians and thinkers were still inclined to consider the respective territories and languages of these groups as incisive foundations pertinent to collective identity.

Prior to their dispersion, many of the Eastern European immigrants who were destined to shape the Jewish centers in Palestine (and later Israel) and the United States had in fact shared a common territory and language.[10] Before emigrating, the vast majority of them resided in the Pale of Settlement in the Russian Empire, a widespread region characterized by a largely distinct, concentrated, richly Jewish environment. One of the defining features of this Jewish population, which also carried great emotional weight, was the Jewish language it shared—Yiddish. Naturally, this was greatly impacted by immigration. In fact, as revealed but one or two generations later, the change immigration yielded was irreversible: once the immigrants settled in their new countries, their children and grandchildren adopted other languages, Hebrew and English, with which they lived their lives and expressed their identities. "Besides sharing a common European origin," literary scholar Ranen Omer-Sherman suggests, "in the early days the new Jews of America and Palestine alike were linked by a giddy sense of fraught potential—a common desire to forget their origins, to break away from the inherent disabilities of the old world."[11] Territory and language, once a common denominator, became the seeds of a deep disparity between the two groups.

Over the years, these territories and languages became vital resources for the formation of identity in each community. Most significantly, the *Yishuv* (and later the State of Israel) drew upon the land of Israel and the Hebrew language as springboards for national identity. Two cornerstones of Zionism, land and language were arguably the most crucial components of the proposed Zionist solution to the crisis of European Jewry in its troubled transition to modernity, facing internal cultural degeneration and external antisemitic attack.[12] The value attached to these concepts was hardly the same among all Zionist thinkers: the founder of modern political Zionism, Theodor Herzl, and the father of cultural Zionism, Ahad Ha'am, for instance, were divided on the relative significance of these two concepts. However, as Jewish settlement in Eretz-Israel grew, the understanding of collective identity as founded "upon two future poles of a national land and a national language"[13] took root as the prevailing zeitgeist. It is impossible to overstate the significance of the land of Israel and the Hebrew language—as reflected in cultural production, political discourse, and both the public and institutional spheres—in shaping the collective ethos of Jewish nationalism. After the foundation of the state, the educational and cultural establishments continued to cultivate the importance of these two components, which in turn became the self-evident pillars of Israeli consciousness. "I tell you, they are still everything. Everything. A land and a language!" Israeli American author Hillel Halkin stated ardently in 1977. "They are the ground beneath a people's feet and the air it breathes in and out."[14] Hebrew literature published in Israel was both a concrete and a symbolic manifestation of this sentiment, even if at its best it dealt chiefly with the difficulties of realizing the Zionist ethos.[15]

Beginning in the late nineteenth century, as large immigration waves arrived from the Pale of Settlement, Jewish American collective identity was transformed by new linguistic and territorial dispositions as well. The crowded ghetto of the Lower East Side played a decisive role as "Jewish territory" in the context of an evolving American Jewish identity[16] and was followed by the concentrated urban areas and later their suburban counterparts, which played a similar role. Literature became a prominent site of expression for these spatial transitions. Surely, the portrayal of Jewish life in these American spaces was often problematized and critical—yet this does not detract from the centrality of the American environment to Jewish identity but rather accentuates it. Sarah Phillips Casteel suggested recently that, as with Hebrew literature in the Israeli Zionist context, "in Jewish writing across the Americas, we can identify a related project of 'bringing a Jew into a landscape'—of constructing a territorialized Jewish identity and sense of belonging to the land."[17] As for language, Jewish immigrants—or at least their second generation—by and large embraced the English tongue with enthusiasm. Abraham Cahan, the legendary editor of the *Forward* who had a profound effect on the integration of immigrant Jews into American society in the early twentieth century, devoted many of his Yiddish editorials to the pragmatic-ideological demand that Jewish immigrants learn English, later turning himself to English literary writing.[18] Mary Antin famously celebrated her new language in sweeping terms, declaring that "in any other language happiness is not so sweet, logic is not so clear."[19] During the 1950s and 1960s, prominent Jewish American writers were met with criticism (its antisemitic undertones scarcely veiled) for blighting the purity of the English language with Yiddishisms. In 1970, writer and essayist Cynthia Ozick went so far as to call English "the new Yiddish" and suggested it be cultivated as the literary, cultural, and even liturgical language of its Jewish American speakers.[20] Recent sociolinguistic research has claimed that American Jews speak a *Jewish* variation of English, which carries phonological, lexical, and metalinguistic characteristics distinct from American English.[21] Thus,

American Jews not only established English as a central component of their identity but also infused it with Jewish features over time, adopting it by "Judaizing" it.[22]

The function fulfilled by the American landscape and English language in American Jewish identity can also be observed from another angle: as a Jewish American response to the territorial and linguistic challenge of Israeli nationalism. National identity in Israel was founded not merely on a different territory and language but on the *historical* land and language of the Jewish people, which carry unique symbolic capital—prompting some Zionist thinkers to go so far as to claim that this land and language are the exclusive foundations of Jewish identity. Assertions such as Amos Oz's claim that American Jews seeking to lead a full and fulfilling Jewish life have essentially two options before them—make aliyah or, at least, study Hebrew[23]—were not foreign to the ears of the American Jewish public. In response to this approach, several Jewish American intellectuals went to great lengths to explain why being an American Zionist had little to do with immigrating to Israel and why life on American soil did not make one a less "authentic" Jew.[24] Others highlighted the spatial dimension of Jewish American identity in literary work. "Zionism has roused the territorial and national awareness of Jews worldwide," literary scholar David Roskies suggests, "[and] resuscitated a new demand for a space or a place."[25] The same held true for grappling with the question of language and the challenge embodied by Hebrew. Saul Bellow's little-concealed rage about the nationalist-Zionist assumption that Jewish literature can be written solely in Hebrew attests to the intensity of emotion that was often involved.[26] It is therefore not only how they adopted English and made it their own but also their rejoinder to Zionist demands to adopt Hebrew that demonstrates the significance of American English to the authors and their identity. It is not merely writing about the American landscape as an act of ownership—the oft-quoted opening of Saul Bellow's *The Adventures of Augie March*: "I am an American, Chicago-born" comes to mind—that demonstrates the centrality of territory to Jewish American thought but also the defensive response to the Zionist demand for aliyah.

Surely it is no coincidence that both communities perceived territory and language to be integral to their identities. Many communities throughout history, including nonsovereign ones, have seen geographical space and a common language as a realization, even a precondition, of collective identity. However, the uniqueness of our case lies in the fact that these are not random or disparate national groups that barely interact or are fundamentally hostile. The opposite is true: for many centuries, the very distinction of the Jewish people was that despite geographic and linguistic dispersion, scattered Jewish communities continued to see themselves as one social entity. Broadly speaking, they perceived themselves not only as members of a common religion but also as organs of *Klal Yisrael*, constituents of a single nation, and, in the words of historian Yosef Gorny, exhibited a "largely persistent subjective desire to uphold Jewish collectivity, despite disagreements upon the latter's content and values."[27] This sentiment has been expressed in acts of solidarity and mutual aid between Jewish communities; but no less important, it was realized in continuous correspondence surrounding issues that were seen as relevant to the Jewish people as a whole.

This correspondence not only utilized written texts—naturally the primary mode of communication between distant communities in previous centuries—but also *revolved* around texts and their interpretation. It was both written and deeply and intensely concerned with the written word. In lieu of other cohesive elements such as a common territory, the text itself became the tribal campfire and a crucial generator of collective identity. "Since inception, our diaspora has undermined its dispersion," Amos Oz and Fania Oz-Salzberger suggest succinctly. "It was centralized by the written word."[28] In previous centuries, most Jewish texts discussed halakhic questions or matters of religious interpretation. In the modern era, the centrality of text to Jewish life has not diminished; *belles-lettres*, in its many forms, became a prominent heir of the religious texts of earlier periods. In light of this long-standing Jewish tradition, twentieth-century thinkers as divergent in ideological orientation as Leo W. Schwarz, Harold Bloom, and George Steiner even defined Jewish literature as an "alternative homeland" for the Jews.[29]

One does not have to accept such contentions at face value to acknowledge that literature has had a unique significance in both the Israeli and Jewish American centers in the twentieth century. These communities, the two most prolific generators of Jewish texts in this era, have historically bestowed preeminent status upon the literary text. The basic experience in the two Jewish centers may have differed greatly, and their cultural and intellectual production has been largely distinct and, of course, expressed in different languages. But if there was any resemblance to the collective expression of these two Jewish cultures, it was in their use of the literary text as a vital sphere of deliberation on the question of identity.

Almost since its inception, modern Hebrew literature has been assigned a leading role in the cultural and national revival of the Jewish people, first in the Jewish hubs of Eastern Europe in the second half of the nineteenth century and later in Eretz-Israel. Ever since the revival generation, Hebrew literature has fulfilled, in the words of Hayim Nahman Bialik, "The authoritative role of governing the spiritual world of the Hebrew audience," has served as a "guide to the nation,"[30] and has accounted for some of the most enduring—and largely influential—representations of developing national life. The work of writers and poets was seen as one of the most profound reflections of change in the life of the nation during both the *Yishuv* period and the statehood years that followed. Baruch Kurzweil's memorable statement upon the publication of *My Michael* by Amos Oz in 1967—that the character of Hannah Gonen was more dangerous to Israel than all of the Arab armies put together—attests to the emotions that often erupted out of the tension between the defiant "autonomy" of literary writing and the collective significance attributed to it in Israeli discourse. The uproar in response to the Ministry of Education's 2015 decision to remove Dorit Rabinyan's *All the Rivers*, which describes a relationship between a Jewish woman and a Palestinian in New York, from the high school curriculum indicates that the social-national significance assigned to literary texts in Israeli discourse, even if diminished, still remains.

Literary texts have constituted vital collective testimony in the American Jewish context as well. Exhibiting immense growth in the decades between the late nineteenth and mid-twentieth centuries, Jewish American publishing was just as ideological a goal as it was a literary or commercial one: to forge a new center of Jewish culture and unite American Jewry "into a nationwide community bound together by a common culture of print."[31] The decades following World War II, arguably the golden age of Jewish American writing in the United States, were not only years of unprecedented individual literary achievement, with Jewish authors integrating into the American mainstream and earning institutional recognition and praise; they were also a time when Jewish writers were considered to jointly form a significant *corpus* of work in contemporary American letters.[32] Despite objections voiced by some of these writers, public and intellectual debates have identified them as Jewish authors and analyzed the characteristics of their works, separately or conjointly, as Jewish, both in real time and in later decades. Following in the footsteps of Arnold Eisen, Ranen Omer-Sherman has described the *communal* role that was, to a certain extent, imposed on Jewish authors in the United States—to articulate the collective essence of Jewish American culture in the absence of a shared daily experience or the public means to do so.[33] Recently, Jewish American literature has been described as a "primary centering force in the lives of American Jews" and has even been reconsidered in collective theological terms as an "American Talmud."[34]

Surely the collective dimensions of Hebrew literature have differed from those of Jewish American literature. I will expand later upon how the distinction between these two forms of collectivity found expression in translation and how these shaped reception discourse in both Jewish cultures. What is most significant for our purposes, however, is that both of these literatures, Hebrew and Jewish American, were often ascribed a representative, communal function. The vehement objection sometimes expressed toward this assumption, particularly among the authors themselves, actually corroborates the extent to which this notion was ingrained in both Jewish cultures.

"Writing itself, for Jews," argues American Victoria Aarons, "has been that center of gravity that has given weight and meaning to their lives . . . storytelling itself the still point in the turning world."[35] "The imperative component or condition that defines us as a nation," Israelis Oz and Oz-Salzberger suggest in their interpretation of Saadia Gaon, "is for him just as it is for us, rooted in books."[36] Yet, although the two most significant and influential Jewish groups in the twentieth century used the literary medium to express and deepen their own identity, and despite "the consistent desire, at least among most of the Jewish nation, to share [one collective identity],"[37] these communities were hardly inclined or even able to read each other's literature in its original tongue. The long-established stature of the text as a collective document of Jewish culture may have been preserved in the twentieth century, thus reinforcing the contention of Oz and Oz-Salzberger that "our [Jewish] nationality is fundamentally textual."[38] But unlike other periods in Jewish history, this era saw no truly shared linguistic platform between the communities in Israel and the United States. The two communities and their literatures were separated not only by thousands of miles but also by a linguistic gulf.[39]

Translation as a Bridge?

By crossing boundaries of language and space, the practice of translation provides an obvious means for bridging, both symbolically and practically, the linguistic and geographic gaps between the Jewish communities in Israel and the United States. It is a medium inherently suited to efforts to connect these societies, the members of which see themselves as one people and seek to maintain mutual ties despite being anchored in different territories and languages. In a century that saw these two societies consistently use literature to redefine their identities, after having shed so many features of traditional Judaism, literary translation can attest, perhaps most effectively, to the connection and discourse cultivated between them.

In the modern era, the concept of translation as a bridge between nationalities and cultures has been familiar at least since Goethe coined the term *world literature* at the dawn of the nineteenth century, hoping that literary translation would help defuse national conflicts and assuage their cruelty.[40] A similar but slightly more sober approach can be found in numerous texts, from the introduction to the translated Hebrew and Arabic collection of poems *A Bridge between Shores* by Israeli intellectual Yeshayahu Leibowitz to deliberations on English-French translation as a way to mend fences in the troubled province of Quebec.[41]

Translation has played a similar role between Jewish communities as well, reaching back millennia. It is true that in certain periods and places, Hebrew could be used as a common mode of communication between dispersed Jewish communities around the world. In other times and places, however, Jewish communities had to rely on translation. A partial but impressively ancient list attests to the extent of this need. In the third century BCE, the Torah was translated into Greek for the Hellenistic Jews of Alexandria, who by then did not understand Hebrew as did their counterpart community in Eretz-Israel; the Septuagint, as the translation was called, would serve the Jewish diaspora for over five hundred years. In the second century BCE, Targum Onkelos rendered the Torah into Aramaic, mainly for Aramaic-speaking Jews residing in Babylon. In the Middle Ages, writings such as *The Kuzari* by Yehuda Halevi and *The Guide for the Perplexed* by Maimonides were translated from Arabic to Hebrew, connecting the Arabic-speaking communities of North Africa and Islamic Spain to communities living in the Christian regions of southern France and northern Italy.[42] In the twilight of the Ottoman Empire, works of the Jewish enlightenment were translated from Hebrew and German into Ladino and from Ladino into Hebrew in Edirne, Istanbul, and Jerusalem as part of the interchange between the Ottoman and German *Haskalah* movements.[43] At the end of the nineteenth and beginning of the twentieth century, the writings of Abraham Mapu and other *Haskalah* writers were translated from Hebrew or German into Ladino, Judeo-Persian, and Judeo-Tunisian Arabic for the Jewish community of Tunisia.[44] These bodies of translation demonstrate that throughout Jewish history, communities separated by great distances and varying languages would not forgo a meaningful connection and relied considerably on translation to that end.

We may think of the corpus examined in this book as yet another layer in this impressive tradition of intra-Jewish translation. In fact, literary translations between Israel and American Jewry have been explicitly described in this manner more than once. "By means of translation," Israeli literary scholar Gershon Shaked reflected on the translation of Hebrew literature in the United States, "a spiritual bridge is built between Israel and the diaspora."[45] Similar declarations have been made not only about what literary translation had been or is but also about its desired future. "Both communities [in Israel and the United States]," claimed political scientist Charles Liebman and Steven Bayme of the American Jewish Committee, "would benefit from broader acquaintance with each other's literature."[46] Dubbing Hebrew and English "the two great languages of Jews in our time," Oz and Oz-Salzberger assert that the number of existing translations of Jewish texts in these languages does not suffice and have urged publishers and translators to "construct more [such] bridges between these two worlds."[47]

However, literary translation in the twentieth century was more than just a bridge between Jewish communities in Israel and the United States; it was also an intriguing and highly revealing site of encounter between them. And the reason why this cultural encounter is so intriguing, and so intrinsically related to the role each community fulfilled for the other, stems from some of its less "connective" features. As demonstrated in the examples at the beginning of this book, it is best not to take the notion of translation as a bridge, with its underlying positive connotations, for granted. This is not to negate the bridging properties of translation—after all, texts have traveled from one culture to the next, reached new readers, and introduced them to entirely different ways of life. Through translation, Israeli and Jewish American readers have been exposed to a Jewish world other than their own, with nuance they would not often encounter elsewhere. Nonetheless, it remains crucial to contemplate the *nature* of this bridge and the contingencies of communication it enables. How were the properties of this bridge determined, and by whom? What were its ideological attributes, and what can be learned from them about the deep undercurrents in the intersection between Israeli and American Jewish culture?

The study of translation has long ceased to treat translation as a strictly linguistic practice. Translation scholars no longer see translation as a transparent or neutral endeavor. Analysis of the formal and stylistic features of translation has vacated center stage in recent decades, making way for increasing focus on its sociocultural aspects. Since the so-called cultural turn in translation studies during the 1990s, and the sociological turn at the beginning of the 2000s, a growing number of translation scholars have removed the spotlight from the text itself, concentrating instead on the people and institutions that mediate, manage, and regulate the social meanings of that text. It has been widely acknowledged that, in the words of translation scholar Lawrence Venuti, "every step in the translation process—from the selection of foreign texts to the development and implementation of translation strategies to the editing and reviewing of translations—is mediated by the diverse cultural values that circulate in the target language, always in some hierarchical order."[48]

Parallel to the sociocultural turn, the role of translation in ideological and power relations between groups and nations has come to the fore. "It can be said that any translation is ideological," Christina Schäffner remarked in 2003, a conception accepted by many today, "since the choice of a source text and the use to which the subsequent target text is put is determined by the interests, aims, and objectives of social agents."[49] Not only is literary translation ideologically implicated, then, but it is an ideological practice per se. Literary debates on translated works similarly serve as a measuring stick for contemporary ideological approaches in the target culture, even as they participate in shaping them. Reviewers, as predominant shapers of these debates, "reinterpret translated texts as a function of the stakes prevailing in the field of reception" and can be perceived as agents "who collaborate in the activity of translation while struggling to preserve or subvert the hierarchy of values within this space."[50] Translation, book reviews, and other mediation processes in the movement of literature across cultures reflect power relations and hierarchies between languages and nationalities and play an active role in their affirmation and reinforcement.[51]

Yet, thus far, studies of literary translation from Hebrew to English and vice versa have hardly addressed the politics of the relationship between the two major Jewish centers. Previous research on translation between the two literary spheres has focused primarily on stylistic, thematic, linguistic, or pedagogical issues.[52] Notable exceptions that address the mediation of translated literature to its readership include the first chapter of Alan Mintz's *Translating Israel*, which touches on the critical reception of translated Hebrew literature in the United States in the 1970s and 1980s,[53] and the unpublished dissertation of Yuval Amit, which maps the institutional factors involved in the publication and distribution of Hebrew literature in English translation.[54] Research devoted to the penetration of Jewish American literature into Israeli culture is even rarer. Some works have focused on the ideological aspects of English-to-Hebrew translation, but these are mainly concerned with Jewish–Christian relations, political correctness, or the censorship of erotica.[55] The sole scholar to have addressed the reception of Jewish American literature in Israel is Olga Zambrowsky, in her two articles on publishers' decisions and secondary-school teaching of Jewish American literature in Israel.[56]

This book is thus the first full-length work to study literary translation in light of the politics of the Israeli–American Jewish relationship during the second half of the twentieth century. It does so by examining both sides of the coin—that is, both directions of the movement of translations. "The social function . . . of a translation can best be located within the contact zone where the translated text and the various socially driven agencies meet," Michaela Wolf suggests, highlighting the ideological aspects of the transfer of text within situated cultural and historical contexts.[57] The forms of mediation of foreign literature this book explores—the contact zones, in Wolf's terminology—are part of the literary, journalistic, and academic fields: the primary arenas where literary discourse occurs. This book takes up such varied channels of mediation as the selection of works for translation, editorial commentary in national anthologies in translation, manipulations in the translation of texts, critical reception and interpretation of translated works in book reviews, and aspects of framing translated literature in university courses. Ultimately, the aim of such an integrated approach is to have a better grasp of the accumulated, sprawling, mediated body of knowledge pertaining to the translated literature in the receiving culture—and its ways of communicating to readers a preferred demarcation of collective identity.[58]

While this book attends to these textual contact zones to study a certain chapter in modern Jewish cultural history, it also considers translation itself as a human and social practice.[59] In particular, this book can enrich our understanding of the unique circumstances of translation between a diaspora and its country of origin or symbolic homeland. In fact, an approach that seeks to compare the transfer of translated literature between national cultures *in both directions* has yet to be taken in translation studies. Translation scholars have almost exclusively focused on unidirectional transfer from a given culture of origin to a given target culture.[60] However, the Jewish communities in question, linguistically and geographically distinct yet belonging to a broad collectivity and seeking mutual connection, and the ongoing history of the relationship between the two, legitimize a *bidirectional* framework for discussing translation. Indeed, although different agents take part in the translation process in each direction, the ideological issues pertinent to the meaning of these processes are similar if not identical, and these issues preoccupy the two Jewish communities on either side of the ocean with a similarly high intensity.

Needless to say, the literary works in translation reached non-Jewish readers as well, in both cultures. In particular, the existence of a non-Jewish American audience for translated Hebrew literature should not be overlooked. Nonetheless, there is a near consensus among scholars as to the primary readership of Hebrew-to-English translations. "Translations from Hebrew," Anita Norich recently noted, "have become something of a staple of the Jewish American bookshelf."[61] "It is only natural," Alan Mintz suggests, "that a large part of the audience for contemporary Israeli literature is, and will likely remain, American Jews."[62] Although we lack quantitative data to support this claim, and although not all English translations appeal exclusively to the Jewish reader, it is hard to doubt the validity of this assumption. The fact that the absorbing language is perceived as a non-Jewish one certainly does not contradict conceiving this literary transfer as a primarily intra-Jewish phenomenon.[63] It is surely not the first time that translation from a Jewish to a non-Jewish language has, in effect, been translation among Jews. The aforementioned Septuagint, the Greek translation of the Hebrew Bible that would later become one of the formative translations of Western culture, as it was eventually adopted by a Christian target audience, was originally one such translation. The decisive argument for a Jewish framing here is not linguistic (in the narrow sense of the word) but rather sociological and cultural: most agents who have mediated modern Hebrew literature to American readers have been Jewish and have often assumed, as implied in introductions to anthologies and in book reviews, that their readers are Jewish as well. Moreover, the prism through which the critics have integrated the works into American discourse has sometimes been that of Jewish identity, inasmuch as they have formulated the major themes of the works in question as "Jewish."

Even when translation agents have assumed a non-Jewish readership, their focus has remained on how the Jewish minority was positioned within the broader American society. That is, even when mediation strategies target non-Jewish readers, they primarily reflect concern with what these readers will be thinking of their Jewish peers. In the English translation of Benjamin Tammuz's novel *Requiem for Na'aman* (1982), the narrator's unqualified accusation against the contemporary Christian world of radical antisemitism was left out in full. Omitting Tammuz's damning representation of the Christian world might indeed attest to cautiousness around offending non-Jewish readers. But even though this interference in translation presumes the existence of a non-Jewish audience, it was primarily done with the social positioning of American Jews—with the place occupied by Jews in American society as a whole—in mind (as will be further discussed in chapter 3). A similar perspective can be readily applied to the interference in translations of Israeli works that offer self-critical representations of Israeli conduct in the context of the Israeli–Palestinian conflict. The choice to provide the American reader with a more palatable depiction of the ambiguous moral reality portrayed in Israeli literature is also a choice to defend the ways American Jews are perceived in the society in which they live, as the moral profile of Israel, the Jewish state, reflects on their own (as will be elaborated in chapter 2).

The movement of text across the two cultures and the collective portrait that ultimately arises from the mediated works are therefore usefully understood in the context of the intersection between the two Jewish groups, and the social significance of this portrait should not be underestimated. Since the 1990s, the social and political impact of literature has gradually diminished worldwide; due to the rise of visual and digital media, the commercialization of literature, and processes of globalization and regionalization, authors and their works have been increasingly marginalized in the cultural field.[64] From the 1950s through the 1980s, however, literary works had, or at least could have, a much more far-reaching social impact; the symbolic capital of authors was considerable, and literary discourse still reverberated through public discourse.[65] Today it is hard to imagine a public frenzy as intense as that which Israeli Amos Oz and American Philip Roth met in the late 1960s, upon publication of the novels *My Michael* and *Portnoy's Complaint* in Israel and the United States respectively. Foreign literature in translation, often perceived as a means of gaining invaluable insight into a divergent social and psychological existence, could also have a meaningful effect. Literary debates in both Israel and America often framed translated works as precious keys to understanding a Jewish experience different from one's own.[66] Indeed, Israeli critics hardly hesitated to draw conclusions about the general state of American Jewry, as did Jewish critics in the United States about Israel, in their reviews of translated works of fiction. As Jewish American scholar Alan Mintz once wrote—and similar statements have been made in the other direction—Hebrew literature is "one of the only ways possible . . . to get at the existential core of Israeli experience."[67]

It is important to note that the mediation of these experiences is mainly, if not exclusively, pursued in this book through the mainstream, rather than academic, manifestations of literary discourse: through reviews in popular dailies and weeklies, say, rather than articles in scholarly journals. These were the domains in which the ideological has been more pronounced, and its expressions the most revealing. It is also worth noting that the selection of titles for translation generally tilted toward the center of the source literary system, as the relative marginality of women writers and writers of non-Ashkenazi origin in the developing canon of each literature during these decades was only further accentuated in the translated repertoire. Whereas women translators and critics did take part in the literary encounter across the two cultures, most translated works were written by Ashkenazi men, who represented the hegemonic voice in both cultures at the time and were at the center of both literary systems. The works whose translation and reception are discussed here are thus not, and do not claim to be, representative of the source literature and culture. Translations, as formulated by theoretician Gideon Toury, are in any case first and foremost "facts of the target cultures"—it is there that they come into being and receive their meaning, according to target-culture values and norms.[68] It is there that they and other forms of mediation charted, through reference to images of the other Jewish community, the desirable contours of what it means to be Jewish in their own.

This book is not a work of literary criticism. Its interest lies less in the literary text itself and more in the function of its reception and mediation in the target culture. It does not attempt a new interpretation of a select number of works and surely does not participate in theoretical discussions on the definition of Jewish literature. Rather, it outlines a wide canvas of phenomena of appropriation and ideological mediation through translation.

It is true that Jewish American and Hebrew literatures each had their own internal history, both of which were independent, to some extent, of the vicissitudes of social and political life; and these will be taken into consideration as well. Yet the patterns of mediation of each literature to the target-language audience are above all indicative of broader historical-ideological trends in each Jewish culture and in the relations between the two.[69]

It is against this backdrop that the ideological orientation of translation, rather than its linguistic and stylistic features, emerges as the most potentially revealing. The processes of literary translation between the Jewish communities in Israel and the United States can be likened to an exchange between family members—at certain times subtle and suggestive, at others blunt and explicit. It is a form of dialogue or negotiation between "siblings in the collective family history of the Jews"[70] that pertains—implicitly or directly or somewhere in between—to some of the most acute questions regarding Jewish collective identity, nationhood, and politics. Although this book deals with the transfer of literary texts, a broader matter is always at hand, and presumably more is at stake. How do American Jews know what they (think they) know about Israel? How do Israelis know what they (think they) know about American Jews? How are perceptions formed and attitudes cultivated toward an alternative way of Jewish life through cultural discourse, and to what ends?

Between Israel and America, Homeland and Diaspora

For both centers of Jewry and their respective literatures, the near-total destruction of European Jewry during World War II and then the establishment of the State of Israel constituted a dramatic shift from earlier decades. The period under discussion in this book encompasses the four decades following this watershed: the 1950s, 1960s, 1970s, and 1980s. This period was distinct not only from that which preceded it but also from that which followed, in terms of the political and cultural trends in each community as well as the relationship between the two.

Let us start with the American Jewish "side," and viewpoint, of the relations. As described by historians and political scientists, the Holocaust and the establishment of Israel had an acute effect in the transformation of the American Jewish relationship to the Zionist idea. In the first decades of the twentieth century, the prevailing sentiment among American Jews was not inclined toward Zionism, and the interest among them in life in the growing Palestinian *Yishuv* was, to a large extent, limited. Until the mid- to late 1930s, the prevalent climate of thought in major parts of the Jewish American establishment was not far off the official stance expressed by the Union of American Hebrew Congregations after the First Zionist Congress in Basel, which strongly objected to political Zionism, polemically asserting that "America is our Zion." There were some exceptions. Institutions such as the Jewish National Fund, the United Israel Appeal, and certain socialist Zionist groups were active in the United States during these years, collecting donations for the *Yishuv* and rallying for its support, and the major Yiddish daily of the time, the *Forward*, cultivated a pro-Zionist position during the 1920s.[71] A few prominent public figures, including Supreme Court justice Louis Brandeis, also worked to expand support for the Zionist cause in American circles. Nonetheless, the majority of American Jews was not engaged with Jewish settlement in Palestine, and many among the intellectual elite and the political and religious establishment, most notably in Reform Judaism, the largest of American Jewish denominations, were even hostile toward it.[72]

Israel in the poststatehood era played a far more central role in the Jewish American ethos. During World War II and subsequent years, as the horrors of the Holocaust were being unveiled, the vast majority of American Jews began to perceive Israel as a symbol of Jewish peoplehood and as crucial for the continuity of the Jewish people, and they showed growing support for the Zionist idea—support that found robust economic and political expression.[73] Against the backdrop of the new social challenges prompted by mass movement to the suburbs and the tide of religious feeling in postwar American society, these years saw American Jews largely return to religion and communal life, which in turn contributed to a growing affinity with Israel and an interest in Israeli life and culture.[74] In the 1950s and 1960s, for instance, American Jews consumed Israeli folk dance, art, and music at a growing rate and assigned them an important role in the cultivation of contemporary American Jewish culture.[75]

The Zionist phase of American Jewish life peaked following the Six Day War. In the months preceding the war and in the years that followed it, most American Jews fervently identified with Israel and showered it with unwavering support. Israel not only was highly important to American Jews during these years but also became a central component of their Jewish identity—in the words of intellectual Conservative rabbi Arthur

Hertzberg, their new religion.[76] The ethnic revival of the 1960s and 1970s, which encouraged American ethnic groups to return to their roots and create separate, communal identities as a form of self-expression, along with growing militant trends within the civil rights movement and the central place the Holocaust began to claim in Jewish consciousness, also played a role in pushing American Jews away from a liberal, universalist identity toward a more separatist, ethnic one.[77] These factors helped cement the bond with Israel as one of the mainstays of American Jewish identity, if not its paramount source.

Some scholars contend that the mid- to late 1980s marked a new chapter in the relationship, in which the strongly felt obligation and identification of American Jews toward Israel began to crack.[78] Others perceive American Jewish criticism of Israel in recent decades as a sign of progress and deepening of the relationship between the two communities.[79] Political scientist Michael Barnett recently described the late 1980s as the point at which the "particularism" or "tribalism" characterizing American Jewish approaches to Israel since the Six Day War began shifting back to a more liberal "cosmopolitanism."[80] Although researchers have not reached consensus on the significance of the change that began in the mid- to late 1980s, most tend to agree that a new chapter was indeed fomented in the relationship between the two communities.

When this relationship is observed from the opposite direction, it is easy to see the relative marginality American Jewry had as a source of inspiration for Israeli culture. During the decades in question, the influence of American Jews on Israeli collective identity, at least in its most evident and direct forms, was far more limited than that of Israel on Jewish American identity. It is no coincidence that research on the impact of Israel on American Jews comes largely from the social sciences, yet only a few studies of the influence of American Jewry on Israel discuss the kind of broad effects typically tested by sociological methodology. Indeed, most scholars who have focused on the role that American Jewry fulfilled, or attempted to fulfill, in Israeli life are political or intellectual historians, who tend to examine the thought or activity of individuals.[81]

During the prestate years, the relationship of Zionist leadership in Palestine to American Jewry was chiefly limited and utilitarian. Although public figures in Eretz-Israel and the United States cooperated on diplomatic matters related to the fate of European Jewry and the growing *Yishuv*, there was not much depth to the mutual relations between the two communities.

Upon the establishment of the state, the years-long limitations on Jewish immigration to Israel were lifted, putting the issue of aliyah center stage and inciting friction between the political leadership of the two communities, largely rooted in the false expectation of Israelis that American Jews would make aliyah by the masses. During these years, the negation of exile, a major tenet of classical Zionist thought denying the feasibility and worth of Jewish emancipation in the diaspora, was still a dominant feature of Israeli public discourse. Collectivist-Zionist criticism also targeted American Jews from a socialist perspective, denouncing individualist American capitalism and predicting that it would "surely evolve into fascism, and American antisemitic fascism will then destroy the Jewish community in the United States, just as it happened in Europe."[82]

From the late 1950s onward, as Israel turned geopolitically to the West and ties between Israel and the United States tightened, the Israeli cultural field underwent a gradual yet persistent process of Americanization. From the rise of advertising and the penetration of supermarkets and private cars into the consumer market, through the change in modes of production and consumption of radio content, American practices and values took root in the Israeli cultural repertoire.[83] The ideological critique of the Left that regarded American society as materialistic and vulgar did not disappear but gradually subsided. At the same time, the presence and impact of the negation of exile in public and intellectual discourse steadily receded, alongside a renewed spiritual quest for the Jewish roots of Israeli identity.[84] During the 1960s and 1970s, writers from the old-guard generation that had fought in Israel's War of Independence, such as Matti Megged and Dahn Ben-Amotz, and even a Canaanite author like Benjamin Tammuz, veered away from the anti-Jewish ethos that guided their early work and sought a kind of reconciliation with the notion of diasporic Jewishness.[85] The Israeli public seemed largely to move away from the classical form of negating exile, and if negative sentiment toward diaspora Jewry still persisted, particularly among the religious right wing, it was no longer related to hostility toward the very existence of diaspora Jewry.[86]

Despite the waning of the negation of exile in Israeli society, it would be an exaggeration to state that spiritual and cultural life in Israel reflected notable American Jewish influences. During these decades, the Israeli political establishment mainly sought technological, financial, and political support from American Jews. This support was indeed granted, and its vital contribution to the continued existence of Israel cannot be underestimated.

However, despite the central role they fulfilled in the economic, military, and geopolitical survival of the Israeli state, American Jews did not often engage with Israeli society and did not have a direct hand in shaping the cultural character of the state.[87] It appears that Israel did not absorb concepts from liberal American Judaism into its collective imagination and drew little inspiration from Jewish American thinkers as it cultivated the identity of a Jewish state. As historian Allon Gal lamented, "The immense potential of American Jewry—its intellectual thought, its experience with democracy and pluralism, and its vision for a deeply progressive Israel—was not realized in the first years and decades of Israeli statehood."[88] The public approach toward Israelis who emigrated to America (labeled as *yeridah*, Hebrew for "descent") never ceased to be one of anger and contempt. Nonetheless, Gal notes that in the 1970s and 1980s, new trends of religious pluralism sprouted that were reminiscent of American pluralism, such as the Schechter Institute's Jewish Studies programs in public schools, the establishment of *batei midrash* for progressive Judaism, and more. According to Gal, even if these did not carry much weight in Israeli society, they "were consistent with other phenomena in the spiritual and cultural life of a 'westernizing' post–Six Day War Israel."[89]

With its focus on the absorption of translated Hebrew literature in (Jewish) American literary discourse, the first part of this book substantiates the general claim that Israel played a central role in Jewish American identity after the establishment of the state, particularly following the Six Day War and through the mid-1980s—yet it does not take this notion at face value. Instead, it seeks to illuminate what *kind* of Israel was mediated to American Jewish audiences—what kinds of representations of Israel were accepted (and rejected) in American Jewish discourse so that Israel could serve as a viable source of collective identity. Anchored in the field of translation studies, it seeks to do so primarily by investigating the Jewish American reception and mediation of images *originating* in Israeli culture. The investigation of cultural aspects of the relationship between the two communities through this research prism has been sparse.[90] A notable exception is Emily Alice Katz's pioneering *Bringing Zion Home*, which discusses the appropriation of Israeli cultural products and practices such as folk dance, art, and music in Jewish American culture from 1948 to 1967.[91] My book, too, examines the American reception of cultural creations dreamed up and shaped in the context and environment of the Israeli sphere—but it extends the discussion to the crucial post–Six Day War years and focuses on the literary field. The latter choice is not arbitrary: in the realm of literature, Israeli self-representation tended to pose a much more complex challenge to American Jewish discourse than the images of Israel that were generated on American shores. The American treatment of these literary works may thus attest to the highly nuanced ideological sieve needed for portrayals of Israel to fulfill their assigned role in American Jewish society during these years.

The second part of the book is devoted to the absorption of Jewish American literature in Israel. Here, my work joins the extensive literature on the negation of exile in Israeli society in the decades following the establishment of the state and the more limited research on the Israeli relationship to American Jewry in the same period. My work does not dispute the prevailing notion that the once-pervasive negation of the exilic Jewish past gradually faded in Israeli public discourse. It does indicate, however, that the relationship to contemporary American Jewish culture was far more complex. The mediation of Jewish American literature in the Israeli discourse gave expression to ambivalent, defensive, often patronizing undercurrents regarding the American diaspora. Here, too, there is much to be gained from examining Israeli attitudes toward works that were written by Jewish American authors, which stemmed from and responded to the cultural conventions and reality of American Jewish life. These works confronted Israeli discourse with American notions of Judaism and Jewishness and intimate depictions of American Jewish experience to which Israelis were not often exposed. Yet, although several works discuss the approach of intellectual discourse in Israel to the political and historiosophical thinking of American Jews,[92] almost no studies have explored this issue from a cultural perspective.

The two parts of this book are not mutually independent. They serve as points of reference for each other and shed light on the findings presented in each part by way of comparison. Taken together, they draw a portrait of an animated dialogue between the two centers of Jewry from the state's establishment through the 1980s, which took on an ideological dimension through its negotiations of collective identity. During these four decades, the transfer of literary texts created a platform for dialogue, and at times downright confrontation, regarding differences of Jewish identity between the two communities. The literary discourse between these groups was asymmetrical, which is unsurprising considering that the history of contact and dialogue between them, though mutual, has been asymmetrical as well—and considering that the features of literary translation, as has long been established, are determined primarily by the predominant norms in the target culture. This is true not only with regard to the ideological content of mediation—but also with regard to its forms, to the ways and places in which it occurred. However, while we find more pronounced textual manipulation in the translations in one direction, say, or richer metatranslation discourse in the other, the varied forms of mediation in both directions shared the common goal of cultivating and influencing what each society knew, felt, and believed about its counterpart.

In both societies, the discourse on translated literature dealt with the most burning questions concerning Jewish nationality, religion, morality, and the ever-present tensions between particularism and universalism, homeland and diaspora. Although the decades in question may have witnessed the peak of the American Jewish relationship with Israel, and the waning of the negation of exile in Israel, mediation between the two cultures actually accentuates the wide gulf between the conceptions each community had fostered about the other—and their practical and symbolic realities. Although translation was meant to serve as a bridge to the culture of the source literature, upon close examination it seems to attest above all to the target-language culture—its expectations and concerns and the symbolic boundaries it sought to establish in response to the challenge represented by its Jewish Other.

The first part of the book, dedicated to the absorption of (translated) Hebrew literature into Jewish American culture, comprises three chapters. Chapter 1 illustrates a nationalist turn in the mediation of Hebrew literature in American Jewish discourse in the 1950s, which reflected a growing Zionist zeitgeist even as it used Israel as a model for a separate yet integrative Jewish identity in American life. Chapters 2 and 3 demonstrate the attempts made from the 1960s onward to adjust and appropriate images of an immoral Israel, particularly in the context of the Israeli–Palestinian conflict, and representations of Jewishness and Judaism that contradicted core values of Jewish American identity, an identity in which conceptions of Israel fulfilled a central role during these years.

The second part of the book is divided into two chapters, both of which exemplify the intrinsic ambivalence of literary debates in Israel toward American Jewish culture, and cast in a new light the prevalent historiographic assumption regarding the decline of the negation of diaspora in Israeli society from the 1960s onward. Chapter 4, which discusses Israeli debates of American representations of Jewish/non-Jewish difference, and chapter 5, which reflects on Israeli metalinguistic and metatranslation discourse, elaborate on Israeli attempts to formulate a hierarchy in the Jewish world that positioned cultural life in Israel as superior to that of American Jews, and Israeli sovereignty as the best and perhaps the only true solution for contemporary Jewish existence.

In his novel *Operation Shylock*, (the character named) Philip Roth discusses his close relationship with Israeli writer Aharon Appelfeld, explaining that their great intimacy stems precisely from their "distinctly radical twoness."[93] According to Roth, it is precisely because he and Appelfeld "each embody the *reverse* of the other's experience; because each recognizes in the other the Jewish man he is *not*; because of the all but incompatible orientations that shape our very different lives and very different books and that result from *antithetical* twentieth-century Jewish biographies; because we are the heirs jointly of a drastically *bifurcated* legacy—because of the sum of all these Jewish *antinomies*, yes, we have much to talk about and are intimate friends."[94]

This delightful definition of Jewish intimacy borne of and nourished by otherness, and sustained by a keen awareness of this otherness, is a useful point of reference in discussing the cultural relationship between the two Jewish centers. By analyzing processes of literary translation, we can explore the extent to which the intellectual dialogue between these Jewish communities answered to Roth's definition or failed to do so. To what extent could "the heirs jointly of a drastically *bifurcated* legacy" residing in Israel and the United States become truly acquainted through their literatures? How did these communities of "*antithetical* twentieth-century Jewish biographies" use literary discourse to fashion their identity and chart its boundaries, in light of the competing Jewish identity across the ocean?

1

The Zionist Transformation

In 1991, literary scholar Robert Alter looked back on the accomplishments of Hebrew literature in English translation from the 1960s onward and reviewed them with an air of considerable amazement. "The presence that Hebrew literature has achieved in English translation over the past two decades," he observed with wonder, "constitutes one of the great literary success stories of our times."[1] According to Alter, the accelerated integration of Hebrew literature in English translation in America, which began in the 1960s, peaked in the 1980s when "it had become the most visible foreign literature in the United States after that of Latin America—actually more visible than French or German or Russian or Italian or the literatures of the Third World."[2] Alter's views are not based on statistical data and were possibly prompted, to a certain degree, by his own heartfelt wishes. A leading American literary scholar, critic, editor, and lecturer in academia, Alter was an active agent in the mediation of Hebrew literature in the United States during these decades. Nonetheless, there is much truth in his claim regarding the unique position that Hebrew literature obtained in the American literary scene from the 1960s onward.

The data collected in UNESCO's Index Translationum project—which maps books translated around the globe—support Alter's enthusiasm. Although Hebrew is not among the hundred most spoken languages in the world, according to Index Translationum it is the sixth most translated language into English in the United States. Although it follows the five principal European languages (French, German, Spanish, Russian, and Italian, in that order), Hebrew precedes all other European languages, as well as important and widely spoken languages such as Arabic, Japanese, and Chinese. According to Index Translationum, the United States is also the largest consumer of Hebrew literature in translation, with 2,343 books translated from Hebrew published throughout the years up to 2008.[3] The project's data, as has been noted in recent scholarly critique, is open to more than one interpretation and is not without error. Yet, even if we question its complete accuracy, the index duly demonstrates Hebrew's disproportionate status in recent decades as a translated language and literature in America—certainly considering the scope of Hebrew readership worldwide and modern Hebrew culture's relatively modest standing in the global hierarchy of national cultures. In light of the traditional, deep-seated unreceptiveness of the American literary market to import from foreign cultures, the presence of Hebrew literature within this market over many decades becomes all the more remarkable.

"The rise and rise" of translated Hebrew literature from the 1960s and 1970s onward, as Alter quipped, catches the eye not only when contrasted with other national literatures but also in comparison to the fate of translated Hebrew literature in the United States during the first half of the twentieth century. In 1937, as translator Israel Meir Lask described with frustration in his foreword to S. Y. Agnon's *The Bridal Canopy*, "the fact of the existence of a modern Hebrew literature is as near unknown [to the average English reader] as makes no difference."[4] During the first four decades of the twentieth century, a mere thirty-six translated Hebrew books were published in America—an average of less than one book annually. By contrast, during the 1970s, 147 such books were published—approximately four times the number in a quarter of the time.[5]

What substantial shift could have transformed Lask's discouraged assessment into Robert Alter's more recent, confident claim? What is the background for the considerable difference in the volume and visibility of translation from Hebrew between its first lean decades of the twentieth century and its later decades—and what can be learned from it? This chapter traces the historical transformation of the movement of literary text from Hebrew to English, Israel to America, in the mid-twentieth century. It also outlines shifts in accompanying but no less important factors related to the increase in the scope of translation, such as the types of works that the American reader could have encountered and the ideological context against which these works were positioned in 1950s literary debates. These, I argue, provide a useful point of reference for the intellectual dialogue and ideological negotiation embedded in translation processes of later decades as well. To better understand the transformations that transpired, however, we need first to return to the earlier decades of the twentieth century for a somewhat broader historical background. In their discussions of the American reception of Israeli literature from the 1960s onward, scholars such as Alan Mintz and Robert Alter have noted the decisive significance of the *Jewish* sociohistorical context in literary translation from Hebrew to English.[6] But if, as Mintz and Alter rightfully acknowledged, the existence of a culturally vibrant Jewish community in the United States has provided a major impetus for the translation of Hebrew literature there, why were translations so scant during the first half of the twentieth century?

Let us first refute a few alternative explanations. It does not seem that we can explain the scarcity of translation in earlier decades in terms of lower intensity in the Jewish cultural scene. The vitality of Jewish creation and activity in America in the early decades of the twentieth century, concentrated in ethnically homogeneous urban enclaves, was arguably more distinguishable in its "Jewishness" than in later decades. Neither can we assume that earlier translations from Hebrew were intended for a general audience and that only from the second half of the century were they principally aimed at a Jewish readership. In fact, translation activity in the earlier decades was conducted mainly in Jewish "channels," such as institutional Jewish publishers—perhaps more so than in later decades—and the assumption that Jewish readers were the natural audience for works translated from Hebrew was widespread during both halves of the twentieth century. Changes in America's Jewish population also do not satisfactorily account for either the increase in translation from Hebrew or its relatively limited scope in the first half of the century. In contrast to the manifold increase in the number of translations between the 1940s and 1980s, the population growth of American Jews was far less dramatic: from 4.8 to 5.9 million—that is, an increase of just 20 percent, as opposed to 70 percent growth in the general US population.[7] Nor can we pin the sharp disparity in the scope of translation on changes in the volume of activity of institutional Jewish publishing in America. From the late nineteenth to the mid-twentieth century, Jewish publishers in the United States experienced considerable growth—growth that was rooted in social and ideological motives no less than literary or commercial ones. Their motivation could even be defined, in the words of Jonathan Sarna, as the consolidation of American Jews nationwide through a "common culture of print."[8] One might have expected such factors to encourage greater literary translation from Hebrew, yet this was not the case.

What, then, is the background, or at least a principal background, for the sweeping changes in the volume of translation and visibility of the translated works? The answer, to draw on translation sociologist Johan Heilbron's terminology, lies first and foremost in changes in the social and ideological relations between the major "language groups" involved in the translation movement: Israeli and American Jewries.[9] More specifically, and as has long been accepted by translation scholars, it is the dominant values in the target-language culture that determine the manner in which a foreign literature is integrated into the local discourse[10]—and translation from Hebrew in America is no exception. Although the translated works almost always originated in Israel, translation processes were shaped and determined mostly by cultural and ideological conventions in America. The explanation for the difference in translation trends between the two halves of the twentieth century is, therefore, predominantly grounded in American Jewry's attitude toward Israel and the Zionist idea.

In the introduction, I touched on the indifference, if not hostility, toward Zionism in the American Jewish establishment in the first decades of the twentieth century. As late as the 1930s and even the early 1940s, political Zionism was seen as a controversial position that for many problematized the attempt to preserve the unity of American Jews in a time of growing internal division. Such reservations were, however, not limited to the political and religious discourses mentioned in the introduction. They were also ingrained, if somewhat differently, in the cultural and intellectual spheres, the spheres with which the literary discourse corresponds and of which it is part. In the left-leaning Jewish literary scene, the reluctance to embrace Zionism in the early decades of the twentieth century may have been particularly pronounced. The critical reception of an author of professed Zionist views such as Meyer Levin, and the ways in which that reception was influenced by his politics, are a case in point. Time and again in the 1930s and 1940s, Levin was "singled out for attack," in the words of Benno Weiser Varon, "because of his consistent pro-Zionism."[11] As Andrew Furman has further suggested, "the Jewish literary left judged Levin's early Zionist fiction [in a hostile manner] largely on political, not artistic, grounds."[12] Anthologies of Jewish literature published in America during these years also evinced, in their selection of stories and their editorial commentary, a certain disinterest in, if not straightforward skepticism toward, the Zionist idea. Leo W. Schwarz, an important anthology editor of the 1930s, made a point of proclaiming that it was Jewish literature, and not the land of Israel, that was the Jewish people's true homeland.[13] And although there were some exceptional and occasionally influential titles on the *Yishuv* published during those years, such as Horace Kallen's *Frontiers of Hope* (1929), it is nonetheless clear that "to be a Zionist in the 1930s and 1940s," in the words of *Tikkun* editor Michael Lerner, "was *not* to be a part of the American Jewish establishment."[14]

This historical background helps us understand not only the limited scope of literary translation from Hebrew during this early period but also the ideological aspects involved in the selection of titles for translation. Works of fiction translated from Hebrew and published in America during the first decades of the twentieth century were not only scarce—they were also hardly representative of the crystallizing Hebrew canon. Although most Hebrew writers of the time were concerned with the challenges and experiences of life in the fledgling *Yishuv*, these themes rarely reached the Jewish American readership. Whether naïvely glorifying the pioneers and their endeavors or presenting realistic and even harshly pessimistic portrayals of life in Palestine, such Hebrew works were not selected for translation.[15] Yiddish literature, press, and theater still represented the foundations and infrastructure of Jewish social life during these years, particularly in New York, Chicago, and other major Jewish urban centers. Yiddish culture's double engagement with themes of New World assimilation and Old World nostalgia seemed to meet the intellectual and recreational needs of the immigrant generation. Rather confined in terms of its cultural production and consumption, it constituted a fairly self-sufficing social milieu.[16] This environment did not cultivate a palpable need for (English or Yiddish) translation from Hebrew literature. Both popular and elitist Yiddish fiction affected local readers much more than literature anchored in the hardships of everyday life in the *Yishuv* and grappling with the unsure implications of the Zionist endeavor.[17]

How the work of S. Y. Agnon fared in English translation during these years is indicative in this respect. Agnon, "dean of Hebrew letters," who remains the only Israeli to win the Nobel Prize in Literature, had always been somewhat anomalous vis-à-vis the developing literary center in Palestine. From the 1910s through the 1930s, Agnon wrote both works that portrayed Jewish life in Europe (from Germany to Galicia and from secular bourgeoisie to piously poor) and allegorical stories with nationalist undercurrents, some of which were set in the *Yishuv*. From this diverse repertoire—and while his reputation was already well established in the 1920s and 1930s—only one work, *The Bridal Canopy*, was published in America through the late 1940s. A deceptively naïve, sweeping epic set against small-town Jewish life in early 1800s Galicia, the novel portrays Rabbi Yudel Hassid's journey from one Jewish village to the next in search of bridegrooms and dowries for his daughters. Hailed as "*the* epic of the old village culture, and as *the* representation of the *shtetl* before its decline," in the words of Baruch Hochman, the novel had little to do with the *Yishuv* in Palestine or with contemporary deliberations of national identity.

It is also telling that at the Jewish Publication Society of America, the major nonprofit middle-of-the-road publisher of Jewish works at the time, books harboring a Zionist orientation gave rise to significant discord among editors up until the 1940s.[18] As Sarna shows, members of the press intervened in the compilation of a collection of poems by Jessie Sampter, an American Zionist and pioneer in Palestine. A fierce anti-Zionist at the time, editor Solomon Solis-Cohen was willing to publish the collection on the condition that he would be given the right to select the poems—and, when he did, he excluded those that dealt with pioneer life in Palestine or had any Zionist undertones.[19] *Aftergrowth and Other Stories*, a collection of short stories by the national Hebrew poet Hayim Nahman Bialik, posed no such challenge for the Jewish Publication Society, which gladly released the volume in 1939, as the non-Zionists on the board of directors considered the stories "free of politics."[20] Another instance of the ideological underpinnings of literary mediation can be found in the English rendering of a Zionist parable by A. D. Gordon, the spiritual leader of Labor Zionism. Gordon's piece was included in *Echoes of the Jewish Soul*, an anthology of modern Hebrew works published by Bloch Publishing Company in 1931—a singular case of a Hebrew literary anthology published by an American publisher before the 1950s.[21] Gordon's was the only text in the anthology with an underlying Zionist understanding of Jewish identity. The story, translated by anthology editor Joseph Cooper Levine, was, however, substantially modified en route to its American Jewish readers. In the original text, the narrator hurls harsh accusations at his readers in the diaspora:

> The destruction [spreading throughout the land of Israel] is the destruction of your soul, and the destroyer is the destroyer in your life, which you have lived in foreign countries and which have so far affixed themselves to you. . . . And if you were to absolutely leave that life, which

> others have created, if you were to leave their country and come here to create a new life, a life of your own—then the embers will be revived and their flame rekindled, and you will be revived, and your people and land will be revived.[22]

In the translation, however, there is no trace of these lines; the English text is neatly "stitched up" around them.[23] In Gordon's text, there is no possibility of a spiritually authentic Jewish existence in a country that is not the land of Israel, and with great pathos the narrator implores diaspora Jews to immigrate to Palestine. Owing to the omission in translation, Gordon's territorial position comes closer to Ahad Ha'am's cultural Zionism, which places more importance on the rejuvenation of Jewish spiritual life than on the resettlement of Palestine, as the entire segment becomes more palatable, and less politically disputable, for contemporary American Jewish readers.

The blurring of the Zionist orientation of a text as it was mediated from Hebrew to American discourse occasionally entailed the obscuring, or universalization, of the source's (national) particularism. Abraham Mapu's *Ahavat Zion* (Love of Zion), published first in 1853 and in many editions since, is considered the first novel in the Hebrew language and a herald of the Zionist movement. Written in biblical Hebrew and set in the days of King Hezekiah and the prophet Isaiah, the novel portrays life in ancient Israel from a romantic nationalist perspective. The novel evoked in its readers "a strong sense of an ancient Jewish national home," and its influence was noted by prominent Zionist leaders such as David Ben-Gurion. Shortly before the novel appeared in translation in New York in 1922, a new Hebrew edition was issued, making the differences in the novel's cross-cultural reception readily apparent. Hebrew reviews stressed Mapu's role in nurturing Zionist consciousness and described him as "the first among our nation's modern visionaries who attained the essential secret of our nation and of the absolute unity between the nation, the language and the land."[24] The American circumstances of the novel's publication and reception could not have been more different. The English translator was pastor Benjamin Schapiro, a Jew who converted to Christianity and established a mission in Brooklyn dedicated to the conversion of Jews. The novel's original title, *Ahavat Zion*, which expresses a longing for the land of Israel, was rendered as *The Shepherd Prince*, a title bearing Christian connotations. Schapiro had to first publish and distribute the book independently, a fact presumably not unrelated to his problematic personal history (from a Jewish institutional publisher's perspective), and then, in the 1930s, the book was republished by Broadside, a Protestant publishing house. When the novel was first reviewed in the *New York Times*, the (anonymous) critic completely ignored the novel's nationalist undertones and never mentioned the Zionist movement or the *Yishuv* in Palestine; Mapu was hailed as the father of the "Jewish"—not the Hebrew or Zionist—novel.[25] Along these lines, the reviewer did not indicate the obvious applicability of the novel's underlying nationalism to the Jewish political awakening of the time. A useful point of comparison, the foreword to the Hebrew edition of the novel from 1918 stated that "the more recent events in our Hebrew world, the new and strong hope to return to the new Zion and establish our home there . . . have now enhanced and elevated the value of the first story in the Hebrew language."[26] Conversely, the *New York Times* critic described the translation first and foremost as bearing the potential to bring Jews and Christians closer together and to carry a universal message:

> The translator is himself a Hebrew-Christian who, by this labor of loving scholarship, has shown a deep loyalty to the oracles of his ancestral faith. And what he has achieved will thus make a double appeal where such double appeal may contribute to unity of citizenship. The learning and genius of a great Hebrew author will enrich the mentality of old and young both in the synagogues and in the Christian churches.[27]

This orientation, somewhat reminiscent of Reform Jewish thought of that period, is very far from the secular stance of political Zionism, whose adherents drew nationalist themes from Mapu's novel. *New York Times* readers therefore encountered an interpretation of the meanings and values of *Ahavat Zion* that was noticeably different from that of contemporaneous Zionist readers.

A nonnationalist approach dictated, to a certain extent, the introduction of Hebrew literature to American audiences in the academic milieu as well. For one, until the late 1930s, the revival of the Hebrew language as a vernacular in Palestine was largely ignored in Hebrew courses at American universities: although Hebrew had by then come to be associated with the Jewish people and its history—in previous centuries, Hebrew studies were still part of Protestant theological scholarship or philological research of Semitic languages—ancient strata of the language were taught, rather than modern Hebrew.[28] Without tenured professors of modern Hebrew, modern Hebrew works could rarely be included in course curricula or taught. The first comprehensive English survey of modern Hebrew language and literature, *Hebrew Reborn*, published in New York in 1930 by Shalom Spiegel, a professor of medieval Judaism, attests to the prevailing views of the time. More up to date in his modernist readings than his peers, and also a passionate Zionist, Spiegel viewed the works of the 1880s–1920s revival generation and of writers of the first aliyot preoccupied with the national awakening as the pinnacle of modern Hebrew literature. In *Hebrew Reborn*, however, he admitted that he had focused on writers of the *Haskalah*, the Jewish enlightenment of the eighteenth and nineteenth centuries, so as to better cater to his readers' expectations:

> A popular approach made it necessary to present the *consensus omnium* even where I myself had gone on to other views. This is the case particularly in the first part of the book, where the true development of Hebrew letters seems to me to run aside from that movement of enlightenment which is accepted as the head and front of modern Hebrew literature.[29]

Even when the scholar himself may have held a differing opinion, then, prevailing notions in the intellectual discourse exerted a powerful influence on the way in which Hebrew literature was introduced to the American reader.[30] By way of comparison, in recent decades, departments for Israel and Jewish Studies in universities throughout the United States have offered a wide variety of courses in contemporary Hebrew literature; in fact, a significant bulk of literary translation from Hebrew, mainly noncommercial literature that might otherwise never have been translated, has been published by university presses, especially since the 1980s.

Reluctance to embrace Zionism may have informed yet another aspect of Hebrew literature's integration into early American discourse: the question of cultural hierarchy in the Jewish world, explicitly or implicitly framed through critical reception. The lukewarm review of Agnon's *The Bridal Canopy* in the *New York Times* in February 1937, by critic Harold Strauss, is a case in point. In his review, Strauss proclaimed an unequivocal hierarchy of Hebrew and Yiddish literatures:

> Yiddish literature has developed spontaneously, and its brilliant history culminates in powerful and artistically sophisticated writers such as I. J. Singer and Sholem Asch. Hebrew literature, on the other hand,

> has been artificially fostered as the handmaiden to Zionism, and even though it can boast of two fine lyric poets, Bialik and Tschernichovsky, it nevertheless is still in its primitive stage, artistically as unsophisticated as "The romance of the rose" or "Morte d'Arthur."[31]

As a reader entirely dependent on English translation, Strauss could not have encountered the modernist achievements of Hebrew letters at the turn of the century, and thus conveyed a very partial portrait to his readers. His stylistic judgment, in turn, reinforced a general conception of Hebrew literature as inferior to Yiddish literature. Strauss's views were a reflection of the era in which he lived. The scarcity of translations into English, and the nonrepresentative nature of existing translations, created a wide gap between the original repertoire of Hebrew literature and its American counterpart. A *New York Times* advertisement from the same year, announcing the publication of Agnon's novel, aptly demonstrates this gap and Hebrew literature's ensuing marginality on the local scene. "[Agnon] writes not in Modern Yiddish," the advertiser saw fit to declare, "but in Hebrew, the language in which the Old Testament was originally written."[32] Anticipating the reader's assumption that, if not specified otherwise, a Jewish writer necessarily writes in Yiddish and not in Hebrew, the advertiser perhaps sought to promote sales by means of this "exotic" detail. The advertisement echoes Israel Lask's cautionary point in his foreword to Agnon's novel that English readers may be unaware of the very existence of modern Hebrew literature.

The sparse and unrepresentative translation of works with an affinity to Yiddishist culture by Hebrew writers such as Judah Steinberg, as well as the *lack* of translations of seminal Palestinian writers such as Y. H. Brenner, Haim Hazaz, Yehuda Yaari, and Yaacov Steinberg, ultimately distanced Hebrew literature's original repertoire from its parallel in America. The critical reception of the works that were translated, coupled with a few manipulations in the translations themselves, further shaped the American acquaintance with Hebrew letters at the time. Hebrew literature, a cornerstone of the national and cultural resurgence in Palestine, was thus transformed and reincarnated as it entered American Jewish discourse, losing some of its most defining, Eretz-Israeli features and preoccupations.

From Invisibility to Tangible Presence

From the mid-twentieth century onward, a considerable ideological shift reshaped relations between the two language groups, gradually leaving its imprint on the ways in which Hebrew literature was mediated to an American Jewish audience. World War II and the founding of the State of Israel fostered a dramatic change in American Jewish attitudes to the Zionist idea, as American Jews were captivated first by Israel's struggle for independence and later by the new state. America's long fascination with the land of Israel, as Peter Grose has argued, proved a fruitful ground for its growing affinity with the new political and cultural life in the State of Israel.[33] More and more, American Jews relied on Israel—its dance, music, and art and the Jewish authenticity its images had come to signify—as a major anchor for their cultural identity.[34] This was manifest as well in the fields of literary criticism and publishing. As early as 1955, prominent critic Harold Ribalow called upon Jewish American authors to focus on Israel's existence and creatively express what he called "The Miracle of Israel."[35] And although canonical Jewish American prose would heed Ribalow's recommendation only some decades later, other areas of the literary field, such as popular fiction, expressed much more immediate excitement. The landmark example is, of course, Leon Uris's 1958 novel *Exodus*—at the time the biggest best-seller in America since *Gone with the Wind*—which popularized the Jewish state and instilled in American Jews a sweeping sense of collective pride "with power and effect," as Matthew Silver suggests, "that far surpassed any Zionist public relations effort that preceded it."[36] As Emily Katz has shown, dozens of reportages and memoirs about Israel, the majority of which were highly sympathetic, were published in America as early as the late 1940s and during the 1950s and 1960s.[37] In the decade following the 1967 Six Day War, during which Israel was transformed into the pillar of American Jewish communal identity, the Jewish Publication Society published more books about Israel, mostly nonfiction, than about Jewish life in America, exceeding the number of books published on Jewish history—ancient, medieval, and modern combined.[38]

Parallel to these publishing trends we also find an increasing number of translations from Hebrew—an importation, so to speak, of literary work from Israel. Agnon's novella *In the Heart of the Seas* (1934; English, 1948) may be seen as marking the end of the pre-Zionist era in Hebrew-to-English translation; this sophisticated fantasy describes the journey of a group of Hasidic Galician Jews to the land of Israel in the early nineteenth century, yet it was widely interpreted through the ideological prism of the contemporary Zionist imperative of aliyah.[39] *Under the Fig Tree: Palestinian Stories*—a collection of stories by Yitzhak Shenhar published in the same year and anchored, as overtly emphasized in its American title, in the experiences and hardships of pioneer life in the struggling *Yishuv*—also reflected this transition.[40] The import of Hebrew literature, therefore, became contingent on Jewish American interest in Israel, an interest that would only intensify with time. Concurrent with the gradual increase in translated literary works in the 1950s, three scholarly overviews of modern Hebrew literature in English were also published, and from the mid-1960s onward, as Robert Alter rightfully suggests, "a powerful momentum built up in the transmission of Hebrew literature to readers of English."[41] This is evident in the general volume of translation and particularly in literary translation: the number of translated works of fiction published in the 1970s (seventy-five) was four times the number published in the 1950s (eighteen).[42]

Other publishing trends accentuate this shifting orientation of translation from Hebrew. From the 1940s onward, the percentage of privately owned commercial presses among all American publishers issuing translations from Hebrew to English grew continuously. It is important to note that the parallel decrease in presses affiliated with Jewish and Zionist institutions did not indicate a lack of interest on the part of readers in the materials these publishers provided. On the contrary: the vital role these institutional presses needed to play in the past as promoters of translations from Hebrew had been diminishing due to a growing interest in these translations on the part of the general public.[43] At the same time, the interval between the publication of a Hebrew book's first edition in Israel and its publication in English translation shortened. Unlike in previous decades, American publishers translated authors whose status in Hebrew literature was established at the time or, at most, a decade earlier. Thus many authors who had become prominent names in Hebrew literature could almost simultaneously establish a position on the American cultural scene. "Several contemporary Hebrew writers," Alter claimed, "have developed a real following in America . . . and there is considerable evidence . . . of a group of readers who eagerly follow these writers book after book." Although they have not achieved best-seller status, according to Alter "their sales constitute[d] a respectable presence."[44]

The number of national anthologies of Israeli literature published in English translation in these years—an often useful way to gauge the interest of a receiving culture in a foreign literature—is also highly indicative in this respect. To compare, during the 1930s, seven anthologies were published, of which only one was of literary fiction; whereas in the 1970s, the majority of the twenty-five published anthologies contained works of fiction.[45] Moreover, the typical discourse surrounding these anthologies discloses that the motives for their publication were not strictly literary in the stylistic sense and attests to an American Jewish interest in Israeli life. In his foreword to the anthology *Firstfruits*, published in 1973 on the occasion of Israel's twenty-fifth anniversary, American Jewish author Chaim Potok likened the stories in the anthology to "deep probes into the psychic soil that supports the land and provides its people with their hopes and dreams and hungers and nightmares."[46] Potok's words typify perceptions of Israeli anthologies in translation as emblematic not only of the national literature but also, to some extent, of the nation itself. In fact, critics often saw this representative quality assigned to the anthologies as one of their major literary assets. This is particularly notable in the critical focus on Israeli stories included in anthologies of Jewish literature by authors from various language and cultural backgrounds. Whereas reviewers in the 1930s of Joseph Leftwich's weighty anthology of Jewish literature, *Yisroel*, did not take any special interest in stories translated from Hebrew, critics of the anthology's new editions in the 1950s expressed their desire for *more* such stories.[47] A piece in the *Washington Post* from June 1953 compared the 1930s *Yisroel* with its 1950s edition and concluded that, unlike stories written in Yiddish, which hitherto had been perceived by American critics as "closest to the traditional Jewish spirit" and which now were part of a dying literature and "disappearing language," the Hebrew stories were themselves the "present" and the "future."[48] As both a topic and a theme, "Israeliness" was perceived as a work's added value, as in Glendy Dawedeit's July 1956 review of Leo W. Schwarz's anthology *Feast of Leviathan*. Dawedeit took a special interest in the Israeli stories because "[although] not so much exceptional in quality as in content, [they] provid[e] a presumably authoritative picture of hardship and courage in the new nation."[49] Like those of other reviewers of the time, Dawedeit's reservations as to the stories' quality did not thwart her admiration for them, on account of her regard for the stories' value as social and historical testimony to the new nation. In a typical vein, critic Philip Rubin, in his review of Schwarz's anthology in the *New York Times* in June 1956, concluded that "it is in the Israeli section that the editor has established the book's usefulness, has given it a *raison d'etre*."[50]

Concurrent with the growth in translation and the increasing interest in Israel as a literary topic, the types of works that the local reader began to encounter were gradually transformed. Unlike those of the first decades of the twentieth century, approximately half the books translated from the late 1940s through the 1950s were either already anchored in contemporary Israeli reality or were historical novels that gave indirect expression to the current national awakening. This does not mean that the works selected for translation were propagandist Zionist tracts—far from it, as is evident from even a cursory survey of the major translated works. In Shenhar's *Under the Fig Tree*, the dominant tone among the pioneer protagonists is one of melancholy and disappointment—in both themselves and the land—and the motif of disillusionment is prominent.[51] Published in English in 1950, David Maletz's *Young Hearts* (1945) portrays life on the kibbutz sympathetically but without pathos and does not spare the reader the inevitable hardships involved in a harshly collectivist lifestyle, which in the protagonist's experience are intermingled with a sense of emptiness. Myths of heroism and determination inherent in the power struggles between brothers during the days of the Hasmonean dynasty are a major theme in Moshe Shamir's *King of Flesh and Blood* (1954), published in English in 1958. Although the novel provides readers with a romantic illustration of the consolidation of the national Jewish consciousness, its explicit theme is the Hasmonean dynasty's downfall due to corruption and imperialist tendencies—an analogy to Israel of the 1950s. Several stories in the 1957 anthology *A Whole Loaf: Stories from Israel*—edited by Sholom Kahn, an American immigrant to Israel and professor of literature at the Hebrew University—present a rather dire picture of the consequences of the War of Independence on Israeli society. Nathan Shaham's and Aharon Megged's stories, for instance, describe the war's lasting effects on young soldiers who are unable to overcome debilitating physical and mental impairments; their bitter tone clearly undermines the new nation's sacrificial ethos.

This is not to say that no works were translated during these years that articulated a deep commitment to the national ethos or spared their readers the individual price claimed by the Zionist enterprise and its wars. Translation of some of these texts was in fact contingent on anthology editors' biased selection practices. Included in Yitzhak Shenhar's 1956 anthology *Tehilla and Other Israeli Tales*, the short excerpt from Moshe Shamir's *With His Own Hands* portrays a young Palmach soldier, Elik, as he falls in love with a girl.[52] Long considered the epitome of the literary oeuvre of the 1948 generation, *With His Own Hands* was engraved on the national consciousness for its conclusion: young Elik's death in a vicious battle on the road to Jerusalem. In the excerpt included in the anthology, Elik (as a young teenager) emphatically expresses his love for the Palestinian sand dunes and immerses himself in the landscape, as expected of a Sabra from the *Yishuv* elite; he also has his first kiss with a girl. The American reader cannot foresee Elik's future as a casualty of the War of Independence, as the short section offers a very selective slice of the novel, one devoid of the ultimate sacrifice that had given it its distinct place in this generation's canon.

The inclusion of Leah Goldberg's short "Growing Up" in the Israeli section of the Jewish anthology *Feast of Leviathan* follows the same logic. In this piece, the narrator marvels at the rapid maturing of her young friend, who now, at seventeen and a half, has become a soldier; the text uncritically reproduces the mythic Sabra character, and it is worth quoting some of its final lines in full:

> He answers our questions unwillingly, with minimum words, in a way devoid of emotion. He knows all types of weapons well. "But I have never hit anybody." And after a long pause, "Thank god." Soon he will get up and leave, soon his mother's merry look will sadden, soon I will begin talking in his absence on the usual topic: our young people.[53]

The mythic image of the Sabra as a quiet, noble soldier unconditionally devoted to protecting the state is replicated in these sentences. Goldberg was known as one of the *Yachdav* literary circle, whose members were criticized for their writing being "insufficiently Zionist in that it does not depict life in Israel forthrightly, and for the closer affinity they felt with world culture than with Hebrew culture."[54] The editor's Zionist bent in his selection of the text for translation stands out, as it had come at the expense of representing the author with work typical of her.

What are we to understand from this mixed picture of Hebrew literature's American repertoire in the 1950s? Can one point to a widespread ideological bias in the selection of works for translation by publishers and editors? Broadly speaking, the answer seems to be no: the works selected for translation in the 1950s did not notably distort the collective portrait of contemporary Hebrew literature. Although many Hebrew works were not selected for translation, including some that problematized the national Israeli narrative more than works that did appear in English translation during these years, there were also many works that went untranslated that did embrace the national ethos with much more dedication and naïveté than those that were translated. We cannot conclude that the relative proportion of these two opposite trajectories changed decidedly in the translated repertoire. Furthermore, the ideological considerations behind the selection of works for translation are not easily isolated from other factors: protocols from most publishing houses are nonexistent or unavailable, and factors whose influence is hard to assess—commercial concerns, considerations of taste and aesthetics, copyright issues, personal preferences—may have played a decisive role in forming the translated repertoire.

Granted, almost none of the translated Hebrew works in the 1950s represented the moral implications of the War of Independence, most notably its consequences for the local Palestinian population, and how ethical wrongdoings might be haunting the Israeli consciousness—a theme that would become evident in the translated repertoire only from the 1960s onward. But even so, the boundaries of the Israeli repertoire were not dramatically traced anew in the transition to an American audience. For although there were works appearing in Hebrew during these years that dealt with these issues, few of them achieved major recognition; most lingered on the fringes of the Israeli literary scene. (This tendency, and the few exceptions from it, will be discussed in chapter 2.) One way or another, the image of Israel that the American reader encountered in fiction translated from Hebrew during the 1950s was often more complex than what we find in contemporary American fiction dealing with Israel. American best-sellers—Leon Uris's *Exodus* (1958) and James Michener's *The Source* (1965) in particular stand out—provided the reader with a popular representation of the Israeli struggle for independence or an auspicious account of Jewish history as spanning the period from ancient times to the redemptive founding of the State of Israel. These popular novels were preceded by some thirty nonfiction works, including Pierre Van Paassen's *Palestine: Land of Israel* (1948) and Isidor Feinstein Stone's *This Is Israel* (1949), that also produced a largely sympathetic and at times naïve portrayal of the Zionist narrative for the American reading audience.[55] This was the dominant prism that shaped the image of Israel for American eyes at the time, rather than complex accounts of hardship and disappointment embedded in the national enterprise, such as those that appeared in some of the translated Hebrew works.

Reincarnation in National Terms

The devoted Zionist orientation of most American fiction and nonfiction about Israel not only exemplifies prevalent approaches to Israel in postwar American culture but also helps us understand the patterns of mediation of Hebrew literature in the mainstream American press. In what follows, I will argue that although the translated repertoire may not be indicative of an ideological "filter" at the level of publishing, the literary discourse introducing the works implied quite a distinct worldview, rendering nationalism the primary prism through which the American reader could understand Hebrew fiction. Book reviews often produced a flatter, more one-dimensional portrayal of the Israeli story than that depicted in the source literature. Lauding what they perceived to be expressions of national sentiment, critics tended to position the framework of nationalism as an effective and desirable resource for good literature. In an effort to draw the American reader closer to Israel and its culture, reviewers also conceived an affinity between Hebrew literature's national underpinnings and American historical myths. Hebrew works were thus associated, quite unproblematically, with Israeli nationalism, and in turn, Israeli nationalism was presented as bearing an affinity to American national identity and culture.

"A Literary Letter from Israel," Alexander Ramati's overview of Israeli literature, published in the *New York Times* in May 1951, was perhaps the first piece in the mainstream American press to offer a survey of contemporary Hebrew letters. A Jewish immigrant from Poland, Ramati was a *Time* magazine correspondent in Israel during World War II, before returning to America, and was the author of a novel set in Israel during the War of Independence. Reading the article, one cannot fail to sense Ramati's appreciation for what he understood as the national underpinnings of the young Israeli literature. This appreciation for the Sabra patriotism of the new generation of authors is matched by reverential adoration, typical of Ramati's time, of their youth and experience in war. "They have grown up relatively without fear or discipline," he writes with some admiration, "and saw in their people's uprising a decisive and dramatic element."[56] The materials of the national struggle and the realization of the national project are presented as fertile terrain and a source of inspiration for the literary endeavor: "events were known first-hand and became a 'usable present.' Many of these young men had become, as Yigal Mossinsohn wrote, 'mankillers before they had reached the age of patting the braids of girls.'"[57] It is true that Ramati echoes literary debates in Israel that strove to find in these authors' works, in Avner Holtzman's words, "an expression of the spiritual world of the 'first generation of redemption' that grew and was nurtured in the interwar period in accordance with the spirit of the Hebrew pioneering ideals of the *Yishuv*."[58] However, Ramati's dramatic choice of words, and the quote he selected from Mossinsohn, rest no less on the mythification of Israel in mainstream American culture. Prevalent images of Israeliness in both fictional and nonfictional contemporary American literature were largely based on stereotypes infused with typically mythic Sabra-esque and "masculine" characteristics reminiscent of heroes in American Westerns. As Michelle Mart demonstrates, the portrayal in these books of strong Israeli fighters pursuing justice established the image of Israel as America's ally in its struggle against Soviet communism during the Cold War.[59] According to Shaul Mitelpunkt, the conception of Israel as a "free-wheeling" yet militarily committed citizen-soldier society was in fact the main prism through which American elite commentators framed Israel for American consumption.[60] The army was a particular touchstone for Jewish American identification with Israel. Moses Zebi Frank, editor of the 1955 celebratory anthology *Sound the Great Trumpet: The Story of Israel through the Eyes of Those Who Built It*, exemplifies this tendency in his reference to Hebrew poet Naftali Hertz Imber, author of Israel's national anthem, "Ha-tikvah" (The Hope): "Long after the author of these verses died a poor man in America," Frank writes in his introductory chapter, "soldiers of Israel's Army of Defense stood at attention when the words were sung or its music played, and Jews in Madison Square Garden in New York rose to sing them."[61] That the metaphorical bridge Frank erects between the two Jewish communities has soldiers on its Israeli end is no coincidence. The "depiction of Jewish strength on the Israeli frontier," as Matthew Silver writes on the roots of the overwhelming success of Uris's *Exodus*, "compensated for lingering feelings of urban vulnerability in America. . . . In the far-off venue of Israel, Jews are seen in heroic roles as fighters who take their fate into their own hands."[62] Thus Ramati's use of popular American imagery of Israel can also be seen as a way to draw his American (Jewish) readers closer to Hebrew literature and Israel—relying on the burgeoning discourse of affinity between the two nations.

Concurrent with these views is Ramati's unconcealed contempt for Hebrew writers of the previous generation who, in his opinion, divert from the national paradigm:

> The new vigor and drive [in Israeli letters] gained momentum by rejecting the "ghettoization" of theme and viewpoint typical of the writers of the older generation. . . . [B]efore this literary reformation, Israeli

> literature was dominated mainly by writers who had come to Palestine from Eastern Europe, who lived pretty generally in the past and who continued to romanticize in their melancholy novels and poems the ghettos of Poland and the backward villages of the Ukraine.[63]

Although Ramati posits the rejection of "diasporic" tendencies in Hebrew fiction as a new revelation, this reference to a generational shift in Hebrew literature in fact reflects his ignorance of Hebrew literary culture in earlier decades. Indeed, the "New Hebrew" themes associated with building the new homeland had already been setting the agenda in Hebrew letters for some decades.[64] The depiction of works from previous decades as guilty of "melancholic" romanticization of the past is yet another unfounded generalization, as modernist Hebrew works in the interwar period testify.[65] Rather than provide an accurate chronicle of literary trends, Ramati's remarks attest to the limited repertoire of Hebrew literature that American critics could have encountered in English, on account of the predominant denationalizing dynamics of previous decades. No less important, Ramati's survey articulates a strong objection to nostalgic Jewish isolationism—"ghettoization," in his words—an objection that complements his disparaging depiction of the former diaspora's "backwardness." Regardless of whether Ramati is dealing here with contemporary Hebrew literature only, or whether his words mask an indirect critique of American Yiddish literature and theater, his belief in the need for Jewish integration, even universalism, is unmistakable. The literary establishment in Israel, Ramati claims, must beware of falling into a trap of regionalism, in order to enable young writers such as Moshe Shamir, Nathan Shaham, and Yigal Mossinsohn to continue to mark a desired paradigm shift for Hebrew literature—one opposite to isolating, local particularism.

Not all American critics shared Ramati's opinion of the dangers of regionalization threatening Hebrew literature. In April 1950, Leo Schwartzman of the *Southern Israelite* also marveled at the pioneering "verve and vigor" of contemporary Hebrew works, yet saw recent literary expression in Israel as meaningfully relevant to the Jewish world as a whole. Moreover, in Schwartzman's view, contemporary Hebrew literature "seeks to interpret the soul of the world, even in moments when it bespeaks the most fervent conviction that Palestine is the ultimation [*sic*] salvation for Jewry."[66] Still, beyond the dispute over Hebrew literature's ability to deal effectively with global Jewish, or even universal, issues, Schwartzman and Ramati's shared perception of the desired purpose of national literature becomes clear: they both see considerable value in national Jewish writing matched by a non-isolationist, universal outlook. Even in more intimately Jewish venues than the *New York Times*, such as Jewish periodicals, then, the added value of universal writing was emphasized. In fact, even when agents of Hebrew literature in America made an explicit address to a *Jewish* readership, they may have appealed to them by pointing to a broadly national, not necessarily Jewish, affinity among the two communities. A fine example is the entreating background offered by Leo W. Schwarz to the "Israelian [*sic*] Fruit" section in his Jewish anthology *Feast of Leviathan* (1956):

> If the reader is a Jewish boy or girl, he must have heard a great deal about an ancient dream that has come true in our days. I mean the birth of the new republic of Israel. There is much that is entirely different in the life of Jews who are building that new country, yet there is a good deal that is akin to our own history and life. Life in the Kvuzoth, the agricultural colonies and especially in the great plains and desert of the Negeb, is remindful of the adventures of the pioneers in the old Wild West. And the huge numbers of immigrants and settlers from all parts of the globe, struggling to bring civilization to rough country and fighting in their War of Independence, read like pages from our own history.[67]

Schwarz's reference to Israel as a "new republic" is quite deliberate: the affinity he delineates between the Jewish American reader and Israel is contingent not on religion or ethnicity but rather on civic nationalism. The kinship he presents is derived not from the particular roots common to both *communities* but from historical circumstances common to both *nation-states*; this kinship, to a large extent, is not between Jews but between Israelis (who happen to be Jews) and Americans (who also happen to be Jews). In American nonfiction about Israel in the postwar years, as Emily Katz shows, authors "presented Israel as essentially analogous to the United States . . . underscor[ing] the compatibility of the two nations, often by invoking shared historical themes such as the settlement of the frontier, the battle of independence, and the absorption of immigrants."[68] Schwarz's address to a Jewish reader follows the same lines. Moreover, this rhetoric of affinity between the two nations helps Schwarz place the Jewish reader within the American national ethos in contexts that were not traditionally engrained in the Jewish American collective memory—fighting in America's War of Independence and pioneering on the Western frontier, among others.[69] It is not coincidental that the addition of "our own history," which appears twice in three sentences, refers not to Jewish but to American history.

Notably, Schwarz's preface does not go into detail about any stylistic or thematic features and hardly even refers to Hebrew literature as an artistic medium. The readers' sympathy for Israel seems much more important to him than their appreciation for the literary works. "As in Bible days," Schwarz says, evoking the Zionist ethos of Jewish continuity and the historic right over the land, "the writers of Israel are telling their stories once more in the Hebrew language, and apart from the excitement of their tales you will discover in them engrossing people."[70] Reading Hebrew literature in translation is presented not as an opportunity to encounter new literary expression but rather as a means of becoming better acquainted with the Israeli people. It is framed almost as a way to express one's Zionist commitment.

Louis Binstock's review of *Feast of Leviathan*, which appeared in the *Chicago Tribune* in July 1956, seems to indicate that Schwarz knew his readership well. Binstock, rabbi of the Temple Sholom congregation in Chicago, mentions two stories—one from the American section, the other from the Israeli—as the best in the anthology. The other two sections in the anthology, which contain mostly Jewish fables and vignettes of East European shtetl life, receive no notice—further indication of the shifting interests in American Jewish discourse. The universal potential, or appeal, that Binstock ascribes to Israeli nationalism is evident in his description of Jesse Sampter's story in the Israeli section:

> In the other [story], an Israeli girl, about to commit suicide because of frustrated love, throws the poison bottle away when she suddenly catches a vision of a greater love. She cries: "He, too, loves Palestine! In the small land, we work for the same love. . . . O my land, my land! You are myself, my body. Let them plow deep that the seeds may grow." . . . We can all, no matter what our country, our class, our color or creed, gather added strength and wisdom in the assimilation of their moral and ethical and spiritual implications.[71]

Although less sophisticated than the other stories in the Israeli section, and surely much more simplistic than major Hebrew works of the time, Sampter's story is presented to the newspaper readers as the anthology's exemplary piece and, consequently, as that which is a prototype for literature written in Israel. The story's underlying values, which reflect a rather anachronistic treatment of the question of the Zionist project, are presented to the reader as Hebrew literature's "calling card." Like Ramati and Schwartzman, Binstock focuses, above all, on nationalistic traits, but nonetheless depicts these traits as a source of inspiration that is not limited to a confined, particular sense of Jewish identity. The nationalism of Hebrew literature is reframed, and celebrated, as a resource for universal identity, an identity that transcends particularity and can speak to the hearts of all American readers.

Of course, the ostensible universalism of this national identity was highly contingent on contemporary cultural and ideological norms. American attitudes toward Arab nationalism in public and diplomatic discourse, as Michelle Mart shows, was largely patronizing if not overtly hostile; it was described as "false," "blind," and lacking "integrity"—especially when compared with Israeli nationalism.[72] In fact, literary debates on the few works translated from Hebrew that revolved around Mizrahi Jews also implied a cultural hierarchy of East and West. Although not on the same scale as in American postwar approaches to Arab nationalism, the attempt to use literature as a way to forge kinship between the American reader and Israel, particularly by employing familiar American or biblical myths, often disclosed underlying orientalist thought patterns—a hierarchical order of cultivation. This is evident, for instance, in American reviews of Haim Hazaz's novel *Mori Sa'id* (1943; English, 1956). Set against the background of an impoverished neighborhood community in Jerusalem in the World War II years, the novel depicts the lives of three generations of a Yemenite family, focusing on the prophecies and messianic dreams of Mori Sa'id, the grandfather. In his review of the novel in the *New York Times* from April 1956, journalist Hal Lehrman postulates a shared foundation for the Zionist project and early American origins by drawing an analogy between the first Yemenite settlers in Israel and the *Mayflower* pilgrims. According to Lehrman, Hazaz's "tale deals with what might be called the colony of 'Mayflower' Yemenites," who in recent years may have

> acquired sophistication from the radios and washing machines from Europe. [Yet o]therwise they entirely resemble their 40,000 kinsmen who have since descended by miraculous airlift upon the new state—"on eagle's wings" . . . as the Scriptures promised. . . . Of the multitude of Jewish nations who have thronged to Israel, none has excelled in piety and merriment as the colorful little folk from the distant Arab kingdom of Yemen, with their exquisitely chiseled faces, their ardor for the land of

> Abraham, lust for living and unlimited joy of the Lord. The distinguished Israeli novelist Hayim Hazaz has caught their juice and flavor.[73]

Alongside his acceptance of the Zionist ethos as resting on a biblical promise, Lehrman obliquely validates the notion that Americanness and Zionism share common roots. At the same time, he reveals his orientalist, patronizing premises, which attribute physical and sensual superiority but cultural inferiority to the East. Such imagery, when applied in the Israeli context, not only echoed the underlying orientalism in Hebrew literature and culture but was also emblematic of Jewish American letters, and American thought, at the time.[74] The exoticization of the East coincided with American conceptions of a religious hierarchy of West (and the Judeo-Christian tradition) and East (and Islam), and is further evident in Jewish American fiction about Israel.[75] In his December 1958 essay "Literary Renaissance Nurtured in Israel" in the *Los Angeles Times*, critic Alexander Holmes similarly compared the Yemenites to America's first settlers. Holmes hailed Hazaz as "a founding father . . . of the new nationalist literature" and explained that the author "went back to the Yemenites (a tribe sometimes called the 'original Jews') somewhat as an American seeker might try for truth by writing about the distant ancestors of the passengers of the Winthrop fleet."[76] Like Lehrman and Schwarz, Holmes aligned Israel's first days with America's early days, with the Yemenites cast in the role of the Puritan immigrants, led by John Winthrop, who landed on the New England coast in 1630. Holmes's use of *nationalist* as a depiction of Israeli literature, like that among most other cultural agents of his time, carries positive connotations only. In this vein, he describes the national awakening in recent Hebrew literature as "something wonderful, even inevitable," and then tries to frame it, for the benefit of his readers, in American terms:

> Suppose that a talented school of creative young writers perceived with sorrow that the American star was sinking toward tragic eclipse. Further, suppose that these writers, in the surge of productive passion, fathered a renaissance that was stylistically, linguistically and emotionally related to historical documents and persons that had given us greatness in the first place . . . [and] that we had writers to recapture the ancient Anglo-American genius which combined to provide for liberty under law, individualism with social restraint, rights of property whether of cottage or castle, and trial by a jury of peers whether churls or earls.[77]

In attempting to draw the American reader closer to Hebrew literature by likening its sources of inspiration to the letters of America's founding fathers, Holmes in fact creates a primordial affinity between the two national entities. He seems to have no reservations about what he views as the nationalist devotion of literary expression, in contrast to what would often be the case in critics' debates in ensuing decades. On the contrary, he views these years in terms of a literary renaissance precisely because the Israeli authors are reviving the ancient Hebrew texts in the spirit of a new nationalism. As in other contemporary reviews, this view is accompanied by the dramatic portrayal of the Hebrew authors' biographical backgrounds: "men, from their 20s to their 60s, who shared experience in sorrow, danger, excitement," some of whom, Holmes adds with admiration, "were outlaws during the British mandate, desert fighters against Arabs, members of the frontier farm collectives."[78] The image of the fearless, masculine "new Jew" easily dovetails with the celebration of nationalism as a literary theme and resource.

Holmes does not stop here, going so far as to bemoan the lack of nationalist undercurrents in American literature, implying that it has much to learn from Hebrew literature in this regard:

> Contrasts rather than comparisons arise when we look for modern American parallels. Our Lost Generation which followed the holocaust of World War I gave us sorrowing rebels—Hemingway, Dos Passos and others. The combat veterans of World War II have gloried in individual problems under stressful conditions and in promiscuous love-making. But we have not come up with *anything* approaching a school of nationalism that communicates the meaning and future of Americanism, its bloodlines, its creeds, its inmost desires.[79]

Holmes's perception of nationalism may reflect notions of American exceptionalism promoted by historiographical schools of thought in America in the 1950s. It perhaps also mirrors strains of conservative patriotism in postwar American culture, as Cold War tensions intensified and while the effect of victory had not yet waned. More important for our purposes, it emphasizes the differences in how Hebrew literature had been introduced and contextualized in American public discourse through the 1950s. When set against the first decades of the century, Holmes's review effectively demonstrates the transformation that occurred in Hebrew literature's mediation to, and reception by, the American reader. Positing the new generation of authors in Israel as a nationalist literary school worthy of imitation constitutes a striking counterpart to Harold Strauss's univocal dismissal, in his review of Agnon twenty years earlier, of modern Hebrew literature as a "handmaiden to Zionism." In their varying references to Hebrew literature in the 1950s, American critics tended to *celebrate* nationalism as a worthy literary foundation—not to invalidate it as parochial. "The intense spirit of nationalism," words used by historian and literary critic Edmund Fuller in a laudatory 1958 review in the *Chicago Tribune* to describe the source of Israeli novelist Moshe Shamir's literary prowess in *King of Flesh and Blood*, usually carried highly positive connotations.[80]

This transformation resonated, even if only slightly, in changes made in the translations themselves. If in the early 1920s the title of Abraham Mapu's proto-Zionist novel was changed from *Ahavat Zion* to *The Shepherd Prince*, in 1950 the name of David Maletz's novel on kibbutz life was changed from *Ma'agalot* (Circles; the word operates in a very literary register) to *Young Hearts: A Novel of Modern Israel*.[81] Maletz's original lyrical title is rendered melodramatically into a trope of an adventurous, daring nation—resonating with the American mythification of life in Israel. The subtitle frames the novel as a means of becoming acquainted with the State of Israel, suggesting what the publisher assumed to be the readers' expectations from a translated Hebrew novel. Another interference in the translation appears in a segment of the novel regarding an incident related to the 1936–39 Arab Revolt, in which kibbutz members go out to plow virgin land nearby, fully aware that the Arabs from neighboring villages may launch an attack on them. When the protagonist, Menachke, asks to be included among the plowmen going out to the fields, his reasons are described as follows (in this citation and those that follow, phrases omitted in the English translation are added but indicated by ~~strikethrough~~, and material added in the English translation is indicated by [**boldface in brackets**]):

> [He] had brooded so long over his imagined inferiority that now he had to prove his fitness to himself. It was not that he saw this as an opportunity for heroism. His desire was modest—to demonstrate to himself that he could face an enemy ~~on this patch, this land, with his own body and soul~~ [**in defense of this land which he called his mother country**].[82]

The rather restrained notions of the original passage ("this patch," "this land") were substituted in translation with a phrase filled with national pathos. The translation represents Menachke's feelings as more patriotic, his motives as more dramatic, than in the source text. Admittedly, such nationalizing interventions are few, and one cannot infer from them the existence of translation norms or even the systematic practice of a single translator. More than the interventions accumulate to form a distinct feature of 1950s translation practices, they provide us with additional supportive evidence for some of the tendencies we have seen in the reception discourse.

When we view the transformation in American approaches to Hebrew literature in the 1950s in historical perspective, we should consider several compounding trends in the target culture. Although the importance of international Jewish kinship should not be diminished, these were not only years in which feelings of affinity toward Israel intensified among the American Jewish community. For American Jews, this was also a time of social and economic prosperity, of increasing migration from urban neighborhoods to suburbs, and of visible integration into the American public sphere. Sociologist William Herberg's influential *Protestant, Catholic, Jew* (1955), which anchored the understanding of midcentury American religion in ethnic terms, came to symbolize Judaism's status as an "equal among equals" among the major religions in America, and the successful assimilation of Jews into mainstream American society. The unparalleled surge in synagogue construction in the public domain, the establishment of Jewish-sponsored Brandeis University, and the meteoric ascent of Jewish American literature in the national sphere are only a few examples of the efforts—and growing success—of Jews to integrate into American society without relinquishing the particular contours of their identity. New patterns of mediation of translated Hebrew works in American Jewish discourse should be read in light of these social changes. The predominantly national framework projected on Hebrew literature, and the linking of the young State of Israel with America's early history, reflected the needs and wishes of the target-culture audience. As Jews felt increasingly at home in America, Hebrew literature, framed as an emblem of Israeli nationalism, served as both a resource to preserve their distinct Jewish identity and as a legitimate way to establish their full belonging to an American national identity.

The understanding and framing of Hebrew literature through a largely nationalist prism did not, therefore, offer a model of isolationist Jewish identity. The ideological underpinnings of its critical reception in this decade rather echoed the Zionism of American thinkers such as Louis Brandeis, Horace Kallen, and Mordecai Kaplan, who saw identification with Jewish nationalism in Palestine (and Israel) as a source of inspiration for Jewish acculturation in America and a proud contribution to a multicultural, pluralistic American society.[83] The polemics of early spiritual Zionist Israel Friedlaender in defense of this conception seem to perfectly anticipate the framing of modern Hebrew writers through the American Jewish lens of the 1950s, even though Friedlaender had originally referenced the biblical prophets, endorsing them as "both universalists and nationalists, believing in the realization of the universal idea through the channel of national existence"; or, as historian Arthur Goren would summarize this Brandeisian form of Jewish nationalism, "identify[ing] Zionism with Americanism."[84] As Emily Katz has demonstrated for the postwar American Jewish absorption of Israeli music, art, and folk dance and Matthew Silver for the reception and influence of Leon Uris's *Exodus*, agents of Hebrew literature in America in the 1950s also aspired to draw their readership closer to Israel by positing American national myths as common to both nations and by drawing similarities between contemporary Israeli reality and historical American narratives and themes. Breaking with the trend of previous decades, Hebrew literature transferred to American culture in the 1950s without shedding its national preoccupations, as Jewish American critics nurtured, and even amplified, a nationalist discourse.

In the late 1950s and early 1960s, the literary discourse began gradually to change. In line with shifting perspectives in American public and intellectual discourse, more doubtful and critical voices were heard that did not endorse the idea of a literature that draws its strength from nationalism. The identification and lauding of nationalist qualities in Hebrew literature became rarer. As we will see in the next chapter, the ensuing decades saw dominant voices on the American scene celebrate Israeli writers mainly for *subverting* accepted conventions of the Zionist narrative. This change of approach was stimulated by the translation of new Israeli writers who dealt in more critical fashion than their predecessors with the charged ideological issues of the time. It may particularly have arisen from, and responded to, the publication of translated Hebrew works that undermined the image of a moral Israel, above all in the context of the ongoing Israeli–Arab conflict. Boosted by the rise of influential new critics of Israeli letters on the American scene, such as Robert Alter, who had published a number of pioneering reviews in *Commentary*, this shift was also increasingly felt in mainstream American outlets such as the *New York Times*.

Nevertheless, even as the American Jewish framing of Israeli works shifted significantly from the 1950s through the 1960s and 1970s, the fundamental premise that crystallized during the earlier years remained the same: the "Israeliness" reflected in Hebrew literature continued to be seen as bearing on Jewish American identity. In the ensuing decades, this would manifest in various ways and would often require a subtler, and at times entirely different, mediation than that found in the reception trends of Hebrew literature in the early postwar years. However, alongside the constant growth in the volume of translation, these new forms of mediation continued to reflect the deep relevance of Hebrew literature, in the eyes of its American agents and reading audience, for American Jewish self-understanding and self-perception. Along the line stretching from Lask's apologetic words in 1937, lamenting American readers' ignorance of the very existence of modern Hebrew literature, to Alter's upbeat 1991 remark on the unprecedented success of translated Hebrew literature in America, the national context has continued to provide a most necessary point of reference for understanding the intellectual dialogue between the two Jewish communities embedded in translation.

2

Ethical Conundrums

In his review of the anthology *A Whole Loaf* in the *New York Times* in January 1962, literary scholar and founding member of Brandeis University Milton Hindus expressed his appreciation for the volume's "unbiased and objective" Israeli writing, particularly praising one of the stories for refraining from "siding with or against [the characters] in the manner of a propagandist."[1] That same year, Robert Alter lauded young Israeli writers in his introduction to the anthology *Israeli Stories* for "[their] integrity and [their] firmness of resolution" to produce admirably independent prose under the harsh national circumstances of a "new state surrounded by enemies."[2] Although this may not have been such a revelation for the Israeli readership of the early 1960s, in American debates on Hebrew literature at the time it was seen as something worth noting—and commending. Hindus and Alter's perspective represented a shift in the dominant values in American Jewish literary discourse from previous years. It also reflected a change in the type of writing that the local reader began to encounter, as the repertoire of Hebrew literature in English translation continued the gradual trend that had begun in the previous decade, to mirror the repertoire of Hebrew literature in real time. In a deeper sense, this trend provided the opportunity for a more meaningful acquaintance of American Jews with contemporary Israeli thought on burning questions of Israeli ethics and morality. Gradually, from the 1960s onward, the books translated from Hebrew testified more clearly to the manner in which Israelis perceived and portrayed themselves and represented for themselves the tense reality in which they lived—not the least with regard to Israeli ethics vis-à-vis its

Arab Others. The American readership was given the opportunity, often unavailable in other places, to be exposed to the manner in which Israel imagined itself, its national complexities and hardships.

This chapter seeks to explore the encounter between the Jewish American discourse and these products of literary imagination. By and large, Israeli titles in English were published during these years by respectable publishing houses and mostly received positive reviews in prominent outlets. The elevated standing of Hebrew literature in translation, and the relatively high visibility that accompanied it, infused local audiences' encounters with the works with additional social significance. However, a fundamental difficulty lay at the heart of this juncture. At times, literary representations of Israel diverged greatly from the prevalent Jewish American imagery of Israel at the time. As historian David Myers points out, the American Jewish community was not usually inclined to critique Israeli moral conduct, particularly in the context of the ongoing Arab–Israeli conflict.[3] However, it is precisely in this context that some of the translated works included uneasy representations of Israeli morals and ethics. At times highly critical, these portrayals posed a challenge to agents of Hebrew literature in the Jewish American discourse, one that may have surpassed cultural or linguistic challenges inherent in the translation. These agents were, by and large, part of the Jewish target audience and well acquainted with the communal consensus. Still, they differed from it in one decisive aspect: they were faced with the opportunity—in the eyes of some, the responsibility—to reconcile these same critical representations for other readers. This was a challenge many were inclined to tackle. The ways in which they chose to mediate the works to their audiences lie at the heart of this chapter.

In what follows, I argue that there are two notable patterns, or discursive strata, in the way cultural agents coped with representations that undermined the image of a moral Israel. These two patterns existed side by side and, at times, were intermingled with one another; yet, on the face of it, they appear largely to disagree. The first pattern, the more overt of the two, created a dominant context for readers to evaluate and understand Hebrew literature by attributing to it a morally critical, humanistic image. In short, American agents of Hebrew literature portrayed its most indicative features, and its choice of representation of Israeli reality, as the ethical expression of moral opposition. Often evident in observations and generalizations on Israeli literature as a collective corpus, this pattern presented Israeli writers as the dissenting voice of the humanistic Left in the country.

The second coping pattern was more covert and subtle, its expressions sometimes hidden within the very same texts that constitute the first pattern. This approach, found primarily in the translation and interpretation of specific works, stood in contradistinction to the images and characteristics attributed to Hebrew literature through the first stratum of mediation. Here, agents sought to soften and blur precisely those literary elements that expressed moral criticism and were celebrated in the American literary discourse as expressions of Israeli moral reflection. Often obscured from sight and unavailable for scrutiny, such propagandistic principles were expressed in the choice of texts for translation, interpretive inclinations in literary reviews, the formulation of editorial commentary, and modifications and omissions in the translations themselves. I would argue that these two patterns, which appear at first glance to be pulling in opposite directions, in truth complemented each other. Together, they enabled Hebrew literature, and Israel as represented in it, to fulfill the central role assigned to it in a contemporary American Jewish identity. The story of Hebrew literature's incorporation into American culture, for quite some decades, was inseparable from the desirable image of Israel sought by American Jews for their internal needs.

Recent scholarship on the reception of Hebrew literature in America may be a useful entrance point into the subdiscourse of the first coping pattern, which remains a dominant framework for understanding this literature's appeal on American shores. Although scholars may be divided on a variety of issues, one metatranslational assumption raises no controversy: any success Hebrew literature had with its Jewish American audience was firmly linked to the relinquishing of the ideological constraints to which previous generations had been bound and to its evolving in the 1960s into a more critical literature. "Hebrew literature in translation began to reach American Jewish readers and make any serious contribution it has made," Gershon Shaked claimed, "only from the 1960s onward, when a new generation began to take over the literary stage."[4] Shaked distinguished between writers of the so-called Palmach generation, who played an active role in the struggle for the establishment of the state and whose literature was bound to the Zionist cause, and the younger generation, led by Amos Oz and A. B. Yehoshua, often dubbed "the generation of the state," who strongly rejected their predecessors' stylistic and ideological principles. In Shaked's view, this generation's undermining of the ethos of redemption in the land of Israel, and its demonstration that "the norms of the 'new Hebrew' were a false front," accounted for the works' relevance for the Jewish American reader. In his entry on modern Hebrew literature in *The Oxford Guide to Literature in English Translation* (2000), Nicholas De Lange, literary scholar and Amos Oz's longtime translator, seems to echo this stance by pointing to the success among English readers of Hebrew poets who are "[the] furthest from the somewhat parochial concerns of the Zionist milieu."[5] In a similar vein, both Robert Alter and Alan Mintz have found the literary achievements of the Palmach generation limited due to this generation's indebtedness to the socialist-positivistic ideology of the time.[6] By contrast, "the explosion of literary talent"[7] of the 1970s and 1980s constituted a peak in Hebrew writing unprecedented "since the time of the Bible and ancient liturgical poets"[8]—literary excellence that had led, in their view, to a surge in English translations. Thus it is implied that the shedding of the ideological constraints of the past fueled the expansion of Hebrew literature's translation into English.[9]

This link between the dissenting voice of Hebrew literature from the 1960s and 1970s and its relevance for the American reader was in fact acknowledged much earlier and outside the academic milieu. Contemporaneously with the emergence of this new literature, influential agents in the American literary field introduced Israeli literature's moral criticism as a core feature that rendered it worthy of translation. The ethical underpinnings of Israeli works were framed in terms of the age-old Jewish literary tradition of bold and unyielding social critique, epitomizing "Jewish morality." In his preface to the anthology *Israeli Stories* (1962), editor Joel Blocker acknowledged that the absence of a "narrowly partisan . . . tough minded ideology"[10] in the stories was a primary consideration for their selection for translation. Regardless of the politicization of Israeli literature, "there is a great deal more to contemporary Israeli writing than mere ideological posturing," Blocker argued, adding, in metatranslational fashion, that it was precisely such works that the anthology sought to offer its readers.[11] In his introduction to the anthology, Robert Alter used ethical terms to describe what he perceived as the new writers' unwillingness to accommodate the nationalistic blueprint:

> If one considers the circumstances in which a young Israeli writes, one must admire his integrity and his firmness of resolution. In a new state surrounded by enemies, compelled to keep up a large military establishment, one might expect the literary output to be marred by frequent displays of well-meaning patriotism or misguided chauvinism.[12]

Alter not only pointed to the fact that the works dealt with moral issues and reflected moral values but also highlighted the very act of *writing* these works within such a complex historical moment as a reflection of a deeply embedded moral code. This morality associated with Hebrew literature was sometimes referred to as a quintessential embodiment of "Jewish character," presumably as a way to bring the translated Israeli works closer to home. In his introduction to the anthology *A Whole Loaf* (1957), editor Sholom Kahn identified three fundamentally "Jewish" traits as basic characteristics of the new Hebrew literature: humor, emotional sensitivity, and conscience, with the latter, realized in "the probings of conscience—in relation to God and one's own self and one's fellow-man and ideals of society," being the most conspicuous of the three.[13] In line with the typical discourse surrounding national anthologies, in newspaper reviews and editors' introductions alike, Kahn looked to the selected texts to draw generalizations about Israeli society. "One of the heartening outcomes of reading these selections," he wrote, "is the picture one gets of Israel's younger generation, in particular, as maintaining the age-old traditions of self-criticism and spiritual search."[14] This identification of "Jewish morality" with Israeli works was perhaps most pronounced in the case of literary accounts that seemed to articulate a nonviolent, forbearing attitude toward Israel's national Others. A case in point is Henry W. Levy's January 1968 review in the *Baltimore Sun* of Hanoch Bartov's novel *The Brigade*. Recounting the journey of a company of Jewish British Brigade soldiers through defeated Nazi Germany at the end of World War II, the novel focuses on Elisha, who not only resists the temptation for revenge against the Nazis but also persuades his comrades to do the same. For Levy, Elisha represents an "unquestionably pure Judaism in its highest moral stance."[15] Similarly, in his 1975 reading of S. Yizhar's "The Prisoner"—an unflinching portrayal of an Israeli platoon's violent harassment and imprisonment of an Arab shepherd during Israel's War of Independence—Robert Alter associated the story's ideological underpinnings, its unreserved moral critique, with Jewish moral values rooted in "the historical memory of the Jewish people."[16]

This emphasis on morality as a cornerstone of Hebrew writing often implied that this literature served as a "truth detector" of sorts. The new generation of writers was seen as providing a porthole through which to view the genuine Israeli reality, a key to Israeli existence as it really was. In his January 1962 review of Kahn's anthology, Thomas Lask of the *New York Times* felt obligated to inform his readers that they would "not find in these tales facile heroics, or hymns to pioneering hardships. No monuments are erected; no scrolls inscribed." He went on to praise the stories for dealing primarily with "the human situation . . . and human personality."[17] This review calls attention to what some American readers may have expected to encounter in literature about Israel—deep dedication to the national cause—precisely by putting these expectations to rest. In this vein, voices in the metatranslational and critical discourse attributed the works' merit to their ability to penetrate Israeli reality and show its true colors. Praising Yehudit Hendel's *The Street of Steps* in December 1963, Rinna Samuel typically wrote: "*The Street of Steps* won't take you into the slick palatable fantasyland of *Exodus*, but it will bring you smack into the very midst of the people who, in the final analysis, hold the future of Israel in their uncertain hands. . . . Hendel has not sidestepped a single puddle nor averted her gaze from any unattractive aspect of her country today."[18] Reading Hebrew literature in translation was in fact sometimes evoked as the best, if not the only, way to balance the superficiality both of news coverage of Israel and of American best-sellers about Israel and was presented as a more profound source of knowledge about life in Israel. The literary works were credited with what Alan Mintz later called a "truth-telling capacity": the ability to reveal some hidden truth—however obscure it might be—about Israel. "When journalism falters and diplomacy fails," literary scholar and historian Morris Dickstein concluded succinctly in 1978, "fiction sometimes rushes in to tell us what we want to know."[19] Depictions of Hebrew literature as a morally critical corpus thus often implied a linkage between moral opposition and a proclivity to portray the *true* Israeli existence; although sometimes appearing independently, for the most part these discursive tendencies were fused and even derived from one another in a causal relationship.

This linkage strengthened in the years following the Six Day War, particularly with the first translations of works by Oz and Yehoshua, as the moral aspect attributed to Hebrew literature acquired a distinctive political undertone. Prominent voices in the American literary and journalistic discourse called attention to the affinity between Oz and Yehoshua and their works and the political Left in Israel. The ethical preoccupations of Hebrew literature were now predominantly described in terms of what they expressed vis-à-vis the Israeli–Arab conflict, the occupation, and Palestinian refugees. Taking a supportive, often admiring tone, these voices highlighted both the undermining of the national ethos and empathy for the Arab Other as standard motifs in contemporary Hebrew literature as a whole. In an essay written in December 1970 for the progressive weekly *The Nation*, following a visit to Israel, Jewish American poet Macha Louis Rosenthal aligned the rise of the Israeli Left with the generation of young authors, but at the same time implicitly assumed a tendency toward subversion and criticism in modern Hebrew literature in its entirety. Rosenthal expressed sympathy for the young authors' public activity and inclination toward "dovish" compromises and, while suggestively mocking Haim Gouri, a member of the older generation, for his "idealistic patriotism," also marked with appreciation the skeptical attitude toward the Zionist metanarrative in Gouri's novel *The Chocolate Deal*.[20]

Outside the literary milieu, articles dealing with Israeli politics and culture marked the new Israeli authors, led by Oz, as the principal voices challenging the institutional hegemony. Meyer Levin's August 1977 review in the *New York Times* of Howard Sachar's *A History of Israel* epitomizes how writers on all matters pertaining to Israel cited these authors: Levin described Sachar's political position as "closest to the socially critical Israeli authors, such as Aharon Megged, Amos Kenan, Yizhar Smilansky, Amos Oz, Avraham Yehoshua, Amos Elon, all of whom illuminate certain strains of guilt toward displaced Arabs."[21] The implied premise that American readers would be more familiar with these authors than with a roster of political figures demonstrates the extent to which Hebrew literature and the Israeli Left were intertwined within the journalistic discourse on all levels, including mundane news items in which authors were identified as spokespersons for the political opposition in Israeli society. Thus, in a kind of self-nurturing pattern, the mention of Hebrew literature in political sections, interviews, news items, and the like guaranteed that the connection between the writers and the Left would catch readers' attention.

Although rooted in American public discourse, the affiliation between Hebrew literature and the Israeli Left was not generated exclusively by the Americans. In the early 1970s, for instance, the *New York Times* provided a platform for left-wing Israelis, including Amnon Rubinstein, a future member of the Knesset from the progressive Meretz Party, and author and *Haaretz* journalist Amos Elon. Associating the recent revival of leftist critique with the writers of the "generation of the state," Rubinstein asserted that "the deepest and most significant expression of dissent is to be found not in the mass media, but in contemporary Israeli literature. There one can find the most stirring, controversial and soul-searching words written on the Arab-Jewish conflict."[22] Rubinstein argued, albeit with an irrefutable bent toward exaggeration, that "the young generation of authors, has, almost without exception, expressed empathy for the Arab side which comes as a shock to the uninitiated," and he went on to conclude that "national values as such have virtually disappeared from the literature. . . . [T]he feeling of guilt toward the Arab is the theme which dominates the latest Israeli literature."[23] Three years later, on Israel's twenty-fifth anniversary, Amos Elon published an article on the cultural climate in Israel in which he argued that Hebrew literature was in fact unique in comparison to other national literatures due to its deeply embedded moral-humanist imperative. Drawing on the theme of guilt toward the Arabs, Elon wrote: "Far from resembling the literature of the other national cultures in the spring of their nationality, the novels and dramas of the past six or seven years are sadder, more politically skeptical, ambivalent and anguished than one could ever imagine."[24] Canadian-Israeli journalist and political scientist Bernard Avishai expressed comparable notions in his piece in *Vogue* from May 1979. Assuming that the authors' political orientation and attitudes toward the issue of the occupied territories not only pertained to their literary oeuvre but also were highly relevant to the American readership, Avishai demonstrated a similar propensity for generalization by stating that "almost every artist and writer in the country's fresh, secular culture is a dove of varying intensity, anxious to exchange land for peace and to settle with the Palestinians on the basis of mutual recognition."[25]

These and other voices in the literary discourse attributed to contemporary Hebrew works the moral capacity to expose the reader to the troubled complexity of Israeli history and reality. However, many did not rely on this point alone in their reviews, ascribing a third powerful quality to the translated literature: the ability to reveal the *collective* Israeli psyche and its hidden complexes. By identifying tropes of a national or political nature in the literary works, and marking them as figurative representations of the Israeli subconscious, these agents framed Hebrew literature as a window into the Israeli mentality. Various reviews of Oz's *My Michael*, for instance, noted its ability to illuminate the "national psyche," "the Israeli consciousness," and "a nation's private soul," among others. In fact, reviews skeptical of such readings also attested to their pervasiveness, as in a *New York Times* article from May 1978, in which Morris Dickstein argued that allegorical readings of Oz's heroine were unconvincing, yet by doing so implied that she was indeed meant to serve as a collective symbol to begin with; Dickstein had to assume that an attempt at national symbolism had been made in order to describe its failure.[26] America's reception of Oz, who has since become Israel's most translated author and an internationally acclaimed figure, seems to have been instrumental in creating Hebrew literature's moral, oppositional image. As in major literary markets, in which canonical authors of minor literatures are represented as agents of, or defining, their national literature, in the American market Oz's works were often perceived as representing Hebrew literature and he himself as a metonym for Hebrew literature.

Literary critiques, news items, pieces on the cultural zeitgeist, and commentaries in national anthologies thus combined to create one of the dominant patterns in the introduction of Hebrew literature to the American Jewish reader. At times, the moral issue framed the polemic on, and interpretation of, translated Hebrew works; it was represented in the American discourse as a challenge facing Israeli literature, which the Israeli authors successfully overcame. Given its canonical writers' dynamic participation in the public discourse, this image of Hebrew literature seemed to become widespread even outside the literary world. This is not to suggest that an alternative perception of Israeli works did not exist or that this was the only prism through which translated Israeli literature was presented to American readers. Indeed, several cases strayed from, and even contradicted, this pattern. For instance, in a January 1974 *New York Times* article, author and journalist Naomi Shepherd alluded to Hebrew literature as evidence of Israel's blindness toward Arabs. A writer of historical monographs on Israel, Shepherd referred to representations of Arabs in Hebrew literature as a symptom both of flaws in Israel's strategic thinking and of the defective morality ingrained in Israeli society.[27] In his review of the anthology *Firstfruits* in September 1973, Arthur A. Cohen claimed that the translated works reflected positions that were anything but oppositional, describing them as conformist and nationalist (though he laid the blame for this on the expectations of the American Jewish audience as well).[28] Still, these were exceptions rather than the rule. By and large, Hebrew literature and the Israeliness it depicted were portrayed in the mainstream journalistic discourse in America as distinctively humanistic and self-critical. Although Israel and its policy in the West Bank were found to be deserving of criticism, critiques tended to focus on the writers themselves, recognizing them for their political boldness, rather than on the problematic situation these writers' criticisms evoked. More often than not, reviewers expressed appreciation for Israel as a country fortunate to have such dissenting, ethical voices to take pride in. As Israeli society's virtual envoy to American readers,

Hebrew literature was thus assigned a representative function: the ways in which it dealt with ethically questionable conduct were infused with collective significance and seen as an emblem of the moral tendencies of Israeli intellectual thought as a whole.

The Propagandistic Trend

Not every ideologically charged issue in the source literature constitutes an identical challenge for the target culture. Representations of sexuality and eroticism in canonical Hebrew literature, for example, were largely restrained, surely far more restrained than those in works by Jewish American authors, and did not seem to pose a great challenge to American Jewish cultural conventions. Comparing Israeli writers' relative puritanism with works by their American counterparts, a reviewer of an Israeli anthology in translation published in 1969—at the time of the scandal surrounding Philip Roth's *Portnoy's Complaint*—drily noted: "It is difficult to imagine a collection of current American short stories with only a few sex scenes—and those understated."[29] Depictions of Israel's moral failings and wrongdoings, however, seemed to present Jewish American readers with a greater challenge. In reference to the plight of Palestinian refugees, which may be extended to other thorny issues of Israeli political and historical ethics, David Myers writes that "misinformation and denial . . . have been more pronounced in the Diaspora [than in Israel]," adding, "Conformity was and remains a prominent value among Diaspora supporters of the State of Israel."[30] A useful backdrop to the encounter of American Jewish discourse with literary portrayals that undermined the image of a moral Israel, this statement provides us with a broad social context for understanding how the discursive pattern outlined in the previous section occasionally stood in contradiction to the ways in which specific Hebrew works were mediated to their American readers.

In what follows, I will demonstrate a pattern of protective mediation whereby translators, editors, journalists, and literary critics moderated the American reception of Israeli literature. Subtly, sometimes furtively, the mediating discourse refashioned and appropriated subversive aspects of Hebrew works, at times even in the very same introductions and reviews mentioned earlier. Through the 1960s, 1970s, and to some extent the 1980s, the moral image of Israeli society, as well as the moral reckonings of the Israeli historical narrative, were appropriated and tempered. The source literature may have been celebrated in the literary discourse as daringly critical and humanistic, but parts of this criticism and humanism were left by the wayside en route to the American audience.

Let us start our discussion of American Jewish mediation patterns by exploring a prototypical character that has been, time and again, charged with symbolic meaning in Israeli cultural and literary discourse—the combat soldier. From the very beginnings of Israeli culture, representations of the soldier's conduct in literature and film were seen as constituting a benchmark for the society as a whole. His own morality symbolized, for better or for worse, the morality of the collective. Likewise, in American literature and culture, and certainly in American Jewish circles, the combat soldier epitomized Israeliness. Ari Ben-Canaan, the protagonist in Leon Uris's best-seller *Exodus*—his film counterpart played by Paul Newman—is but one well-known example. Images of tough, disciplined Israeli soldiers abounded in popular nonfiction books about Israel, as well as in contemporary issues of *Time*, *Life*, and the *Saturday Evening Post*, among others.[31]

Extending beyond the individual soldier, this linkage rendered the Israeli military a metonym for Israeli society as a whole and was therefore particularly significant in the mediation of Hebrew literature for American audiences. The national anthology *Firstfruits* is an effective example. Published on the occasion of the twenty-fifth anniversary of the State of Israel by the Jewish Publication Society of America, the anthology was, in the words of author and chief editor of the publishing house Chaim Potok, "our gift to the new land on its twenty-fifth birthday."[32] Inflected with this celebratory tone, the introduction by Pulitzer Prize winner and American author James Michener included a section on the Israeli army, which he referred to as a moral yardstick for the Israeli people: "Israel used the necessity of its army as a heaven-sent excuse to educate its young people to a higher standard than they might otherwise have attained. This is one of the brightest successes of Israel's first twenty-five years, and one least appreciated in the outside world."[33] Referring to the military service of authors included in the anthology, Michener in effect created a link between the Israeli author and the image of the combat soldier: "I was struck by the number of writers in this anthology who had some of their education in uniform. I doubt if they liked it at the time, but the system of which they were part seems to me the finest in the world, a prime example of converting necessity to virtue."[34] In light of the representative role assigned to the Israeli soldier in American popular discourse, Michener's attribution of high moral values to the Israeli army—assuming in fact that military service transforms Israelis into better people—carries a broad significance: its morality implies the morality of the collective.

The connection between the representation of soldiers and warfare and issues of collective morality was perhaps most salient in the major protest stories of Hebrew literature. The military incidents and contexts depicted in these stories were often seen as trenchant commentary on hegemonic narratives of Israeli history and ethics. This subversive stance renders their mediation to the Jewish American audience all the more revealing. Let us look, for instance, at S. Yizhar's "Khirbet Khizeh" and "The Prisoner," both published in Hebrew in 1949. These two stories, particularly "Khirbet Khizeh," are perhaps the most painfully self-critical and poignant stories about the Israeli–Palestinian conflict and the results of Israel's War of Independence in 1948. "The Prisoner" describes Israeli soldiers who capture an innocent Arab shepherd, steal his livestock, beat him, and then, presumably, pack him off to jail—or worse. The more important and controversial "Khirbet Khizeh" describes the expulsion of Palestinians from their village by an Israeli detachment during the War of Independence. Yizhar depicts the Palestinians as authentic dwellers in the land and pins their expulsion on an immoral Israeli policy based on disingenuous national rhetoric.

Awarded the Israel Prize in Literature in 1959, Yizhar was arguably the most prominent writer of his generation. Apart from the novel *The Days of Ziklag*, "Khirbet Khizeh" and "The Prisoner" are his best-known works and surely his most widely read. Despite, or perhaps due to, the controversy they caused, these two stories "have come to occupy an exceptional, almost mythical place in the Israeli literary canon."[35] But regardless of its seminal importance in the history of Hebrew literature, "Khirbet Khizeh" was not translated into English until 2008; it was passed over for six decades following its publication in 1948—decades of significant growth in the translation of Hebrew literature, including the publication of various literary anthologies containing far less influential works. Especially conspicuous is the story's absence from the first collection of Yizhar's stories, *Midnight Convoy and Other Stories*, published in 1969 by the Institute for the Translation of Hebrew Literature.[36] In addition to "Khirbet Khizeh," Yizhar's "The Prisoner" was also excluded from this collection, although it did appear in English in the 1962 anthology *Israeli Stories* and later in two other anthologies of Hebrew literature published in America. Given that factors such as commercial considerations and linguistic challenges did not prevent the translation of other stylistically demanding, less marketable Hebrew stories for the American reader, the causes for the prolonged abstention from translating "Khirbet Khizeh" can be traced to the particularities of its subversive ideological underpinnings. Unlike "The Prisoner," the events in "Khirbet Khizeh" directly touch on what is still one of the most charged issues in the conflict's historiography and politics—namely, Israel's responsibility for the expulsion of Palestinians from their villages in 1948. Over the years, this volatile topic became a near taboo in mainstream Israeli public discourse and among American Jews as well.[37] This may be why the translation of "Khirbet Khizeh" constituted, as we will see shortly, something of an exception in terms of its decades-long "filtering" already at the publishing stage, if an important exception worth discussing.

The ways in which American readers may nonetheless have heard of "Khirbet Khizeh" are indicative of the gap between the construction of Hebrew literature's image in the American discourse as morally critical and the protective mediation of the works themselves for the American audience. In 1978, following Israeli censorship of the story's film adaptation and the ensuing public outcry, the American press covered the story outside literary supplements. Thus American readers encountered recaps of the story's controversial content in the *Washington Post*, *New York Times*, and *Chicago Tribune*[38] and became aware of its critique of Israel's moral ethos and the Israeli public's outrage over its censorship. The story itself, however, could not be read, as it had not yet been translated. Another revealing instance involves mention of the story in an article by Levi Gertned about Yizhar, published in the *Jewish Advocate* as early as 1957. Gertned, who described Yizhar as the literary moral compass of his generation, also provided a brief recap of the story. In this recap, Gertned avoided using the word *Arab*, instead choosing "the enemy" and "[the enemy] of the people."[39] Such denationalizing and dehistoricizing measures—presumably meant to cloud the backdrop of the Israeli–Arab conflict and obfuscate the story's pertinent national context—undermine Yizhar's major themes and, to some degree, eclipse the story's purpose and potency.

Even as late as 2008, when the story finally appeared in English translation—some forty years after Yizhar's first collection of stories was published in English and sixty years after "Khirbet Khizeh" was first published in Hebrew—its publication was a politically charged act. One of the more important translations from Hebrew literature in the past few decades, it was published by the Jerusalem-based nonprofit Ibis Editions, in Nicholas de Lange and Yaacob Dweck's English translation, and was distributed in the United States and widely reviewed in the American press. Noting explicitly that the content of the works they select for publication makes it hard for them to receive funding, the publishers express their goals in plain ideological terms: "to build bridges of various sorts, between Arabs and Jews, the communal and the personal, America and the Middle East, and more."[40] Interestingly, even in a translation that represents moral reckoning, and aims at, indeed performs, a discursive act of dissidence, some omissions occurred in the translation; here, in the story's climactic ending, the nameless narrator witnesses the restrained agony and anger of a Palestinian woman and her child as they are uprooted from their homes:

> Everything seemed to mean something different, more precisely: exile. This was exile. This was what exile was like. This was what exile looked like. ~~We brought exile upon them~~. I couldn't stay where I was. The place itself couldn't bear me. . . . I had never been in the Diaspora—I said to myself—I had never known what it was like. But people had spoken to me, told me, taught me, and repeatedly recited to me, from every direction, in books and newspapers, everywhere: exile. They had played on all my nerves. Our nation's protest to the world: exile! It had entered me, apparently, with my mother's milk. What, in fact, had we perpetrated here? ~~We, Jews, had created an exile.~~ There was nowhere to wander or distance myself.[41]

Although the story was otherwise faithfully translated and its depictions of Israeli forcefulness retained, the two omissions somewhat subdue the narrator's explicit assertions of *collective* Jewish-Israeli blame for Palestinian exile. These omissions notwithstanding, the text's powerful account of these grim aspects of Israel's War of Independence was largely retained—as indeed acknowledged and further elaborated in the American reception of the work in varied essays and reviews.[42] Also worth noting is the very political afterword to the translation, written by Israeli professor of Indian Studies and peace activist David Shulman, in which the Israeli activist speaks of the relevance of Yizhar's story to our time. Shulman describes taking part in human rights activities in the West Bank and draws a direct parallel from the story to the present day and Israel's current occupation. He concludes on a personal note, stating that the next time he demonstrates with the villagers, "maybe I'll make [a sign] for myself: 'No More Khirbet Khizehs.'"[43] The cause that kept publishers from translating

Yizhar's story into English for six decades seems to be the same reason that led Ibis Editions finally to do so in 2008.[44]

This is not to say that Israeli portrayals of dubious, morally flawed conduct did not appear in English from the 1960s onward. The lack of a translation of "Khirbet Khizeh," as mentioned earlier, was more an exception than the rule in terms of its "filtering" in the publishing stage. Alongside works that embodied the hegemonic national narrative—such as popular accounts of the Six Day War that tended to attribute mental pain and moral superiority to the victors rather than the victims, or nostalgic historical novels about the British Mandate that portrayed Arabs as cruel and culturally inferior[45]—important critical works were made available to the American audience. First anthologized in English in 1957 (and again in 1969), Nathan Shaham's story "The Seven" portrays the moral and mental collapse of a platoon of soldiers whose mission is to hold an army post surrounded by undetected land mines.[46] As fear of detonation spirals, the soldiers send two Arab prisoners running around the post to detonate the mines, finally shooting one in the back as the second hits a mine. Aharon Megged's surrealist social satire *Fortunes of a Fool*, published in English in 1962, depicts social reality in Israel as governed by bureaucracy and aggression.[47] The novel's principal chapter, "White City," deals with Gaza's occupation during the Kadesh campaign in 1956 by focusing on the anonymous narrator's refusal to kill a young Arab in the harsh context of the population's suffering under the Israeli soldiers' callous hostility. As a testament to the chapter's import, it was selected for an anthology of short stories published in English in 1965 by the Institute for the Translation of Hebrew Literature in Israel.[48] The depiction of contemporary Israeli life and values is no less ambivalent in Yoram Kaniuk's novel *The Acrophile*, published in English in 1961.[49] The story of an Israeli living in New York and struggling to adapt to American life, *The Acrophile* delves into the details of the protagonist's compulsive guilt over accidently killing an Arab child as a soldier during the War of Independence. Within the Israeli literary discourse, this tormenting sense of guilt not only was understood as motivating the protagonist to leave Israel but for some also represented a subversive attitude toward the fundamental Zionist principle of the moral claim to the land.

In the early 1970s, American readers could also encounter A. B. Yehoshua's and Amos Oz's important early works, which presented characters pathologically afflicted by a nagging sense of individual guilt over acts of aggression taken for the national cause. This guilt was largely associated with the abrupt historical transition of the Jewish collective in Eretz-Israel from a society in a mode of self-defense to a sovereign state that, in its struggle for independence, banished part of the Arab population. Anchored in the framework of the complex relationship between Arabs and Jews, Oz's and Yehoshua's works revolve around the perverse pathologies of their Jewish protagonists: a forest ranger's desire to set fire to a Keren Kayemet forest planted on the ruins of an Arab village in Yehoshua's "Facing the Forests"; a young kibbutz woman's fantasy of being raped by a Bedouin in Oz's "Nomad and Viper"; and Hannah Gonen's often-cited fantasies of sadomasochistic sexual encounters with Arab twins and the devastating terrorist attacks on Israeli targets in Oz's *My Michael*.[50] Although these works do not deal with the Palestinian calamity directly and do not bear the historical significance of a work like "Khirbet Khizeh," they express, in Avner Holzman's words, "an alienated, critical attitude toward the foundations and fixtures of the Zionist project"[51] and as such reverberated throughout the Israeli public discourse.

Although Yizhar's "Khirbet Khizeh" and a few other incisive stories about Israel's combat morality were not selected for translation, these works by Kaniuk, Megged, Yehoshua, and Oz presented Jewish American readers with a reality that was far more ambiguous and complex than that which they had encountered until then in the mainstream American press, commercial best-sellers, or even nonfiction books on Israel. The American reader could otherwise hardly encounter novels and stories that engaged with the moral implications of the Zionist metanarrative as a central theme and treated it so critically. However, an examination of the ways in which critical aspects in Israeli works were mediated to the American readership may curtail the impression of bold dissent arising from the decision to translate them. As it turns out, the Jewish American cultural discourse was not as open to a critical image of Israeliness as it had perhaps initially seemed.[52]

In what follows, I provide examples of a protective tendency that underpinned the enterprise of mediating the Hebrew works and the portrayals of the Israeli military that they offered. I begin with ideological manipulations of the translations themselves. These pertained mostly to descriptions of violence perpetrated against Arabs by Israeli protagonists—mainly by soldiers but also by pioneers and educators, Israeli figures expected to be exemplary in their conduct. I have identified these interferences through comparison of the translations of Hebrew fiction published in America with the original works, implementing a close reading of the texts while focusing on ideological issues rather than stylistic or aesthetic ones. Of course, just as literary form and content are not independent entities, so the aesthetic and ideological may also be intertwined. In this respect, a methodological consideration should be emphasized in advance. Although the difference between aesthetic and ideological interference is not always clear, the decision to omit one passage from the text rather than another, even in cases where cuts might have been made primarily to eliminate repetitions or overwriting, might be ideologically determined—whether consciously or not—and in any case may definitely carry ideological implications for the translation. My criteria for an ideological interference, therefore, are first and foremost its immediate effects on the text. Although some of these interferences are shorter and some longer, some independent and some part of large-scale omissions governed mostly by stylistic considerations, all modify the text and make it less politically charged and less morally critical.[53]

The cases of interference in the texts presented here are organized chronologically according to their year of publication in English and span the period from the 1960s through the mid-1980s. Although not all works containing contentious matter translated during these years were subjected to some form of ideological manipulation, the findings here do indicate this tendency's consistency over several decades. At the risk of appearing to be a list, the following will demonstrate this with representative examples and make a case for the existence of such an ideological trend.

We begin with Nathan Shaham's "The Seven," in which the soldiers' merciless attitude toward Arab prisoners—notwithstanding the circumstance of mortal danger in a minefield—contradicts the image of the Israeli purity of arms. In both of its English translations, we find subtle discrepancies from Shaham's representation of at least one aspect of the soldiers' combat ethics. D. Briskman's translation in the anthology *A Whole Loaf* (1957) tempers the soldiers' conduct after occupying the hill: unlike the source text, here the soldiers show respect for the Arabs' bodies by covering them in dirt.

> After taking the ridge, we were posted into the positions deserted by the enemy, in readiness for an all-out defense. We ~~hurled~~ [**buried**] the enemy dead in a pit which had been dug, apparently, for garbage.[54]

The soldiers' treatment of the dead is similarly mitigated in Israel Meir Lask's translation in the anthology *The New Israeli Writers* (1969):

> [A]fter the occupation we took up position for an all-round defense in

> the posts the enemy had left. We ~~hurled~~ [**placed**] his dead in a trench that had apparently been cut as a cesspit.[55]

Although differing in most of their stylistic choices, both Briskman's and Lask's translations facilitate a somewhat more ethical portrait of the Jewish soldiers than the source text.

Another, more canonical work whose English translation presents a less ambiguous image of Israeli morals than the source text is Aharon Megged's *The Living on the Dead* (1965) in Misha Louvish's 1971 translation.[56] The novel's narrator, Jonas, plans to write a biography of the legendary Third Aliyah pioneer Davidov and goes on to interview Davidov's many old companions and fellow pioneers. In the following paragraph, a friend of Davidov's from the early settlement days tells Jonas about the part played by Davidov in the establishment of upper Hanita in the Western Galilee. After he mentions an affair Davidov was having with the wife of another worker, the man describes the Jewish settlers' forceful evacuation of the Arab farmers who lived and worked there (note that the first sentence refers to Davidov's affair, not to the expulsion of the Arabs):

> "Look, I don't take it upon myself to decide what is moral and what isn't, but there are some things, how should I say, that are like defying the order of nature, if I can put it like that."
>
> ~~There was a large stone house in upper-Hanita where Arab farmers dwelled. They refused to evacuate it before being compensated with large sums of money. Every day the men from the detail came to negotiate with them, they would ask for more. One day, Davidov suggested they take the place by force. Twenty men were sent up there, equipped with hoes, hammers, barbed wire, sacks. They entered the inner yard and started to turn it into a stronghold, surrounding it with a fence and trenches, and fixing its walls. The Arabs still would not leave, so all their things were taken out; the inhabitants and their possessions were mounted on donkeys and sent across the border. This was how upper-Hanita was conquered. A spotlight was then placed on top of the roof, and the two Hanitas would signal each other every night, from the stone house to the tower within the stockade.~~
>
> [**When upper Hanita was taken**] Davidov moved to the top of the hill. From then on he would set out from there to accompany the surveyors, the truck that maintained communications between the two points, the tractor that reaped the disputed fields.[57]

Whereas Davidov's affair with another man's wife, and other portrayals of his immoralities, were not deemed problematic enough to be omitted from the translation, the novel's only scene testifying to any violence in the Jewish acquisition of land in Mandatory Palestine was eliminated, and the English passage was neatly stitched around it. As a result of this omission, the image of Davidov and his fellow settlers is more ethically sound with regard to the story of the establishment of Hanita, in which the Arab farmers are now not even mentioned. The translation spares the reader unpleasant facts about Third Aliyah pioneers and some of the dire consequences of the Zionist settlement enterprise for the local population.

Nicholas de Lange's 1973 translation of Amos Oz's first novel, *Elsewhere, Perhaps,* done in collaboration with the author, omits several instances of aggression on the part of its characters as well.[58] The novel offers an ironic and unflattering portrayal of communal life in the fictional kibbutz Metsudat Ram and was perceived by some critics and scholars as representative of 1950s Israeli society. In various places in the novel, Reuven Harish, an outwardly wholesome kibbutz educator, immerses himself in wild delusions of brutality. The following passage is a case in point. As the tension rises between the kibbutz and the Syrian forces on the other side of the border, Harish imagines a violent outburst. While Israeli forces exchange fire with the neighboring Arab village, Reuven lets his thoughts roam:

> He was still feeling happy. That powerful feverish flush that grips weak men when they suddenly have a ringside view of violent fighting. Let the struggle wage on to the utter end of its final destiny.
>
> ~~Grab them. Tighten your fingers around their throat. Smash them. Crush. Pierce. Slice. Little hills like lambs. Tear them into shreds. Dash in pieces those that grow up against thee. . . . Fling at them. Crush their soft, delicate innards. Aim at their belly. Jab with a white-hot knife, with the stabbing hand of a drunkard. Wipe out mountain dwellers. Create a wasteland. Slay by the sword. Eliminate passers-by. Fill his mountains, expanses, hills, valleys and all of his ravines with the dead, slain by the sword. Form eternal wastelands with your wrath and fury. Mount Seir shall become a wasteland, and Mount Edom will come under your curse forever, so that all may know. . . . And you shall eat flesh and drink blood until you are satiated and inebriated, perched on a very tall mountain. In the eyes of the flesh. A sickly flow in Reuven is about to disgorge.~~
>
> Reuven stood at his window, his mouth open wide to scream or to sing. But his innards rebelled and he vomited again and again.[59]

The middle passage, with its ferociously violent stream of consciousness, full of murderous connotations as well as several biblical allusions (Exodus 15:6–7; Psalm 114:4), is omitted altogether, presenting the reader with a less pathologically haunted Reuven Harish. The kibbutz educator's inner fervor, here aimed at the Arab enemy, starts out concrete and specific but quickly unfolds into a frenzy of full-scale imagined destruction. Harish's unrealized violent fantasy, which serves to illustrate the influence of militarization on the Israeli collective unconscious, is left out in full.

The translation also omits the sadistic inclinations of Oren, one of the kibbutz's young members. Although this omission is part of a larger elision, which seems to stem mostly from stylistic considerations, the consequence for the translation is a more wholesome portrayal of a representative Israeli youth. Not only are depictions of Oren's perverse pranks—such as leaving carcasses of cats and dogs to rot in hidden spots about the kibbutz or rubbing the penis of a shy boy-poet with antirust paint—left out, but omitted as well is a description of Oren's attraction to the nearby Syrian border, where he performs vandalism on the marker flags on the line of demarcation.[60] Oz may be intimating that Oren's inward and outward violence is a reaction to the strain of militarization in Israeli life and to the prevailing chauvinistic expectations of 1950s Israeli society. "Cleansing" Oren of his aggression, the translation thus circuitously exonerates Israeli society from its responsibility for this volatile violence, fostering a more palatable picture not only of the youngster but also of the society that shaped him. Although the motivation for these omissions may have been to tame Oz's associative style, temper his stream-of-consciousness technique, or simply render the text accessible by shortening it, we cannot ignore the implications of these exclusions—exclusions that provided the American reader with a different, softer version than that encountered by the Israeli reader.

Israeli military ethics were represented differently in the source and target texts later in the 1970s as well, as is evident in Richard Flantz's 1977 translation of Yoram Kaniuk's *Rockinghorse*.[61] In this case, the translation omits a description of barbaric behavior performed by an Israeli commanding officer during the War of Independence. In the original text, Kaniuk relates a scene on an Israeli ship sailing from the United States to Israel, as the narrator makes his journey home after many years abroad. At some point during the cruise, the onetime commanding officer, now a (drunken) sailor, is persuaded by his fellow shipmates to retell "that funny story of his" from the war; he goes on to describe how he shot down a defenseless, elderly

Arab man, who nevertheless kept standing and "refused to die." Eventually, the soldier approached him and filled his body with holes "like buttons." Only then did the old man finally fall to the ground. The sailor suddenly breaks down in tears, muttering, "I just wanted to tell the story, like I tell it on every Independence Day." This sharply critical scene in Kaniuk's novel, which stains the notion of purity of arms, a mainstay in the ethos of the Israeli army, is omitted in the English translation.[62] Apart from the brutality of the actual killing, the reader of the translation is also spared the barbarism of the sailor's retelling of the story as a joke every Independence Day. As with the previous examples, the translation improves the image of a literary character who is expected to be an exemplary representative of Israeli society.

For the final example in this section, let us turn to Hillel Halkin's translation of Amos Oz's *A Perfect Peace*, published in English in 1985. The translation of this novel, too, includes some large-scale omissions, some of them of passages that depicted a sadistic element in the Israeli consciousness stemming from and related to the ongoing conflict with the Arab enemy. A case in point is a scene from the beginning of the novel, where some men and women from Kibbutz Granot take a stroll to a nearby abandoned Arab village, Sheikh Dahr. As in other English translations of Oz's works, the stylistic difficulty may have largely motivated the abridging. Nonetheless, even if the purpose was to mitigate the reader's difficulty with the wild stream-of-consciousness shifting among the characters of Yonatan, Azaria, and Udi, this does not take away from the ideological effect of the omission. The omitted passages include a vivid fantasy of Jewish brutality, without which the translation is more ethically palatable than the Hebrew source. In the omitted passage, for instance, Azaria imagines the untold fantasies of Udi, a hotheaded kibbutz member from the younger generation:

> ~~This Udi guy, for instance, if he ever let it all hang out he would tell me, Zaro, until you stick a spear a hand-grenade pull a machine gun on some Muhammad's guts you'll never know what it means to be alive, you'll never feel that pleasure in your stomach for which we are born.~~[63]

Later in the same scene, the ruins of Sheikh Dahr, the professed destination of the stroll, are described as follows:

> Above the ravaged village rose its shattered minaret ~~which was severed by an accurate mortar fired by the commander of the Palmach, so people say, with his own hands during the War of Independence.~~[64]

Without this description of the deliberate destruction of the village mosque during the war, the English translation lacks the explicit reasons and context for the abandonment of the village in the original. In addition, the omission improves the image of a leading figure who may be seen as representative of Israel's military ethics, the commander of the Palmach. Along the same lines, a full paragraph is omitted later, in which the character Yonatan is reminded of a dream he had at night. The dream expresses Yonatan's guilt over an Arab he had killed even though the latter had thrown up his hands in defeat. The emotional toll of the incident becomes evident when Yonatan turns the "~~punctured body~~" of the slain soldier over in his dream, only to see the face of "~~the Yonatan Lifshitz I know from the bathroom mirror when I shave.~~"[65] Here and elsewhere in the novel, vivid depictions of brutality are omitted altogether and, with them, the author's implied criticism for this brutality and an intimation of the individual and collective guilt it conveys.

Such interferences as we have seen here, which "cushion" critical aspects of the texts and make them more easily acceptable in terms of their political implications, prompt an inevitable set of questions: Who is responsible for these textual shifts? Who among the translators, editors, publishers, and even authors are responsible for the translation's final version? And given that these translations were published decades ago, is this at all determinable? When asked in personal correspondence about the shifts in their translations, the translators who could still be contacted responded that they did not clearly remember the fine details of the translation process, which had indeed taken place more than thirty years before, but they strongly believed that they had not introduced, of their own accord, any ideological alterations to the original texts.[66] This may very well be true and is reminiscent of translation theorist Gideon Toury's concept of the translator as a "conjoined entity": "sometimes there is no way of knowing how many different persons were actually involved in the establishment of a translation, playing how many different roles. . . . [T]he common practice has been to collapse all of them into one persona and have that conjoined entity regarded as 'the translator'; this would appear to be the only feasible approach."[67] The authors who could still be contacted similarly rejected the idea that they ever introduced changes for political considerations.[68] In a lecture given by Amos Oz at the 2017 annual conference of the Israel Translators Association, Oz mentioned editorial changes to the American edition of his 2004 *A Tale of Love and Darkness*, of which he did not approve.[69] My own intuition, based on my correspondence with translators and authors, is that the manipulations indeed occurred during the editorial process; but, admittedly, this can never be verified. The guidebook *Translation in Practice*, published following a symposium of English translators and editors on literary translation held in 2008, provides a peek behind the scenes of the publishing world that may lend support to this assumption; in it, we find the expressed notion that the editor of the translation should "look at the overall book, not the 'translation,' and edit it as an original book."[70] One of the editors at the symposium even stated that "copyeditors have to look out for unacceptable or controversial usage. . . . [T]horny issues might be references to Israel, Palestine and the Occupied Territories, or Kurdistan being referred to as a country."[71] Such inclinations may have existed in previous decades as well, impacting the final versions of English translations of major Hebrew works.

The obfuscation of moral critique in the translated works was also manifest in the next crucial stage of integration into the target-culture discourse—the critical reception in articles and reviews in newspaper literary supplements. Unlike publishers' decisions or manipulations in the translated text, here it was no longer about materials that could be kept from the American reader. The work had already been translated and published, and any mediation had to occur on the level of interpretation. Perhaps less dramatic in terms of its conspicuous censorial outcomes—it does not include the blunt omission of entire sentences or paragraphs—this stage may have had even more impact than direct interventions in the translations. Through its extensive circulation, the literary discourse in the mainstream American press reached a wide audience, constituting a relatively effortless and accessible way for Jewish American readers to stay updated on Israeli life and culture. Considering that many readers must have read the reviews without reading the books themselves, one can argue that literary supplements in the major American newspapers instilled in readers, to a large extent, the decisive images of the books and their meanings.

The literary supplements of leading newspapers such as the *New York Times*, *Chicago Tribune*, and *Washington Post* are, therefore, the main discursive sites explored in this section. Journals with limited intellectual readerships such as *The Nation* and *Commentary*, and more specifically targeted publications such as the American Library Association's *Booklist*, serve as another frame of reference. Obviously, these varied platforms differed not only in terms of the scope of their readership but also, and more relevant to the discussion here, in their overarching ideological orientations. However, it is precisely for this reason that the features they *did* share, even if not completely or exclusively, enable us to point to a common denominator in the response of American Jewish discourse to challenging literary portrayals of Israel. In other words, it is the exploration of such differing platforms that allows us to outline the broad contours of common ground. Referring to the interpretation of works from the past, sociologist and semiotician Pierre Bourdieu noted that "the text serves [the pundit] according to the manner in which he uses the text; however, this is only under the condition that he is seen by himself and by others as serving the text, and not as serving his own interests by means of the text."[72] The reviewers discussed here, from newspapers and journals alike, represented themselves, and were most likely perceived by their readers, as "serving the text." The examples that follow demonstrate how their ideological orientations were nonetheless reflected in their interpretations and how their readings contributed to the construction of the contemporary image of Israeli morality.

Primarily anchored in a political-ideological context, my focus will be on the reception of works in which the Israeli literary discourse tended to find dissenting, subversive collective meaning. These pieces naturally differed in their themes and modes of expression, as well as in their sense of urgency. In some of the works, the moral injustice caused by an Israeli soldier was inscribed as a momentous trauma that disrupted his life, and the historical circumstances of this injustice were charged with profound symbolism. In others, the pathological fantasy of a detached, estranged protagonist stemmed from guilt associated with the destruction of Palestinian villages in the War of Independence. And still, the important point common to all—from S. Yizhar's "The Prisoner," Megged's "White City," and Yehoshua's "Facing the Forests" to Kaniuk's *The Acrophile* and Oz's *My Michael*—is that they were perceived as communicating a subversive message that pertained not only to a character or event in the text but also to the Israeli *nation*, its history, and its moral image; a message that, in short, undermined the ethical foundations of the Zionist metanarrative. The mediation of these works in the Jewish American literary discourse, however, sometimes took a different interpretive direction. American critics obliged their readers by ignoring the works' subversive materials, blurring their symbolic meaning through selective analysis, or explicitly contending their validity.

American reviews of Yoram Kaniuk's *The Acrophile*, which appeared in English in 1961, are indicative of this tendency. Kaniuk's novel follows the life of Daan, a young Israeli living in New York and trying but failing to integrate into American life as a university professor, as he debates whether to return to Israel, toward which he is ambivalent. As mentioned earlier, one of the main themes of Kaniuk's work relates to the obsessive guilt that haunts Daan for accidentally killing an Arab boy in the 1948 War of Independence, implied as the underlying factor in Daan's withdrawal from Israel to America. However, reviews of the novel in the *New York Times*, *Commentary*, and *Booklist* stripped the killing of its particular historical circumstances and immediate national connotations. The critique by (Jewish) literary editor Rollene Sall in the *New York Times* does briefly note that the protagonist's emotional anguish may be related to guilt over the killing and mentions the victim's Arab identity, yet in her final interpretation of his character, Sall downplays the crucial national context: "Man's savagery was too much for him," she broadly states, "and he has tried to resign from the human race. Airplanes, tall buildings, mountains, the freedom of a fly attract him. Human life he denies."[73] Ignoring the different outcomes of the war for the peoples involved, she does not reveal to her readers the symbolic dimension of the scene, so pertinent to Kaniuk's novel, in which a person of one nationality is responsible for the catastrophe of a person of another nationality. Jane Hayman's review of the novel in *Commentary* refers to the incident in passing, tucked in a dependent clause, yet never reveals to her readers that it was an act of killing or that the victim was an Arab: "Daan, who took part in a bloody incident in Israel, longs to rise above his sense of sin. He divorces the human race and becomes a child symbolically."[74] The anonymous review of the novel in *Booklist* states very generally that "[Kaniuk] illuminates an individual's search for self-identity and emotional independence, and, in some degree, mirrors the apartness and loneliness of modern man," yet never refers to the central scene of the killing of the Arab boy or attests to its symbolic meaning in the novel.[75] The undertones of this scene, subtly undermining, or at least hinting at the possibility of undermining, the Jewish moral right to the land, never come across.

We find a similar approach in Gertned's previously mentioned review of Yizhar's "Khirbet Khizeh" from April 1957 and in Sylvia Rothschild's review of "The Prisoner" from July 1963, both in the *Jewish Advocate*, in which the word *Arab* is avoided, although it is pertinent to both stories' thematic core and symbolic connotations.[76] Similarly, yet in a much more explicit manner, Robert Alter articulated opposition to a political interpretation of Oz's *My Michael* in his May 1972 review in the *New York Times*, titled "An Apolitical Israeli," by downplaying the work's national-political implication. Alter argued that Oz's novel "manages to remain so private, so fundamentally apolitical in its concern, even as it puts to use the most portentous political materials," and claimed, in regard to the character Hannah Gonen, that "any consideration . . . of a Palestinian question is irrelevant to her conjuring with the Arab twins."[77] Although Alter's review offers a meticulous, well-articulated reading of the novel, his assumption that the Palestinian identity of the twins carries no representative meaning shares with the other reviews an underemphasis on the political. Such clouding of the particular national context in oppositional scenes was one way in which the interpretation suggested by critics assuaged challenges to the hegemonic Zionist narrative—challenges that were daring and dissenting for their time.

Another approach was simply to disregard the existence of the most dissenting, oppositional aspect of the novels. This is evident, for instance, in reviews of Aharon Megged's aforementioned *Fortunes of a Fool* in the *Washington Post* and the *New York Times* in September 1962. The chapter in the novel titled "The White City," in which Megged describes the Israeli conquest of Gaza in the 1956 Sinai campaign as unnecessarily brutal, is one of the few examples of early Israeli literary works that empathize with the suffering of Arabic characters.[78] Nonetheless, the reviews of *Fortunes of a Fool* in the *New York Times* and *Washington Post* never mentioned this chapter.[79] This is particularly striking in critic Rinna Samuel's rather long appraisal of the novel in the *New York Times*, as Samuel noted that the work's "greatest merit, perhaps, is the way in which, without ever mentioning that the background is Israel, Megged manages to flash before the reader portrait after portrait of Israel, her people, their most characteristic moods and postures."[80] She indeed goes on to detail some of the latter, yet the aspect of Israeli reality that elicited Megged's chief protest—the needless brutality of Israeli soldiers during the military invasion of the Sinai peninsula in 1956—receives no mention. Readers of these critiques who had not read the novel itself would have never known of the chapter's trenchant portrayal of Israeli conduct in the Sinai campaign.[81]

A subtler protective tactic involved acknowledging the works' politically subversive meanings, sometimes even noting them with the highest regard, while describing their plots and meanings in a manner that undercut their subversive subtexts. Jewish American poet Masha Louis Rosenthal employed this strategy in an article he wrote recounting his experiences on a visit to Israel, published in *The Nation* in December 1970. Rosenthal celebrated the critical tenacity of the new Israeli literature, yet when addressing its themes and subjects, he elegantly sidetracked those involving morally and politically charged questions, preferring instead to concentrate on less provocative issues. Hence he chose to discuss, at some length, Yehuda Amichai's "The Battle for the Hill"—a satire of heroic war literature whose theme is the institutionalized Israeli discourse on warfare, not the battles themselves, which therefore lacks unpalatable representations of Israeli soldiers' aggression.[82] However, when Rosenthal described more morally fraught works such as Yizhar's "The Prisoner" and Bartov's *The Brigade*, which portray barbaric behavior on the part of Jewish soldiers in the Israeli army and British Brigade, respectively, he did so very concisely, while largely downplaying their acerbity:

> The novel by Palestine-born Hannoch Bartov, *The Brigade*, about the Jewish brigade in World War II, focuses on one of the most deeply troubling issues of Israeli sensibility: the problem of reconciling the ancient role of the Jew as the wise, saintly, suffering victim with his new role as man of action and victor. So does the nausea-filled story, "The Prisoner," by S. Yizhar, another native Palestinian. The new role of "Victor" is manifestly precarious and tentative, or is it only Jewish self-irony that makes it seem more so than it would be for other peoples?[83]

By merely describing the "new role" of the Jew in *The Brigade* "as man of action and victor," while avoiding some of the Jewish soldiers' vindictive and violent behavior, including an attempt to rape German women, Rosenthal evaded dealing with the pertinence of these incidents to Bartov's novel. Likewise, he avoided addressing the moral failing in "The Prisoner" by not mentioning the abuse inflicted on an innocent Arab prisoner by a group of Israeli soldiers—a key scene in the narrative. Instead, Rosenthal referred obscurely and noncommittally to the "self-irony" with which the Jews perceive their "new role of 'Victor.'" Thus his piece concurrently realized both coping patterns in the Jewish American discourse, as mentioned earlier in this chapter: the tendency to link Hebrew literature with leftist principles and present it as humanistic and self-critical, on the one hand, while safeguarding the reader against the immoral and inhumane reality often rendered in it, on the other.

Not all responses to condemnatory representations of Israeli morality in the translated works were, however, indirect and subtle. Nor were they always confined to the literary text, its description, and its interpretation. There were also other reviewers who took a less oblique path and directly assaulted the works' credibility as authentic representations of Israel, its society, and its culture. This is a sort of photographic negative of the tendency to attribute to Hebrew literature the moral daring to expose genuine Israeli reality without embellishment; here, unpalatable portrayals were simply dismissed as untrue. In his review of an anthology titled *The New Israeli Authors* in the *Saturday Review* (1969), Jewish scholar, author, and translator Curt Leviant, for instance, explicitly opposed the critical representation of the Israeli army in the collection's stories:

> The three stories that focus directly on army life give the impression that Israeli soldiers are small-minded sadists—a gross distortion of a citizen army that has no time for spit-and-polish soldiering, and which has a special feeling of dedication and affection between officers and men. Although we must respect a writer's private vision—indeed, give it preference over so-called national or political aims—and although anti-army stories are fashionable everywhere, it was unfair of the editor to have chosen only stories that depict the Israeli army unfavorably, especially if the ostensible purpose was to give the reader an honest experience of Israel.[84]

Taking a rather emotional tone, Leviant defended the Israeli army's image as reflected in the stories while delivering his subjective perception as *the* authentic view of army life in Israel. Leviant's adherence to the established narrative regarding Israel's military is all the more conspicuous considering that he later criticized the anthology's failure to reflect Israeli society truthfully as divided both ethnically and religiously. Leviant's acquaintance with Israel's domestic problems far exceeded the norm in mainstream American journalism during that period; he in fact displayed a rather deep understanding of the inequality inherent in Israeli society and did not shy away from criticizing it. However, this also demonstrates that the interethnic tensions in Israel were, for him, a far more legitimate topic to criticize than the army, whose negative representation, in his view, was practically taboo.[85]

Such a defensive standpoint regarding Israeli reality, which maintains that this reality is not as immoral as its fictional representations, can also be found in Robert Alter's commentary on S. Yizhar's "The Prisoner," published in the anthology *Modern Hebrew Literature* (1975), which he edited. Although Alter did select this scathing story for the collection, he tempered its discordant message in two ways. First, he set it against his description of the *real* Israel: "One need not assume that the beating of an Arab prisoner is in any way typical Israeli behavior (as predictably, Arab protagonists, capitalizing on the story, have done)."[86] Second, he historically contextualized the soldiers' violent behavior (even though he had just described it as atypical): "It takes only a little historical imagination to see what in the experience of young Jews growing up in Palestine of the 30s and 40s, repeatedly subject to murderous Arab incursions, would prompt this sort of feeling."[87] The representation of prisoner abuse as atypical, as well as the historical background that Alter proposes as its motivation, moderate the problematic image of the Israeli soldier emanating from the story. Alter later linked the story's ideological underpinnings to moral values rooted in Jewish history: "The crucial point is that the plea on behalf of the conscience is made here on the strength of values embedded in the historical memory of the Jewish people; a Jew knows from bitter experience what it means in concrete terms to be the helpless target."[88] Like Rosenthal, then, Alter mediated the Hebrew text for the American reader both by generating a humanistic, morally informed discourse to facilitate its understanding and by mitigating the image of an immoral Israel that it presents.

We find similar ambivalence in a course taught by Alter in 1970 at the University of California, Berkeley. The course, titled America and Israel: Literary and Intellectual Trends, was documented in a booklet published by the Hadassah Education Department.[89] In past decades, sociological thought has given special attention to the academy as a discipline of knowledge that organizes and governs discourse, noting that the field of social sciences (along with other academic disciplines) shares with the journalistic field and the political field the "claim to the imposition of the legitimate vision of the social world."[90] American universities, as institutions of knowledge invested with symbolic capital, thus distribute what are perceived and accepted as "authoritative" representations of Israel and so play a role in determining the position Israel occupies in the taxonomy of images in elite American culture. In this case, most relevant to us are Alter's notes for the last class of the course, called "Confrontation with the Arabs." In what follows, I will touch not on Alter's literary interpretations but rather on those places where Alter commented on the "character" of Jews and Arabs as revealed in the conflict—or, in other words, where he partook, and indirectly took sides, in contemporary political discourse.

During this class, Alter described war experiences that were recounted by Israeli soldiers in the seminal 1967 *Siach Lochamim* (translated into English as *The Seventh Day* in 1970), a compilation of interviews with kibbutznik soldiers who fought in the Six Day War. The compilation was notable for providing a more thoughtful and self-critical narrative of the war at a time when popular photographic albums depicting the war heroically were proliferating. As later research has shown, the collection of interviews was also carefully constructed so as to project a sensitive, humane image of the Israeli soldiers: Alon Gan has demonstrated the tendentious nature of the editing of the original book, as the editors left out instances of professed Israeli brutality, among other things.[91] In his class, Alter relied on interviews from *The Seventh Day* to deduce a generalization about the asymmetry between Jewish and Arab ethics: "One of the most disturbing 'asymmetries' in this whole terrible confrontation of Arab and Jew is the fact that so many of the Arabs, even women and children, have been thoroughly brutalized by their own propaganda."[92]

In one of the incidents Alter cited from *The Seventh Day*, an Israeli soldier is murdered by an Arab family begging for bread, as he hands them his own rations. Alter draws from this story a generalization about the difference between Arab and Jewish mentalities and ethics and ties this difference to the "Jewish character": "Perhaps the saddest aspect of this story is not the tragedy of the murdered soldier but of the Arab family, which had effaced its own humanity. In stark contrast, the degree of moral conscience Israelis have managed to preserve, the degree of their resistance to brutalization, is quite remarkable. And this moral conscience seems to me to have a peculiarly Jewish character."[93] It is important to note that although Alter drew generalizations about "Arab mentality" from stories depicting Arab barbarism, he refrained from generalizing about "Jewish/Israeli mentality" from stories depicting Jewish/Israeli brutality. The latter, unlike the former, were not deemed representative or a sound basis for a generalization on Israeli ethics. This changed, however, when it came to positive generalizations, as Alter stated that mulling over hard moral issues was something essentially "Jewish" (note the aforementioned remark of his on Yizhar's "The Prisoner"). It is true that Alter later hinted at the proximity of his views to the Israeli left wing's willingness to consider a territorial compromise and sharply criticized American Jews' tendency to readily adopt the right-wing narrative of "the Jewish right to the land" without giving attention to its Arab inhabitants.[94] The overtones of his final remarks for the class, which also ended the whole course, are, however, quite similar to those of his earlier commentary: "Israel's peculiar predicament may be representative, situated as it is as a sophisticated technological society, a parliamentary democracy, a country with humanistic and humane traditions, encircled by enemies, some of whom are even self-styled Maoists and many of whom stand for nothing more meaningful than destruction, or personal aggrandizement, or the lawless lust for power."[95] In his conclusion for a course in literature, then, Alter chose to participate and take sides in the charged political discourse of the day by presenting a sharp opposition between the two peoples with regard to their morality and ethics. Even as he promoted the values and general viewpoint of the moderate Left, Alter felt the need to protect the image of the Israeli army and Israeli/Jewish morals. It should be stressed that this does not take away from the moral sensibility expressed in Alter's (and others reviewers') disapproval of militant tendencies in Israeli policy over the years, or from the sophistication of Alter's readings of Hebrew literature—which were as profound as any scholar of Hebrew literature of the time. It nonetheless shows that even a left-leaning intellectual such as Alter may have subdued, to some extent, Israeli self-criticism, in the mediated absorption of Israeli works into 1970s American Jewish culture. Alter's arguments coincided with the translations, reviews, and anthology annotations that dealt, each in its own way, with literary depictions of Israeli existence as tainted with moral failings—representations that challenged the dominant image of an ethical Israel within American Jewish discourse. Due to these mediations, various portrayals of the immoral aspects of Israeli reality, as well as the subversiveness they embodied, were moderated en route to their American readers.

Moderating (Imagined) Palestinian Perspectives

As entailed in Alter's course notes, a complementary aspect of the ideologically implicated introduction of images of Israel to an American readership had to do with the representation of Palestinian fate and Palestinian identity. Even though works dealing directly with the fate of the Palestinian population in Israel were few and far between, and they too did not always provide an authentic depiction of Palestinian otherness, their public significance cannot be underestimated. Against the backdrop of the prevailing national zeitgeist, they played a central oppositional role in Israeli discourse, through two main thematic alternatives. Some authors gave a Palestinian character a voice of its own as a means to infuse its identity with a sense of national otherness while anchoring it in particular historical circumstances of the conflict; others focused on the Israeli sense of responsibility and guilt over the destruction of Palestinian villages—guilt that was highlighted as having a traumatic effect on Israeli identity in both individual and collective terms. However, when mediated for the American reader, both literary designs were sometimes adjusted to provide less complex and contentious representations of Palestinian identity on the one hand and more morally acceptable renditions of modern Israeli history on the other.

Let us return to the form of interference perhaps most hidden from sight: manipulations implemented in the translations of the literary works. As in the shifts in the English renderings discussed earlier—and based, again, on my correspondence with translators and authors who could still be contacted—it is my impression that here too most modifications of charged subject matter occurred at the editing stage. At whichever stage the changes were introduced, they often affected the depicted role of the Palestinian historical calamity in the making of individual Palestinian identity. An interesting example of a novel dealing with the effects of the national conflict on Palestinian life, while employing a Palestinian protagonist who narrates in the first person, is Amnon Jackont's political thriller *Borrowed Time* (1982), translated into English by Dorothea Shefer-Vanson and published in 1986. In the following example, Katherine, the Palestinian lover of ex-Mossad agent Arik Ben-Dor, who had defected, remembers her family's expulsion from Jaffa in 1948, when she was a little girl. When she describes her fleeing from the war, it is with words taken from Lewis Carroll's Alice in her journey through the looking-glass:

> The Looking-Glass, from that day, was the fine border between sanity and madness, ~~both a shelter and reality, a thin, shaky barrier between the horrors of the outer world and the anxiety that prevailed in the inner one. Page six in the book—below the picture with the broken lines—was my private "Sura": "in another moment Alice was through the glass. She was quite pleased to find that there was real fire blazing away in the fireplace, as brightly as the one she had left behind. "So I shall be as warm here as I was in the old room," thought Alice: "warmer, in fact, because there'll be no one here to banish me from the fireside. Oh, what fun~~

> ~~it'll be when they see me through the glass in here, yet can't reach me!"~~ [**as well as between the country we abandoned and the new one we craved to think of as ours.**] In Uncle Shafik's store, in Hamra Street, the names of distant places rang out: Caracas, Buenos Aires, Asuncion, La Paz. Half of the Shazli family lived in South America. The other half ~~lived in Jaffa. Now we are all~~ [**was starting a new life**] in Beirut. Father was to work with Uncle Shafik in the store.[96]

Katherine's childlike perspective on her family's expulsion is omitted and replaced in the translation with a single sentence that mirrors the wishful thinking of the hegemonic Jewish narrative following the war. The translation nullifies the Palestinian experience represented in the source text by putting a description of the family "abandoning" their country and arriving at a new one they "craved to think of as [theirs]," in Katherine's own words. Similarly, the explicit mention that before the war, half of the Shazli family had lived in Jaffa was omitted, and the translator incorporated into the text that the family was "starting a new life" in Beirut. In other words, the Palestinian family of the English translation conveniently wishes to leave the past—that is, their homes in Jaffa—behind. Crucially, in the original text, Jackont, who was otherwise faithful when quoting and translating Carroll, politicized the sentence "scold me away from the fire" by rendering it *yegaresh oti min ha-esh* (banish/expel me from the fire; compare with Aharon Amir's faithful 1951 translation, available to Jackont but unused by him, *yarhikeni bi-ge'ara me-etzel ha-esh*). The use of the politically charged *yegaresh* (banish/expel) seems to create the necessary context for Katherine's identification with Alice in this passage and is perhaps the main reason for the existence of the passage in the novel, just as it is the main reason for its omission from the translation.[97] In other places in the novel, explicit reference to the expulsion of Palestinians from Jaffa and Ramle during the War of Independence and to other aspects of the Palestinian refugee problem were omitted and the translation neatly stitched around them.[98]

Another work that gave voice to a Palestinian character, and whose references to the Palestinian refugee problem born in the 1948 war were not retained, was Yoram Kaniuk's *Confessions of a Good Arab* in Dalya Bilu's 1987 translation. Kaniuk's novel tells the story of Yosef Sherara/Rosenzweig, son of a Jewish mother and Arab father, who indeed embodies the Israeli–Palestinian conflict and is inwardly torn as he is rejected by both worlds. In the following paragraph, Yosef's father, Azouri, asks Hava, his Jewish wife, why he should make any effort to understand Jewish pain:

> Why do I have to understand him and who asked me to be his doorman to paradise, he asked himself~~, with words taken from the way it had used to be back then, from present absentees who were outside the Israeli borders on May 15th, 1948, and now could not return to their houses, houses in which refugees lived and cut down lemon trees. Hava looked distressed, yet beautiful~~; he looked at Hava and was flooded with sadness, he didn't want revenge but he didn't not want it either.[99]

This reference to the Palestinian refugees who fled or were expelled from their villages in Israel's War of Independence was not preserved in the translation, nor was the following one, in which Azouri debates with Hava whether they should raise a son in Israel:

> Hava said, I have to have your child Azouri, and he said, and where will we bring him up, how? ~~This whole country is full of nightmares, transit camps, screwed up Jews, Arabs looking for their homes, do you want to create a curse we could never escape?~~ They sat in the intoxicating fragrance of the orange trees and caressed each other, they surrendered to their love because there was nothing else to surrender to.[100]

Though some references to the Palestinian *Nakba* were kept in the translation, these and similar omissions create a more homogeneous discourse between Kaniuk's characters in the English version of the novel, keeping it closer to the institutionalized Zionist narrative that tends to exclude mention of Palestinian fate in 1948. In both cases, the passage is neatly joined together around the charged references to the Palestinian refugees, omitted from the translation. Although the translation includes some stylistic changes, presumably meant to make the impressionistic, loose language of Kaniuk's narrator less vague, it seems that ideological rather than stylistic considerations motivated the interferences noted here. As in Jackont's novel, the Palestinian catastrophe became less prominent in the formation of Azouri's identity than it was in the source text. Complementing these manipulations in translations of passages dealing with the trauma of the *Nakba*, interferences in other novels subdued the ethnonational otherness embedded in the voice of Palestinian characters—yet in a more mundane way and without direct reference to the 1948 war. Such, for instance, is Philip Simpson's 1978 translation of the monologue chapters of the Palestinian teenager Naim in A. B. Yehoshua's *The Lover*. Here, Naim describes the journey he makes to work every morning from the West Bank into Israel proper:

> At first I really did sleep the whole journey and I used to ~~reach the Jews~~ [**arrive at work**] dead tired. . . . So I just look out at the road, seeing the darkness disappear, the flowers on the mountains. I never tire of this route, the same route day after day, an hour and a half there and an hour and a half back. ~~You leave and enter Palestine and it's always most pleasant on the way back~~.[101]

For Naim, the main feature of the auto repair shop where he works is that it belongs to "the Jews"; in the translation, this distinct ethnonational otherness is not evident. The translation also spares the American reader what is for Naim the land's genuine name, Palestine, by which Yehoshua gave expression to Naim's disparateness and obvious rejection of the Zionist perception of the land. Neither did the English translation keep Naim's explicit preference to go back to his own people rather than remain among the Jews. Another expression of the foreignness of Palestinian identity moderated in the novel's translation is a number of instances in which Yehoshua incorporated (transliterated) Arabic into the body of the text. Such phrases in Arabic stood out in transcription in the Hebrew text as markers of disparate identity, either with or without a footnote that translated them for the Hebrew reader.[102] These aspects having been moderated or omitted in the translation, the American (Jewish) reader encountered in Naim a Palestinianness that was less threatening as it was emptied of its national otherness.

Direct and indirect references to the Palestinian *Nakba* and other repercussions of the national conflict on Palestinian life were not only manifest in Hebrew literature in the construction of Palestinian characters. They also marked a collective traumatic experience that threatened to corrode Israeli consciousness and identity, leading to its demise. Both Oz and Yehoshua, for instance, highlight the Palestinian calamity as a source of Israeli guilt eating away at the basic premise of the Zionist discourse—the moral right to the land. In what follows, I will demonstrate how such themes were mediated for the American reader in Hillel Halkin's English translation of Oz's *A Perfect Peace* and in an interpretation of Yehoshua's "Facing the Forests."

Admittedly, as in Bilu's translation of Kaniuk, the changes introduced to Oz's novel were perhaps intended to restrain the fluidity and looseness of the narration rather than to reconstruct the text ideologically.[103] However, some of the original passages that were left out of the translation include recurring references to the ruins of Sheikh Dahr, an Arab village destroyed during Israel's 1948 War of Independence, not far from Kibbutz Granot, where the novel takes place. As Ranen Omer-Sherman shows, the internal crisis of the protagonist Yonatan Lifshitz is greatly determined by the existence of the abandoned nearby village, "for when a young man raised in the certitude of Zionism wakens to the reality that his comfort hinges on the dispossessed Arab Other, he suffers a violent existential shock, causing him to flee toward an uncertain fate in the desert."[104] This lends significance to the fact that Yonatan's recurring thoughts about Sheikh Dahr, which imply that it was a source of ethical stress, were lost in translation.[105] As is evident from the following examples, smaller segments with mostly concrete information related to the village of Sheikh Dahr were also left out, subduing aspects of the original text that subtly undermined the selective hegemonic perspective in Israel on the Palestinian role in the conflict:

> At ten o'clock, Udi and Anat had joined Yonatan, Rimona and Azariah, and they had all set out together for ~~the ruined village~~ [**Sheikh Dahr**]. Udi was sure that the floods must have unearthed some of the ancient facing stones of the biblical Jewish village~~, that the Arabs had used to build their own village in the 8th century A.C~~. [106]

> A grindstone fragment that Yonatan came across had to be left for drier weather when a tractor and a wagon could be used to haul it back. ~~Seventeen years after the death of the village, the ruins of Sheikh Dahr still produced remnants of life, and like an abandoned orchard they gave anything to he who wanted to take.~~ Suddenly, Azariah started and grabbed onto Udi's shirt.[107]

Troubling allusions to the War of Independence and its devastating consequences for the village were thus not always retained in the translation. In the first example, the inference that Sheikh Dahr had existed for twelve centuries before its ruin in 1948 was left out. As Sheikh Dahr is representative of the history and fate of other Palestinian villages, the connotations of this sentence within the politically charged discourse on "the historical right to the land" are clear and may be the reason behind its omission. In the second example, we can see that the translation also left out a suggestive reflection about the "afterlife" of the Arab village. This short meditation seems to accentuate Sheikh Dahr's actual devastation and the dispersion of its people. It may also be hinting at the continuous presence of the ruined Arab villages in the Israeli psyche and particularly in Yonatan's obsessed consciousness. Further in the novel, yet another crucial reference to Sheikh Dahr is left out, as Srulik, the kibbutz secretary, speculates about why Yonatan left his wife and his life in the kibbutz and where he might have disappeared to:

> Is he looking for a streetwalker in the alleys of south Tel Aviv? Or is he navigating by the stars in the wilderness of Judea or the Negev? ~~Walking aimlessly about an old agricultural colony? Hiding in the ruins of Sheikh Dahr, not far from here? Is he talking to himself, or has he finally been engulfed in winter night silence? Is he confused?~~ Is he serious, or just playing a practical joke on somebody?[108]

Admittedly, the translation omitted quite a few of Srulik's guesses concerning Yonatan's whereabouts and methodically condensed this passage, which had originally been much longer. However, the most significant exclusion is Srulik's reference to Sheikh Dahr. Something of a logical conclusion to other omissions of Sheikh Dahr in the novel, this instance leaves out Oz's explicit connection between Yonatan's flight from the kibbutz and the haunting presence of, as Omer-Sherman put it, "the destruction of the previous occupants of the land in the form of a ruined village."[109]

In Yehoshua's "Facing the Forests," the Israeli trauma rooted in the Palestinian demise and its symbolic implications for the Zionist project as a whole were not obfuscated in the translation itself. Rather, ideological mediation took place at a later stage, in the context of interpretation and commentary in the American literary discourse. In this way Yehoshua's story, a cornerstone of the Hebrew canon, loses some of its subversive edge. For instance, by completely ignoring the eradication of the Arab village that led the Jewish protagonist to help set the Keren Kayemet forest on fire, Hugh Nissenson, in his *New York Times* review from October 1970, circumvented any discussion of how this event symbolically challenged the Zionist claim to the land:

> [A] graduate student takes a job in a forest planted over the ruins of an Arab village. He is studying the crusades: "from the human, that is to say, the ecclesiastical aspect." Gradually, he is confronted with the agony of Jewry during that period. . . . [T]he Jew, increasingly obsessed by oppression, his head filled with monks, cardinals, mass suicides and blurred kings, shows the Arab how the forest can be burned down. When the Arab fulfills his will, the Jew disavows him. He has surrendered to the evil impulse and compounded humanity's crimes.[110]

As Gilead Morahg points out, "there is an almost complete critical consensus that 'Facing the Forests' constitutes an assault on the dominant national narrative in Israel."[111] Nonetheless, whether for lack of knowledge of Israeli history or due to a conscious decision to defend Israel's image before the American reader, Nissenson attributed the forest ranger's act of self-destruction to his obsession over the plight of the Jews at the time of the Crusades. Considering that Nissenson lived on a kibbutz for a few years in the late 1960s and later published stories that take place in Israel, we can assume that he may have been familiar with the domestic literary discourse. Even so, his American readers encountered a rather unconventional interpretation that, instead of highlighting the Palestinian *Nakba*, stressed the persecution of the Jews in earlier periods.

Like the approach taken in his reading of Yizhar's "The Prisoner," Alter's commentary on "Facing the Forests" in his 1975 anthology undercuts the story's affinity with Israel's reality and actual historical circumstances. Although he briefly mentioned Israeli guilt over the Palestinians' devastation in the context of the narrative, he questioned the story's historical accuracy, claiming that its cause was more imaginary than factual: "The national forest that has been planted over the site of a destroyed Arab village suggests, with the symbolic aptness of a guilt-ridden psychology though not necessarily with historical accuracy, the State of Israel itself."[112] Alter also appealed to the reader, asking that the story not be read only as a political allegory. Adhering to his own directive, Alter focused almost entirely on other dimensions of the story; his analysis of its poetic and psychological aspects fills two full pages, whereas his discussion of the ideological-political element is limited to a mere two lines.[113] By contrast, scholarship and public discourse in Israel continued to pay special attention to this dimension of the story, which seems to be the decisive reason behind its central place within the Israeli canon as a work that is repeatedly taught in high school and institutions of higher education. Alter's important anthology, which served generations of students in Hebrew literature courses at American universities, thus contributed to a meaningful difference between the story's reception in Israel and its reception in America—and, perhaps, to differences in the way the story was taught as well.

Naturally, the ideological worldview that served as the background to American mediations of Israeli portrayals of the Palestinian calamity was not formulated explicitly in the literary discourse; such practice would defeat the purpose. Translation editors and literary critics could not very well offer reasoning for textual alterations or interpretive tendencies; ideological mediation, as Bourdieu has shown, must appear devoid of ideology for it to be effective. However, we catch an interesting glimpse of the discursive undercurrents regarding the question of Palestinian existence in Israel in James Michener's introduction to *Firstfruits*, the anthology of Israeli writing in translation published by the Jewish Publication Society in 1973. At the beginning of the introduction, Michener speaks fondly of the years he lived in Haifa and of his visits to the Negev desert. Michener describes Israel's agricultural, technological, and artistic accomplishments with admiration and compares them to the way "the desert bloomed" before him one day and produced "a rug of many colors" following some rare rain showers: "I think of Israel in those terms. It was a land long dormant which sprang to abundant life. It was a desert of sorts which waited sleeping, for the awakening rain. It was arid, but it held the secret of vitality. Mysteriously, it was summoned back to life."[114] The hegemonic Zionist discourse of "progress" adopted here by Michener excludes reference to the Palestinians who had been living on the land before the pioneer Zionist settlements. Later in the introduction, Michener acknowledges that the land was not empty before the Zionist enterprise, but his reference to the native Arab population is largely paternalistic: "I do not believe that prior to 1948 all was barrenness, with the Arabs and the British having achieved nothing. From what I could see of Haifa when I lived there I suspect that both the Arabs and the British accomplished a good deal and that if they had retained control of the Jewish homeland they might have accomplished a good deal more in a quiet, desultory sort of way, with swamps still swamps and water still wasting itself on its way to the sea."[115] Michener's "compliments" for the Arab population reveal an orientalist attitude that refutes the Arab (or British) ability or willingness to bring any "real progress" to the land. Moreover, when he refers to it he makes use of the exclusive term "the Jewish homeland," implying doubt of the Palestinians' right to claim any part of the land.

At the end of his introduction, in quite an unusual manner for anthologies of Hebrew literature in English translation, Michener mentions (what remains) a charged political issue: the question of the occupied territories in the West Bank, captured from Jordan in the Six Day War:

> I have never been a Nile-to-Euphrates man, for mere territorial aggrandizement is repugnant, but I used to feel strongly that the former arrangement on the road from Tel-Aviv to Jerusalem was an abortion that simply had to be corrected. I am gratified that it has been. I felt the same way about the narrow waist northeast of Tel-Aviv, and I am equally glad to see it repaired. I speak not as a nationalist but as a geographer.

> Geographical monstrosities ought to be corrected, and history usually takes care of the matter, for it does not like to see them indefinitely prolonged. The land is therefore in better *shape* than it used to be.[116]

Although Michener's argumentation is somewhat unconventional, the viewpoint he expresses on the loaded issue of the occupied territories in the West Bank is explicit and unambiguous. He notes that the land is "in better *shape* than it used to be" and that he is "glad to see it repaired." This case of taking sides in the political debate coincides with the underlying approach of Michener's introduction in general, and it is evident in many of its passages. In fact, it is revealing to compare these remarks to an article Michener himself published in the *New York Times* in 1970 about the Israeli–Palestinian conflict. In that article, titled "What to Do about the Palestinian Refugees?," Michener expresses sympathetic concern and criticism over the difficult humanitarian conditions in the Palestinian refugee camps.[117] Michener's criticism of Israel's policy following the Six Day War is also evident in his earlier, otherwise supportive letter to the editor in the *New York Review of Books*.[118] In his introduction to *Firstfruits*, Michener states that there is no use going over what he has already written elsewhere on the subject, but he does not refer the reader to these articles. This seems evasive, as most of the readers of the anthology would be unlikely to know them. In any case, it is clear that the difference in the medium and, crucially, the difference in the assumed target audience influenced the ideological underpinnings of what Michener chose to share with his readers. Michener and his partners at the Jewish Publication Society did not see allusions to Palestinian refugees or any politically critical stance as appropriate matter for an introduction to an anthology published to salute Israel's twenty-fifth anniversary. They preferred instead to present the Jewish American reader with a more palatable image of Israel and its history, military, and culture and by doing so not only reflected the prevalent trend in Jewish American discourse but also made yet another contribution to it.

What, then, is the broader context for understanding the encounter of American discourse with the more contentious works of Hebrew literature, and how might we make sense of this protective mediation in the larger framework of the relationship between the two major Jewish centers? First, things must be put in the proper perspective by acknowledging that Hebrew literature could still fulfill an eye-opening role for its Jewish American readership, even beyond the screen of mediation. In decades when attempts from within the American Jewish community to pass judgment on Israel were usually met with severe objection, translated Hebrew works could provide readers with a more complex image of Israel, while articulating a more critical alternative to the prevailing discourse. The assumption that "works of Israeli novelists and poets in translation have worked to counteract the stereotype of Israel as an idyllic and morally untroubled land,"[119] common in both scholarly and public discourse, is thus not disputed here. The translated works still constituted a balancing factor to the dominant, uncritical image of Israel in the largely naïve, more supportive than skeptical Jewish American community from the establishment of the state through the mid-1980s.

That said, we have seen that one cannot simply assume that works harboring an oppositional stance had crossed the linguistic and geographical boundaries between the two cultures "untouched." Although moral critique was framed as a principal "Jewish" quality of contemporary Hebrew literature, and despite the common notion that this literature exposed readers to Israel's complex reality, literary representations that undermined the construction of the Zionist narrative as morally sound were sometimes obscured. The growth of Zionist sentiment among America's Jews, which provided a useful context for the reception of Hebrew literature in the 1950s, helps us to better understand the nuanced politics of negotiation over images and ideas that were part of translation processes from the 1960s onwards. Apparent in a wide variety of textual and extratextual phenomena, the obfuscation of the critical dimension in literature translated from Hebrew points to the difficulty that Jewish American cultural agents faced when confronted with a perspective that undermined the moral foundations of their Zionist disposition and, perhaps no less important, with the threat of exposing these failings to their fellow Americans. Viewed through a broad social, even national, lens, the varied forms of mediation in the literary discourse can be seen as practical efforts to defend Israel's image in the eyes of not only Jewish American readers but also American readers at large. Agents of Hebrew literature in America thus chose to assume a social-ideological role that extended beyond the literary domain: filtering and modifying the collective image emanating from the translated works.

And yet we cannot fully understand this inclination if we do not also place the Jewish American consumption of these images of Israel within the framework of another major strand of Jewish identity in America. Aside from Israel, an important component in Jewish American identity and self-perception has historically been the moral dimension. In Jewish American intellectual thought, ethical principles and moral reflection are traditionally considered central features of American manifestations of Jewish identity, both in actual political practices and in media of imaginative creation.[120] The notion that the humanistic imperative is at Judaism's core is part of the formal theology of the Reform movement and constitutes a prominent motif in Conservative and even Modern Orthodox thought. In this context, the protective mediation of Hebrew literature in America could be seen as rooted in the perceived necessity to produce a certain image of Jewish American identity, of which Israel is a constituent. From the 1960s through the mid-1980s, different Jewish American thinkers had discussed Israel, particularly its relation to and significance for diasporic Jewry, in religious terms. Arthur Hertzberg and Leonard Fein even suggested that Israel became *the* religion of American Jews following the Six Day War.[121] Against this backdrop, the expectations of American Jewish students that Hebrew literature will "reflect some ideal reality that corresponds to the readers' perception of their own self-identity"[122] can indeed be easily understood. However, given that Israel was assigned a quasi-religious role as a mainstay of Jewish American communal identity and that this identity was seen as deeply rooted in moral principles, images of Israel in Hebrew literature sometimes had to be aptly appropriated. In order for the Israel of the literary discourse to partake in constructing Jewish American identity, the humanistic image of Hebrew literature had to be bolstered, even if this involved obscuring unpalatable depictions of Israeli society. The translation and mediation of Hebrew literature in American culture call attention, therefore, to the inherent, unresolved tension between two crucial components of Jewish American identity—Zionism and morality—that did not always go hand in hand. These practices also exemplify the subtle yet relentless effort, on both overt and covert levels of the literary discourse, to diffuse this tension.

3

Israeli Jewishness for American Eyes

In 1990, Israeli historian Yosef Gorny's seminal study on the State of Israel in Jewish public thought was published in Hebrew, under the title *Ha-hipus ahar ha-zehut ha-le'umit* (The Quest for National Identity). The book outlines the competing ways in which Jewish intellectuals and political leaders, mainly in Israel and the United States, philosophized over the meaning of a sovereign Jewish state in the post-Holocaust era, primarily against the backdrop of the flourishing existence of the Jewish diaspora in the United States, in their unresolved search for a global definition of *Klal Yisrael*. When the book appeared in English translation, the original Hebrew title was slightly changed: rather than *The Quest for National Identity*, it was rendered *The Quest for Collective Identity*. In a personal conversation, Gorny told me that the decision to revert "national" to "collective" was made by the American editors: perhaps, he noted, not without reservation, they disliked the idea of nationhood.[1] Even without delving into a semantic or historical discussion of the two concepts, it is clear that the nuanced shift in translation is telling—and not only with regard to the difference in the self-perception of each Jewish group. It also alludes to the difference in the principal meaning they ascribe to being Jewish, to belonging to the broad entity of Jews, in modern times.

The transmutation of Gorny's title may be seen as emblematic of the challenge embedded in the English translation of any Hebrew text that related, in one way or another, to the question of the desirable contours of Jewish identity. As noted in the previous chapter, this challenge was further enhanced by the fact that, since the 1950s and 1960s, Israel (or rather, images of Israel) was increasingly construed in both popular and institutional frameworks as a mainstay of Jewish identity in America. Set in this context, we saw how moral reflection was represented in American Jewish discourse as an inherent feature of Hebrew literature and how, concomitantly, Israeli society was portrayed in a more positive moral light than in the sometimes self-critical source texts.

However, the challenge—and potential inspiration—posed by Hebrew works to American Jewish identity discourse had to do not only with constructions of ethics and morality but also with other essential aspects of Jewish self-definition. It involved not only the image of Israeli society and ethics but also the basic contours of (American) Judaism and Jewishness. "Just as ancient Hebrew literature is being translated into English to make it part of the cultural heritage of American Jews," literary scholar Gershon Shaked suggested, "so also modern literature is being translated for the same purpose."[2] Shaked further assumed that translated works of Hebrew literature, at least from the 1960s onwards, "have become part of their Jewish identity . . . because the protagonists of these stories and their plots are close to their hearts."[3] Shaked's claim is, perhaps, not too farfetched with regard to these decades, considering the omnipresence of Israel in American Jewish life at the time. This trend had trickled, to an extent, into the literary sphere: notably, not only were most reviewers of Hebrew literature in American newspapers Jews, which in itself "Judaized" the field, but Hebrew literature was sometimes framed or contextualized in Jewish terms, implying that Israeli works could have a bearing on the readers' self-understanding—individual and collective—as Jews.

One way in which the collective Jewish significance of Hebrew literature, and American Jews' ensuing affinity for it, was implied in reviews was through projecting that the translated work would appeal to a specifically Jewish readership.[4] In other cases, this was indicated in the critic's participation in what had been a largely internal Jewish discussion (for instance, American Jewish debates on Zionism).[5] Israeli works were also sometimes specifically described or formulated as *Jewish* or as exploring Jewish themes[6] or compared to other works or writers that were already marked as such in contemporary Jewish American discourse. Some critics, for instance, pointed to similarities or emphasized differences between the thematics of contemporary Israeli and Jewish American authors.[7] A more subtle way in which Hebrew literature was predetermined, or contextualized, as Jewish was through the use of language with predominantly Jewish connotations, which implied that the intuitive way to make sense of the works was by placing them in a Jewish context.[8] References by critics to Jewish places of symbolic consequence (such as Jerusalem) in the translated Hebrew works carried the same assumption and had similar undertones.[9] Although some of these passing references were anecdotal or self-evident—and may indeed have been no more than a casual attempt to connect readers to the work under review—they obliquely constructed a broad Jewish frame of reference for the meanings and values of the translated works for American readers of the reviews.[10]

This framing was perhaps the least implicit in national anthologies in translation, in which editorial introductions often emphasized, in one way or another, aspects of Jewish collectivity as finding expression in the selected Hebrew works. The portrayal of the issuance of the national anthology *Firstfruits* in 1973 by the Jewish Publication Society as "our gift to the new land on its twenty-fifth birthday," in the words of editor Chaim Potok, can in itself be seen as testimony to a collective Jewish meaning ascribed to Hebrew literature.[11] In the introduction to his seminal 1975 anthology *Modern Hebrew Literature*, Robert Alter asserted this in unambiguous terms: "It is hard to think of another field of modern Jewish cultural activity that provides, as does Hebrew literature, such a luminous mirror both of the creative élan and of the deep perplexities of Jews trying to define some relationship to an age-old heritage in a radically unfamiliar new world."[12] Although diverging from one another in the tone and meaning of their discourse, then, different agents of Hebrew literature shared a common assumption of this literature's relevance to American Jews and, more obliquely, of its potential claim on collective definitions of Jewishness. For our purposes, it does not matter whether this was expressed explicitly—it most often was not—or whether any reference was made to what makes a literary piece or corpus or writer *Jewish*. Scholars such as Dan Miron and Hana Wirth-Nesher have convincingly demonstrated the reduction inherent in any such criteria.[13] The framing of the Israeli works in question as Jewish may have been better reasoned in some reviews and less so in others, but this is not our main point of inquiry. The features of the literary works are only the means and stimulus here, whereas the ideological underpinnings of the American Jewish cultural discourse vis-à-vis Israel are the object of study.

As studies have shown, the impact of Israel on American Jewry has often had less to do with the actual ties between Israelis and American Jews, within or without the cultural and political establishments, than with the realm of ideas, images, and historical narratives—the realm of collective identity. However, such abstract entities are usually not simply borrowed or taken from one culture to another "as is" but rather, as posited by cultural theorist Itamar Even-Zohar, they may be imported and appropriated as "goods"—material or semiotic—into the target culture's repertoire, *without* maintaining their source-culture functions.[14] From this viewpoint, it is the Jewish American appropriation of Israeli notions of Jewishness that may have had the most lasting effect on Jewish American cultural discourse. As we have seen in previous chapters, cultural agents played a crucial role in the movement of literary text across these two cultures, which should not be overlooked.

How, then, did agents, mostly translation editors and literary critics, mediate, even modify, images and narratives related to notions of Jewishness and Judaism in Israeli works on their way into Jewish American discourse? What configuration of Jewish identity surfaces from these processes of mediation?

In what follows, I will show how Israeli representations of Jewishness that contradicted core values of Jewish American identity were mediated and adjusted. Literary expression that accentuated Jewish/non-Jewish boundaries through representations of antisemitic persecution or antagonistic portrayals of the non-Jewish world was sometimes obfuscated. We find further mediation of Hebrew literature in American Jewish literary discourse, which promoted a more progressive, yet not secular, notion of Judaism than that depicted in the source works and rejected, or at least subdued, a nationalistic, territorially centered understanding of Jewish identity. Antagonistic portrayals of the diaspora or of representative characters of diaspora Jews were also minimized. The desirable boundaries of Judaism reflected by American mediations of the translated works thus corresponded with the image of liberal American Jewry at the time and helped shape a form of Judaism easier to stomach than the one introduced in the source texts, a notion of Judaism that could serve to reinforce some of the tenets of contemporary American Jewish identity.

It should be reemphasized that the works whose mediations are discussed here are not, and do not claim to be, representative of Hebrew literature. Nor should we presume that their depictions of Judaism captured the complex competing notions of Judaism within Israeli society, even as these notions did surface from more or less nuanced portrayals. Translations, as I noted in the introduction, come into being and receive their meaning first and foremost according to target-culture values and norms.[15] Thus the organizing principle for the focus on the reviews, translations, and other forms of mediation considered here is that they communicated a discursive demarcation of (American) Judaism in some way or another. Their common denominator has less to do with the Hebrew source works they dealt with (or their authors) and more to do with the ways in which these works were appropriated for the American Jewish reader.

De-Emphasizing Jewish/non-Jewish Boundaries

One of the defining aspects of Jewish history and thought in America has been the community's existence as a minority group in a non-Jewish world. Negotiations on the preferable contours of American Judaism were inextricably bound to questions of Jewish/non-Jewish relations and to the particularities of a Jewish identity intermingled in non-Jewish—mainly Christian—life. Indeed, much of the creative thought of important American Jewish figures, from political leaders to writers, rabbis to secular intellectuals, was devoted to the tensions—as well as potential inspiration—faced by American Jewish culture in this environment. Against this backdrop, it is interesting to examine how the representations of Jewish/non-Jewish difference that appeared in translated Hebrew works were mediated to American readers. As we will see, bitter portrayals of Jewish/non-Jewish boundaries as insurmountable, or offensive descriptions of non-Jews that were seen as reinforcing these boundaries, posed a challenge to the American Jewish audience—and may have been appropriated accordingly.

Let us start with the modification of translated Hebrew works in which it was implied that extreme antisemitism, though realized to the utmost in Nazi Germany, was in fact typical of all nations of the world throughout history—and perhaps still is. As literary scholar Naomi Seidman shows, there was a tendency in American Jewish representations of the Holocaust, from the 1950s through the 1970s, to universalize the Jewish particularity of the Holocaust and to play down antagonistic references to the Christian world. Seidman demonstrates this with regard to the English translation of stories by American Yiddish writer Isaac Bashevis Singer, in which anti-Christian sentiments were censored, and to the universalizing approach of the Broadway production of *The Diary of Anne Frank*.[16] The omission from translated Hebrew works of sweeping accusations of antisemitic persecution on the part of contemporary (Christian) nations can be understood in the same vein. The following example is taken from Ben Halpern's English translation of *Mori Sa‘id* by Haim Hazaz, published in 1956. This paragraph, part of a chapter that was omitted in full from the original text, has the protagonist, Mori Sa‘id, charge the nations of the world with antisemitism on par with Nazi Germany. (For the sake of clarity, citations of passages removed in their entirety from the English translation are not indicated by ~~strikethrough~~.)

> The nations of the world saw the suffering and destruction that came upon the people of Israel and looked the other way in silence—good bye and good riddance. For such is the way of the world, that the Jewish people suffers, and not only at the hand of that most evil one but at the hand of all nations, and there is no difference between him and them but the difference between thieves and archthieves; the former plunder you little by little whereas *he* plunders and takes everything away from you en masse; they strangle you bit by bit, whereas *he* strangles you all at once.[17]

Mori Sa‘id's assertion that Hitler and other nations of the world are comparable in terms of their attitude toward the Jews is followed, later in the same omitted chapter, by his conviction that the catastrophe of Nazi Germany was a punishment imposed on the world for its deep-seated antisemitism and historical persecution of the Jews. Here, Mori Sa‘id envisages George V, king of England, being visited one night by the archangel Michael, who recounts to him all the forms of suffering that were inflicted on the Jewish people by different nations. When Michael informs the king of the scale of destruction soon to be unleashed by Hitler, not only upon the Jews but upon the world, the king

> became utterly frightened and asked: "what is the reason and cause for this predicament?" Michael, archangel of Israel, replied: "Ah, don't you know? Don't you know? It is because you have persecuted and enslaved the Jews in ways that are worse than hell, yet considered yourself off the hook. Now, it is eye for an eye, tooth for a tooth: what you did—will be done back to you. You will now eat from the same stew and come to know its taste!" When the king heard this, his spirit left his body and he died; he only managed to briefly instruct his son: "Beware of reigning over these heretics!" which is why his son gave up the monarchy, renounced the throne, and let his younger brother reign in his place.[18]

Even though Hazaz put these perspectives in the mouth of an ostensibly naïve, uneducated protagonist, the broad generalization that all (Christian) nations of the world are not only deeply antisemitic but antisemitic to the point of wishing total annihilation on the Jews was presumably seen as potentially offensive. Although considerations of style and length perhaps contributed to the editorial decision to omit the chapter, agents of Hebrew literature may also have wished to avoid non-Jewish readers' antagonistic reaction to such a sweeping and damning portrayal.

A similar case in which unqualified accusations of antisemitism were omitted in the translation can be found in Mildred Budny and Yehuda Safran's 1982 translation of Benjamin Tammuz's novel *Requiem for Na'aman* (1978). The short and extremely bitter chapter 28, in which the narrator bluntly accuses all nations of the world throughout history, and particularly the contemporary Christian world, of radical antisemitism, was left out in full. Here, too, the Christian world is juxtaposed with Hitler, with whom it ostensibly shares the wish to annihilate all Jews:

> From the dawn of civilization, the nations of the world have delighted in a little gift granted to them: the Jews. Assyria and Babylon, Greece and Rome—and then the Christian world—have all made the most of enjoying the Jews. . . . Then came Hitler and put a spoke in their wheels. He just wanted to fulfill the ancient dream of eliminating the Jews with his German thoroughness and meticulousness; however, apart from this blessed idea of his, he had some other wishes too, which did not go hand in hand with the leanings of the other nations. His fine services were well appreciated as far as they concerned the Jews; however, he had to be fought, for other reasons. And so the dream of the Christian world had once again come to nothing.[19]

As in the translation of Hazaz, the original text may have been perceived not only as potentially offensive to a Christian reader but also as politically volatile from an insider's Jewish perspective, within the context of Jewish–Christian relations in America—thus leading to the omission, in a translation otherwise rendered faithfully. Subtler interferences in the translation of similarly charged subject matter are found in Dorothea Shefer-Vanson's 1986 translation of Amnon Jackont's political thriller *Borrowed Time*, already mentioned earlier. Here, the reader is spared a statement about contemporary Germany that accentuates its Nazi past, as an explicit reference made in passing to the German crematoriums was not retained in the translation.[20] Interestingly, not only was a bitter reference to Jewish persecution tempered in the translation of Jackont's novel, but so were much less charged indications of antisemitism, as if any mention of antisemitism were politically untactful for overly stressing the boundaries between Jews and non-Jews.[21]

Another way in which translations de-emphasized social or religious boundaries between Jews and non-Jews was in the rendering of Christian symbols, such as the figure of Jesus Christ or the church. These interferences in translation, though not many in number, are telling in that they attest to a certain cautiousness in representations of the Christian world. Yigal Mossinsohn's *Judas*, a historical novel about the figure of Judas Iscariot, deconstructs the Christian myth of Jesus and substitutes a nationalistic, secularly inclined reinterpretation of the Christian story. In Mossinsohn's version, Jesus is primarily concerned with the war waged by the Jewish underground against the Romans.[22] Mossinsohn's novel, which originally appeared in Hebrew in 1962, was published in the United States in 1963 by the commercial St. Martin's Press, with a translation by Conservative rabbi and liturgist Jules Harlow, yet several interferences in the text made the translation more unambiguously benign than the source text in its portrayal of the figure of Jesus. When the character of Andigones first encounters the scrolls from Roman Judea that recount the story of Jesus, for instance, he describes them as "tales about a strange, ~~outlandish~~ [**amazing**] man from a village called Nazereth."[23] The Hebrew adjective *timhony*, used in the original text to describe Jesus, carries largely negative connotations of peculiarity and was substituted in translation with an adjective of predominantly positive connotations. Later in the same chapter, when Andigones expresses his surprise about Pontius Pilate's decision to free Barabbas instead of Jesus, the image of Jesus in the text is similarly modified to a chiefly positive one: "whom did he put into prison and crucify instead of the rebel? ~~One who lives in a fantasy world~~ [**A visionary**], Jesus of Nazareth. This man from Nazareth, the son of a carpenter, ~~a naïve~~ [**an ordinary**] man."[24] Mossinsohn renders the Hebrew *hoze hazayot*, which carries connotations of an eccentricity out of touch with the real world, with the positive and grounded "visionary." Moreover, the more neutral "ordinary" is substituted for the Hebrew *tamim*, which is not necessarily negative but can be readily interpreted as "gullible" when preceded by *hoze hazayot*.

Later in the text, when Andigones expresses his admiration for Jesus based on the stories he encounters in the scrolls, the translation delicately shifts again:

> "when I read about Jesus in the first version, I was filled with an enormous joy," said Andigones. "I discovered a human being, a marvelous, ~~trusting~~ human being. I said in my heart that finally ~~a story about someone flesh and blood~~ [**a flesh-and-blood story**] had been created, ~~someone~~ complete, both foolish and wise, ~~in~~ a story about faith in people and in the destiny of man upon earth.[25]

The translation subtly misconstrues Andigones's original assertion that Jesus was sometimes "foolish" by changing "flesh and blood" from a noun to an adjective that describes the story rather than the person. Consequently, in the translation, the story, not the man, is described as "foolish," whereas in the source text, Jesus himself was referred to as "foolish." As in the previous examples, the modification subdues what readers might consider an irreverent approach to the portrayal of Jesus.

Another Hebrew work whose passing reference to the Christian world had been deemed religiously insensitive was Jackont's *Borrowed Time*. Here, in a conversation between the narrator (a Jewish double agent in Teheran) and a Franciscan priest, the narrator offers an acerbic critique of the wrongdoings of colonialism and then goes on to claim that the church has been a driving force behind it all:

> "And the church, wasn't the church the spearhead of colonialism?"
>
> He became silent, veils of bluish smoke rising from his pipe.
>
> A distant loudspeaker summoned believers to the evening prayer.
>
> "You know your material well," he suddenly said, "—the church." . . .
>
> "You are right. A couple of years ago it would never have crossed my mind. This past year, living in solitude, with all the suffering and mayhem around. I don't know how much good we did for these people," he sighed. "We sent missionaries, who brought army men with them, and then came the merchants and clerks and treasure hunters and adventurers, and finally—politicians."[26]

The exchange was, however, removed in its entirety from the translation. In the source text, the narrator lays the responsibility for the destructive effects of colonialism, even if unwittingly, on the church and its missionaries, in a passage that could easily be perceived as religiously offensive. Furthermore, Jackont has the priest, first silently and then explicitly, agree with the accusations. The omission of the charged dialogue is, therefore, largely self-explanatory.

The rather vulgar generalizations about "all American women," made in passing by the male Jewish narrator of Yehuda Amichai's *Not of This Time, Not of This Place* in the context of his affair with a Christian American woman, were similarly left out of the English translation (1968).[27] Although these shifts may have adhered to normative editorial expectations of American publishers, they perhaps also reflected a heightened sensitivity, on the part of the translators or translation editors, that derived from the Jewish–Christian dimension of the relationship—which is a prominent theme in the novel. Translation agents might have assumed that the Jewish identity of the protagonist would inform the audience's response to his degradation of American women in the text, and modified the translation accordingly.

Along the same lines, we find omissions of racial language. Substituting inoffensive language for derogatory vocabulary occurred in a number of contexts, but was perhaps most significant in sections that had to do with Israeli–Arab relations and represented Israeli approaches to the conflict. A telling example is found in Amos Oz's *Elsewhere, Perhaps* from 1973, in which the word *black* was put in the mouth of a Jewish character to describe Arabs derogatorily. In a dispute between kibbutz members on whether to retaliate for attacks from the neighboring Arab village, Oz has a young kibbutznik proclaim that "there's one language they're perfectly at home in, without a crushing blow, a really juicy blow, as they say, we'll never stop the ~~black rascals~~ [**bastards**] and their ~~black~~ [**blasted**] nuisance."[28] Oz uses racial language to reveal the underlying orientalism and militancy of his character, representing 1950s Israeli society as a whole, yet his stylistic and thematic choice was curbed in the translation. This and similar omissions are perhaps best understood in the context of increasingly strained Jewish–Black relations in America from the late 1960s onwards. The shifts in translation further resonate with the growing identification of Black activists with the Palestinian cause in the 1970s and 1980s, a trend that led to tension with the Jewish establishment and distanced Jewish members from the civil rights movement.[29] The cleansing of racial language thus joins the previous examples of interferences that are usefully interpreted against the backdrop of Jewish/non-Jewish relations in the United States.

Finally, although this section focuses on the rendering of Hebrew works that originated in Israel, I will touch briefly on the English translation of Hebrew literature written by two American writers, the Hebraists Reuben Wallenrod and Ephraim Lisitzky. The two novels, translated in the late 1950s, highlight the rendering of material that deals directly with Jewish life in non-Jewish American settings and thus crystallize the question of appropriation of Hebrew works in that particular context. Both Wallenrod's *Dusk in the Catskills* (1946; English, 1957) and Lisitzky's *In the Grip of Cross-Currents* (1949; English, 1959) take place in the United States and have little or nothing to do with Israel.[30] Both were published by institutional Jewish houses, *Dusk in the Catskills* by the Reconstructionist Press and *In the Grip of Cross-Currents* by Bloch Publishing Company.

What both English translations do have in common with the translations of Israeli works discussed earlier is the de-emphasizing of text that stresses or might otherwise contribute to the bolstering of social boundaries between Jews and non-Jews. In Wallenrod's *Dusk in the Catskills*, the translation tempers mention, and implied critique, of American antisemitism targeting Jews living or vacationing in a New England village in the Catskills during World War II. Several representative examples are the altering in translation of a dialogue in which a Christian woman laments the fact that her younger friend "preferred the company of ~~young Jews staying at the hotel~~ [**young hotel people**]";[31] the omission of observations made by a non-Jewish train-station attendant attributing certain physical traits to Jewish passengers, which, though they are made without malice, echo antisemitic tropes;[32] and the editing out of a reference to the growing wealth and upward mobility of Jews in those years.[33] The subtext of these interferences is made explicit in a conversation between the protagonist Leo Halper, a Jewish hotel owner, and Stevens, his Christian friend and neighbor—and, most revealingly, in the ideological shifts in the dialogue's translation. In the source text, Stevens levels criticism at Halper that he, and the Jews in general, have turned to tourism and the entertainment business at the expense of the biblical values of manual labor and tilling the land.[34] "The biblical people are making us forget the Bible," he tells Halper, a sentence that was left out of the translation, as were other generalizations and accusations similarly made in the plural. Stevens thus makes use of much less essentialist language to describe the character of the Jews in the English version. And whereas Halper defends himself in the original text—"I don't understand this division into 'us' and 'you.' . . . [I]t is neither our fault or yours"—in the translation, this becomes "it is neither my fault or yours."[35] Other, similar interferences in the translation make the exchange less charged and, more important, less *representative* of a broader dispute between Jews and Christians than its counterpart in the original work. Elsewhere in the novel, the translation leaves out not only instances of antisemitism but also passing mentions of Jewishness in uncharged, neutral contexts, as if these mentions might suffice to stir uneasiness in the reader or suggest the existence of a problematic disparity between Jewish and non-Jewish identities in America.

Similar instances of interference can be found in Lisitzky's *In the Grip of Cross-Currents*, which describes the author's life from his childhood in Slutsk, Belarus (at the time part of the Russian Empire), to his adulthood, wandering between different cities in North America. Here, too, sections that accentuate Jewish/non-Jewish difference are revealing. References to "Jewish looks," whether expressed by the Jewish protagonist or his non-Jewish peers, and expressions of antisemitism were blurred in the translation, as in a description of Lisitzky standing in line among other men looking for a job in Boston: "my shrinking posture ~~and Jewish facial features~~ and the foreign accent in which I answered the interrogating official made me a butt to my companions in line."[36] In the translation, the attitude of the other men toward Lisitzky does not emanate from antisemitism as inevitably as it does in the source text. Elsewhere in the translation, the narrator describes meeting a woman on his voyage to New York, as she is pestered by other travelers on the ship: "I looked hard into her eyes—they were honest eyes. ~~Their deep sorrow testified that she was a kosher daughter of Israel.~~ I invited her to sit down beside me."[37] In the source text, the narrator feels an affinity with the woman and assists her primarily because she is Jewish; in the translation, his help stems from universal empathy. The implied possibility that she was harassed for her Jewishness, and the critique it entails, are also left out. Another ideological interference is found in the translation of the title of the fifth chapter, *Bein ha-goyim* (Among the Gentiles), which was substituted with the ethnically transparent "In a Strange World."[38] The religious and ethnic boundaries between Jews and non-Jews alluded to in the title were also de-emphasized occasionally in the chapter itself, as in Lisitzky's description of his students, the sons of a Jewish family in the Canadian village of Ahmic Harbor:

> My two pupils in Ahmic Harbor were Willie and Hymie Brown~~, two children taken captive by the gentiles~~. Hymie, the younger, was a seven-year-old, and he was still at home, most of the time, [**under his mother's influence**]~~, so the Jewish mark left on him in his home environment was not yet lost from his eyes~~. Willie, who was about eleven, went to public school, and moved in a gentile environment~~, so the Jewish mark left on him in his home environment was already fading~~.[39]

The interferences downplay Lisitzky's implied isolationist stance: compared to the Hebrew original, the non-Jewish influences on the children and the possibility of assimilation are represented as less of a threat. Moreover, the changes emphasize the motherly influence in the upbringing of the children at the expense of the broader familial, religious, and cultural impact of the Jewish home. As a result, the narrator's exclusivist language and wish to preserve the boundaries between the boys and their non-Jewish surroundings are subdued.

Interferences in the translation of Wallenrod's *Dusk in the Catskills* and Lisitzky's *In the Grip of Cross-Currents* reflect a negotiation inherent in the self-positioning of Jews in American society broadly: whether with a Jewish or non-Jewish reader (or both) in mind, the texts were altered to the effect that the English version drew less attention to Jewish/non-Jewish difference—and problematics—than the Hebrew source. In this, they epitomize the shifts in the translation of Israeli works discussed earlier. Whether the boundaries between Jews and non-Jews, and their respective identities, were accentuated in the Hebrew text from a Jewish or a non-Jewish perspective, they were blurred en route to American readers.

It should be noted that, as with other types of interferences, one finds inconsistencies not only between texts but also within each text. Some translations involved ideological interference whereas others did not, and in texts that were altered, some charged material was tampered with and some left untouched. Nor should we overestimate the influence of the manipulations on the major themes and underlying meanings of the original works. The translation of *In the Grip of Cross-Currents*, to take one example, may have subtly underplayed barriers between Jews and non-Jews, but the novel's core story line, in which Lisitzky decides to leave the woman he loves because she is not Jewish, remained intact. The differences between the source text and the translation, as discussed in the previous chapter, are of quantity rather than quality: changes in the text subdued it, but did not dramatically alter it as a whole.

The usefulness of the findings presented here therefore lies first and foremost in how they help reveal the ideological underpinnings of American Jewish cultural sensibilities. As mentioned earlier, the tendency to downplay Jewish/non-Jewish difference was not unique to Hebrew-to-English translation. As literary scholar Anita Norich recently suggested, the inversion of a text in order to articulate a "universal, sympathetic message" by erasing anti-Christian intimations was "a central, repeated trope in the movement from Yiddish to English."[40] In light of the major role of Yiddish culture in the shaping of American Jewish collective consciousness, the fact that translations from Hebrew exhibit a similarly cautious approach in rendering references to historical Christian antisemitism and Jewish/non-Jewish difference further anchors the basic claim that the appropriation of Hebrew literature helped chart the preferable contours of Jewish identity in America.

Along these lines, although the manipulations in translations from Hebrew surely attest to a practical wish not to stir antagonism in non-Jewish audiences, they can at the same time be seen as indicating a desired orientation for the demarcation of Jewish identity in America that differed from that implied in the source texts. The late 1950s were "a moment when ideological concern passed . . . to the planting of American cultural roots in *Judeo-Christian Civilization*"—an ostensible trend of interfaith harmony to which Jewish American thinkers and writers, from William Herberg to Leon Uris, contributed.[41] As part of "the talk in America of a Judeo-Christian tradition," writes Arnold Eisen, summarizing Israeli philosopher Nathan Rotenstreich, "repeatedly Jews attempted to convince gentiles and themselves of their shared culture."[42] In 1966, Reform rabbi Arthur Gilbert called for a Jewish identity that goes hand in hand with, and can grow from, Jewish–Christian dialogue, and lamented that "there are some Jews of exclusivist bend of mind . . . who have defined their existence as Israel or as the New Israel in such delimiting terms as to prohibit all others from the promises and responsibility of God's election, unless they fulfill certain racial or creedal qualification."[43] Compounded, then, the changes in translation can be also seen as signifying an ideational principle not to withdraw into Jewish particularity and not to allow the symbolic and practical boundaries between Jewish and non-Jewish life to have an isolating effect on Jewish American self-definition.

(American) Boundaries of Judaism

The desirable boundaries of Judaism, as a religion and blueprint for a collective ethos, also shaped the way Jewish identity was appropriated through the integration of Hebrew literature into American Jewish culture. Reviews of translated works formed the literary discourse in ways perhaps best understood in the context of the internal debate within American Jewry regarding its identity as a religious and ethnic group in the wake of the religious revival of the 1950s. Jacob Neusner's influential 1978 anthology *American Judaism: Adventure in Modernity*, an eclectic sample of writings by Jewish American thinkers mostly from the 1960s and 1970s, reflected contemporary intellectual and theological trends.[44] It includes two recurring themes pertinent to our study: the expressed fear of the loss of a distinct Jewish identity through secularization or through a rupture with the Jewish past[45] and, at the same time, a distancing of American Jews from the traditional observance of classical Judaism.[46] Similar anxieties are reflected in segments of the literary discourse around Hebrew literature. The inclination of reviewers to accept or reject conceptions of Judaism that arise from the translated Hebrew works essentially hinted at the boundaries of a "preferable" form of Judaism for their readership.[47]

The critique of translated works by S. Y. Agnon following his receipt of the Nobel Prize in 1966 is particularly revealing. Agnon's works were increasingly translated and published in the late 1960s and 1970s. In fact, his Nobel Prize may have been an "early catalyst" in the process that led to the substantial rise of translated Hebrew literature in America in the 1970s and 1980s.[48] Agnon's translated oeuvre was also extensively taught in English-speaking university programs and at major Jewish institutions such as Hebrew Union College in Cincinnati, perhaps more than any other author during the 1970s and 1980s.[49] As Sylvia Barack Fishman has argued, "translations of classical, poetic, tradition-steeped works by S. Y. Agnon tend to intensify feelings of the mystical connection that Jews around the world may feel toward Jewish tradition and the Jewish homeland."[50]

Yet Agnon's works, which relate to questions of religion and faith in an oftentimes suggestive and ambiguous manner, also provided a platform for reviewers to express views on contemporary religious issues in America. Two general responses, outlining opposite boundaries of liberal American Judaism, were the dismissal of classical observant Judaism on the one hand and the renunciation of an ultrasecular approach to Jewish identity on the other. The first response—the implied rejection of (Ultra-)Orthodoxy as a "primitive" system of beliefs and way of life—was more prevalent in reviews of Agnon's works anchored in Hasidic surroundings. For example, in his review of Agnon's *The Bridal Canopy* in the *New York Times* in May 1967, writer and journalist Richard Elman stated that the novel is flawed because of the way it celebrates the Hasidic Judaism of early nineteenth-century Galicia.[51] Elman connected his unabashed objection to the "naïve" conventions of culture presented in the novel to the historical circumstances and eventual fate of European Jewry. Elman sharply reminded readers that "just a few years after *The Bridal Canopy* was written, they were being herded into gas vans and before fusillades" and went on to assert that "the fact of God's failure to 'minister justice' to his 'peoples with equity' does set limits on our ability to appreciate such celebrational works."[52] As a result of his preference for a more skeptical and less traditionally observant form of Judaism than Hasidism, Elman denied the literary value of Agnon's novel. "I'm sure [the book's translations] will be great successes," he wrote sarcastically, "on the coffee tables and in the Judaica shops of Jewish suburban communities."[53] Elman seems to have missed the subtle irony Agnon directed at his pious characters, some of which was perhaps lost in translation. What is more important, however, is that Elman's description of the Judaism of *The Bridal Canopy* as folkloristic and historically irrelevant enables him to chart the boundaries of the Judaism he finds desirable for his American readers.

A few months later, in December 1967, a review of Naftali Chaim Brandwein's *In the Courtyards of Jerusalem* in the *New York Times* by historian Laurence Lafore was grounded in similar principles. Brandwein's stories are situated in socioreligious settings comparable to those of Agnon's work, rather uncharacteristically for translated Hebrew literature at the time, whose prevalent narratives revolved around secular mainstream Israeli society. Lafore seemed unable to hide that his uneasiness with the stories, which are anchored in the Ultra-Orthodox community in Jerusalem, stemmed to some extent from the "backwardness" of Jewish life presented in them. "Some of the stories are moving," he wrote, "but the deeper human relationships do not often emerge from the theological and sociological details of ritual butchering, pillars of fire, shaven earlocks and sacrificial urges."[54] Lafore's estrangement from the stories cannot be separated from the alienation he felt toward Ultra-Orthodox life, the features of which he listed with irony and aversion. By discarding the "primitive" sociology and theology of the "orthodox and rather archaic residents of the quarter-of-the-walls,"[55] Lafore implicitly hinted at his preference for a more progressive form of Judaism.

Whereas some reviewers, such as Elman and Lafore, did not separate the discussion of a work's literary merits from their own socioreligious inclinations, others implied their preference for a certain form of Judaism in literary discourse in other ways. Henry W. Levy's review of Agnon's *The Bridal Canopy* and *In the Heart of Seas* in the *Baltimore Sun* in May 1967 indicated his viewpoint more subtly. Levy declared the target audience of these books to be limited: "This is specialized reading," Levy wrote, "for Jews of piety and knowledge, and for all others who are knowledgeable and interested in biblical lore and Chassidic legend."[56] By removing Agnon's novels from the modernist canon and locating them in Jewish folklore, Levy, like Elman and Lafore, implied a distance not only from the literary works themselves but also from the kind of mystical Judaism they depict, underscoring the irrelevance of (Ultra-)Orthodox Judaism for the contemporary educated American Jewish reader.

Discussions of Agnon's works also touched on topics far removed from Hasidic or more traditional Judaism. Agnon's work, perhaps paradoxically, also provided an opportunity for reviewers to express reservations about secularism, the other extreme of Judaism. And although they wrote explicitly about Israeli secularism, their critiques may also be seen as pertinent to the religious blueprint of American Jewry. The socioreligious judgments implied in such literary critiques therefore helped outline additional boundaries of liberal Judaism in the American context in a period when American Jews, as Jacob Neusner argued, had grown more secular but had not lost their need for traditional and historical particularity, the need to "remain Jewish." As Neusner wrote, "The archaic 'holy people' has passed from the scene. In its place stands something different in all respects but the most important: its manifest and correct claim to continue as Jews, a different, separate group, *and* the claim that that difference is destiny."[57]

After Agnon won the Nobel Prize in 1966, literary critic and Jewish Studies scholar Curt Leviant described Agnon's work in a piece in *The Nation* as something that "has little in common with the often cosmopolitan and consciously un-Jewish contemporary Israeli literature." According to Leviant, Agnon suggested that "Judaism in exile is not complete without Zion, and that Jews in Zion are not complete without faith and Torah."[58] Leviant expressed appreciation for the Jewish foundations of Agnon's poetics and for what he perceived to be Agnon's message for contemporary Israelis about the persistent need in Israel for "faith and Torah." Significantly, he not only dubbed Agnon "the representative Jewish artist of our time" but also described him as "a literary expatriate in his own homeland."[59] Two years later, in his review of the literary anthology *The New Israeli Writers* for the *Saturday Review*, Leviant regretted Agnon's absence from the anthology and explicitly bemoaned the lack of Jewishness in most of its stories, which he saw as a distinct weakness in these works, and which he connected to the loaded opposition between diaspora and homeland: "Alienated from the religious tradition, these young Israeli writers are so rooted in their land that their Jewishness is no longer evident." Leviant continued, "In the Jewish state young writers are seeking a chic cosmopolitanism that strips their world of all identifying elements. The Jewish problem is equated with the despised Diaspora."[60] In making this proposition, however, Leviant himself assumed an affinity between secularism and the negation of the diaspora he so painfully ascribed to Israeli culture. That is, inadvertently, he himself seems to have adopted the dichotomy (Canaanite, in essence, as will be elaborated later) that sets "land" and "Judaism" as two antithetical alternatives, the gulf between which cannot be bridged. The undertones to his claim are both social and religious: Leviant not only deplored the marginal status of Judaism in Hebrew literature but also obliquely dismissed secularism as a viable foundation for Jewish identity.[61]

In a similar vein, Richard Elman's April 1968 review of S. Y. Agnon's *A Guest for the Night* in the *New York Times* related in passing to what he saw as a spiritual void in Israeli culture. The review contrasted this void with Agnon's oeuvre, which, as celebrated by Elman, draws profusely from classical Jewish sources. Elman does not refrain from taking sides, suggesting that "one can see Agnon's chosen style and subject matter only as an implicit commentary on the narrow, behavioristic pragmatism which is at the center of so much Israeli life and thought."[62] Parenthetically, in the 1990s, avid Agnon scholar Alan Mintz expressed similar disappointment, in reviews of David Grossman and A. B. Yehoshua, with the secularist tendency of Israeli writers to draw little, if at all, on the wealth of historical Jewish sources.[63] Emphasizing that his outlook was one "viewed through American Jewish eyes," Mintz later emphatically regretted, in what could be seen as a summation of this viewpoint, that "Israeli culture often views the spiritual achievements and imaginative creations of Jewish civilization over the ages as so much poison fruit" and warned that this denial of access to "the imaginative reservoir of the Jewish past" runs the risk of "desultory shallowness."[64] Speaking of Hebrew literature in past decades, he voiced his fear that at least "around the margins there are signs of cultural insufficiency that may signal more serious problems if a deeper connection to the past is not made."[65]

This Israeli approach to the Jewish past, perhaps most explicitly manifested in the Zionist tenet of the negation of the diaspora alluded to by Leviant, may have diminished with time in certain areas of public and intellectual thought.[66] Yet the Israeli view of contemporary diaspora existence, as we will see in the second part of this book, remained largely ambiguous. This, of course, was nothing new to American Jews, as is evident in the circumstances of the Ben-Gurion–Blaustein exchange of the late 1940s and early 1950s, to give one well-known example from the political arena.[67] Its mediation in the literary field, however, was different in tone, as the Jewish American response to the challenge seems to have been less "head-on."[68]

Such an approach could be found, for example, in academic circles, where modern Hebrew literature was gradually treated more seriously as a subject for teaching and learning.[69] A short 1959 book by Eisig Silberschlag, professor of Judaic Studies and then dean of Hebrew College of Boston, titled *Hebrew Literature: An Evaluation*, provides a short introduction to Hebrew literature from biblical times to the present day. Discussing contemporary Hebrew literature, Silberschlag writes with aversive irony about the anti-Jewish Canaanite movement, which was somewhat influential in Israel during the 1940s and 1950s, and which discarded the connection between Judaism and the new nation being built in Palestine. Canaanitism called on Hebrew youth to disaffiliate themselves from Judaism, believing the nation should be rooted in territory and language alone, not religion.[70] "In creating an artificial dichotomy," Silberschlag concludes, "the Canaanites have succeeded in branding all Jews who are not native to Israel as total strangers and foreigners. But their ideas and ideology are no longer in vogue. Jewish consciousness—*todaah yehudit*—is the current aspiration and slogan. And it emphasizes identification with total Jewry, historical continuity and knowledge of Jewish classics rather than exclusive veneration of a very remote past."[71]

By ridiculing the Canaanites and depicting them as marginal, Silberschlag reflected, perhaps more than anything else, the Jewish American apprehension and dismay at the negation of the diaspora in Zionist thought. Silberschlag's claim about the centrality of "Jewish consciousness" and the "identification with total Jewry" in contemporary Israeli literature and thought, too, mirrored his own desire, and the desire of other contemporary American Zionists,[72] more than Israeli reality at the time. As famously posited by scholar of Jewish thought Eliezer Schweid, the tendency of major Israeli writers of the 1950s to search restlessly for new subject matter can actually be ascribed to the spiritual crises experienced as a result of these writers' growing *distance* from Judaism and Jewish tradition.[73] As for Silberschlag's claim about Israeli "identification with total Jewry," in fact, Israeli literary discourse was rather disinclined to see contemporary diaspora culture as a living source of Jewish identity. As we will see in the next chapter, Israeli literary critic Yisrael Cohen, for instance, assigned the translation of Israeli works into languages of the diaspora a redemptive significance;

Cohen saw such translations from Hebrew as a crucial means of breathing new life into the withering diaspora and helping save it from its imminent and total cultural assimilation.[74]

Although most Israeli works selected for English translation did not deal with the issue of the contemporary diaspora directly, some diasporic characters in Hebrew works were portrayed extremely unfavorably; in these cases, we find literary reviews that rejected what they felt to be a demonization of the diaspora. David Stern's review of Amos Oz's *Elsewhere, Perhaps*, translated into English by Nicholas de Lange in 1973, is a case in point. In his review in *Commentary* in July 1974, Stern protested that "Arabs and Diaspora Jews are forever being straitjacketed into Oz's embodiment of the power of Evil" and declared that "Israeli literature, if it is ever to mature, will undoubtedly have to confront the critical issue of the relationship of Diaspora Jewry to Israel and the relation of Israel to Diaspora Jewry, in all its troubled complexity."[75] Stern's tone may be condescending,[76] but his rhetoric is revealing. By defining the capability of "successfully" dealing with Israel–diaspora relations as a mandatory step for the full growth of Hebrew literature, Stern presupposed Hebrew literature almost as a proxy of Israeli society, communally representative of Israel and bearing some kind of social responsibility for its American Jewish readers. In fact, it was not that rare for Hebrew literature to be equated with Israeli society in such a way by Jewish American critics. Often, the line between literary autonomy and social claims was readily blurred. It is clear that for works of Hebrew literature to be accepted within Jewish American literary discourse, at least as viable contributions to Jewish identity, it did not work in their favor to be perceived as outright antidiasporic.[77] If they were, some mediation was required on the part of the agents, so as to deal with this competing—and perhaps threatening—conception of Jewish identity.

A more direct strategy for appropriation, which interfered with the literary work but at the same time stayed hidden, unavailable for scrutiny, was to deal with critique of diaspora Jews through the manipulation of the translation itself. One such case appears in Dalya Bilu's 1980 translation of David Shahar's novel *His Majesty's Agent*, in which, as noted in the opening paragraph of this book, methodical interference in the translation subdued Shahar's acerbic depiction of an American Jewish icon. The character of Abie Driesel, who represents Jewish writer and thinker Elie Wiesel, is caustically portrayed by Shahar as a pompous and self-indulgent media star who knows little about Israel and, against the backdrop of devastating scenes from the

Yom Kippur War, cares only about his own comfort. On a deeper level, as suggested by Dvir Tzur, Driesel's character allows Shahar to juxtapose Israeli and American Jewish alternatives for representing trauma through writing and to imply that the American mode of expression is inherently flawed in rendering collective Jewish trauma.[78] To subdue the unambiguous satire of Elie Wiesel, the editor of the translation first changed the character's name from Abie Driesel to Jules Levy, blurring his identification with Wiesel. More substantial interferences in the translation include large-scale omissions of passages and scenes that ridicule the character's moral fiber, in an otherwise faithfully translated book. In the following (omitted) passage, Driesel's assistant describes him as a man of modesty and elevated ethics, while Shahar is actually implying that he is concerned first and foremost with his own fame:

> "He is so modest and unassuming, that the average Joe will meet him on the street or talk to him at the grocery shop and never even imagine who it is that is standing before him. . . . It is hard for ordinary people to fathom his greatness, his uniqueness. He experiences the torments of each and every one of us, feels the pain of all the depressed and the wretched and the poor, he . . . he is the very conscience of humanity."[79]

The passage is followed by a cynical description of Driesel electrifying a crowd of students at Brandeis University—which was similarly excised in full from the translation:

> "Some call me 'Drasell', some call me 'Driesel', and some call me 'Drizzle'—but who is the man behind these names? And what is that singular essence of his, unique only to him?" As the speech ended, the crowd roared. The auditorium shook with applause. The male students pushed through the crowd to see him close-up, to ask questions. The female students shoved their way through to touch the tips of his fingers, to stroke his arms, to feel that singular essence unique only to him. Many—especially among the younger generation—perceive him as something far beyond a moral human-being; they see him as the last of the Tzadikim, and even, if one may say so, as the Messiah, the earthly embodiment of God Himself.[80]

Neither Driesel nor his young admirers come out well in this ironic passage. The section not only undermines Driesel's value as a thinker and, indirectly, as a recorder of Jewish trauma, but also ridicules his American

Jewish following at Brandeis. Having been cut out of the translation, however, the passage never reached the American reader. Shahar caps off this sardonic episode with an Israeli diplomat from the Ministry of Foreign Affairs, who wishes Driesel to portray Israel favorably in the American press, worrying about the high price of Driesel's coveted services:

> How could we recruit Abie Driesel to our cause? Such a spiritual leader costs a lot of money, and the Ministry of Foreign Affairs is, alas, broke. For one lecture—if he concurs—Abie Driesel asks for no less than three thousand dollars; and the more morally elevated the topic of the lecture—and thus the more spiritually taxing—the higher the price.[81]

This passage, too, was left out of the English translation. The scornful portrayal of Abie Driesel and the ideal of American Jewish ethics and thought that he represents are, of course, decidedly moderated by the elimination of these passages. However, the most substantial interference in the translation is the omission in full of a scene of some five pages in which Driesel meets an attractive female Israeli soldier who happened to attend his classes at Brandeis, where she wanted but never had the chance to ask him a few philosophical questions. Driesel accidentally sees the soldier naked in the showers of the military base before she approaches him, which has a pronounced effect on his reaction to her intellectual interest:

> Of course, he readily and eagerly agreed to her request, and set a meeting in his room within a half an hour, once he had finished his shower. As he returned to his room, he began preparing himself meticulously for the visit. He wrapped his stark-naked body with nothing but a robe, gargled an assortment of colognes, hid all used underwear in the closet, changed the sheets and the pillow cover, laid a clean towel on the bed for tidying up after the act, turned off all lights but the dim shaded desk lamp, and even gulped some French cognac to elevate his spirits before the endeavors awaiting him. However, fearing that the scent of alcohol would spoil his colognes and mar the spiritual aura surrounding him, he quickly hid the cognac and rinsed his mouth once more. . . . Unlike Lilly [Driesel's American assistant], she did not fall into his lap but rather sat on a chair far away from the bed. He urged her to come closer, and sit on the bed, or else his spirit would be lacking and he would not be able to prophesy. His features in agony, his eyes rolling up piously, he explained to her that before she touched his hallowed sanctified scorching flesh, she could not hear the divine word of God emerge from his mouth.[82]

This sarcastic scene, in which Driesel's character is as morally questionable as he is ridiculous, was fully omitted, thus conveying to readers of the English translation a much less contemptible Driesel than the one met by Hebrew readers. The sarcastic likening of Driesel to Jesus is also lost, much as potentially offensive references to Christian symbols were omitted from other works. The concluding description of Driesel as "no more than an advertisement agent for holy Coca Cola," as the harassed Israeli soldier ultimately calls him, encapsulates Shahar's ridicule of an American way of life and the ensuing invalidation of an icon of American Jewish collectivity—and was similarly left out of the English translation.

Critique or mockery targeting diaspora Jews was similarly softened, if more subtly, in Jackont's *Borrowed Time*. Varied, sometimes even contradictory critical references to diaspora Jewry (which, though not explicated, implied American Jewry) were moderated in the translation. In the following dialogue, Arik, an Israeli Mossad agent, painfully describes his shame and regret for leaving Israel, while his Palestinian lover, Catherine, tries to console him:

> "He's all right. He lives [there] together with three million other Israelis. He's not afraid. Only I, the deserter, ran away . . ."
>
> ~~"And so did half a million Israelis and several million Jews who live in other countries . . ."~~
>
> ~~"That's not . . ."~~
>
> ~~"It is. It's exactly the same."~~
>
> The plane dipped into the air-pocket.[83]

Whereas Arik sees himself as a deserter, Catherine, for the sake of argument, adopts a hard-line Zionist stance implying that diaspora Jews should also be classified as defectors from the state. In the translation, the framing of life outside Israel as an unethical evasion of a collective obligation to the sovereign Jewish state was neatly edited out of Catherine's response.

Elsewhere in the novel, Catherine makes several references to the role played by diaspora Jews in the geopolitics of Israel. Whether recounting her family history against the backdrop of the Six Day War or arguing with Arik about Israeli nationalism, her mention of diaspora Jews and the effect they had on the Palestinian side in the conflict was not retained in the translation:

> The hatred grew too. There was war again. The Israelis ~~received lots of money from their brethren Jews and~~ took more land. This time the big

> house in the hills near Ramallah passed into their hands and we could no longer go there in the summer.[84]
>
> [to Arik:] There's something obsessive about your nationalism. You give it as much attention as an adolescent boy does to sex. You vest it with supreme importance and ostracize anyone who doesn't regard it in the same light. ~~You have even mobilized Jews from all over the world to be engaged with your national issues.~~[85]

The careful omission of any reference to the help Israel received from Jews around the world—American Jews being the main "culprit" here—spares the novel's Jewish readers a perspective that lays partial responsibility for the Israeli occupation and ensuing Palestinian suffering on them. Although the underlying charges expressed in these passages are in essence contradictory—the former for not sharing enough of the burden of life in Israel and the latter for *over*participating in the country's affairs—no chances were taken, and both forms of critique were eliminated. To sum up, even as Israeli thought and literary expression were integrated into Jewish American cultural discourse, and even as translated Hebrew works were being read, as Robert Alter presumed, not only by Jewish readers indiscriminately committed to Zionism but also by "more independent and more unpredictable Jews who are deeply curious about Israel, critically or passionately concerned about its complex fate,"[86] unflattering portrayals of the diaspora or of American Jews, as represented in certain works of Hebrew literature, were appropriated or moderated for the American Jewish readership.

This tendency should not be seen only as a practical attempt to help maintain ties between the two major centers of world Jewry by making the translated works less potentially objectionable. Rather, it may be understood in the context of the need to reassert the viability of Jewish nationhood and collectivity without sovereignty,[87] as well as the viability of the Americanized version of Zionism.[88] In other words, these forms of protective mediation should be seen as a negotiation of ideas about Jewish identity and, implicitly or explicitly, as a demarcation of a desirable form of Judaism for the American readership. If postwar Jewish American collective identity was founded primarily on notions of religion and ethnicity, whereas Israeli identity was more closely tied to ideas of nationality,[89] it is not surprising that the American mediation of Hebrew literature suppressed negative portrayals of diaspora Jews and expressions of territoriality based on nationality, or that approaches to religion were tackled in a way that accommodated the receiving culture's needs. The appropriation of Hebrew works by softening expressions of antisemitism or de-emphasizing boundaries between Jews and non-Jews, and by safeguarding the moral image of Jewish collectivity (as predicated on the morality of Israel), can be similarly understood in the framework of American Jewish cultural needs and self-perception.

Ultimately, then, the findings presented in this and previous chapters combine to illuminate our understanding of the mediated role of Israel in American Jewish discourse. If Israel "emerged as a significant cultural touchstone in American Jewish life in the immediate postwar years,"[90] as Emily Katz points out, and following the Six Day War became a paramount source of Jewish meaning, and if Hebrew literature can be seen as one of the more refined ways of discussing questions of Jewish identity, and even considered in theological terms,[91] then we can indeed think of these negotiations, borne by and about literary translation from Hebrew, as assertions of, or claims on, American Jewish identity. Both communities, to return to Gorny's book title from the beginning of this chapter, may have been pursuing their Jewish identities—yet, as implied in the way his title was rendered from Hebrew into English, they have been looking in quite different directions. It is precisely in this context of divergent communal identities that some translation agents perceived themselves not only as practitioners of literature but also as social mediators filling an ideological role, charting and maintaining the contours of American Jewish self-understanding.

4

Jewish American Literature Makes Aliyah

In an oft-quoted anecdote about two Jewish Nobel laureates in literature, Israeli author S. Y. Agnon asked American writer Saul Bellow, in an amiable conversation on the occasion of Bellow's first visit to Israel in 1960, whether he had already been translated into Hebrew. As Bellow had not as yet, Agnon urged him to see to it immediately, for his works "would survive only in the Holy Tongue."[1] When Bellow cited Heinrich Heine as a poet who "had done rather well in German," Agnon replied, "Ah, we have him beautifully translated into Hebrew. He is safe."[2]

Agnon's quip, presumably only half serious, raises a smile by turning the well-known hierarchical order between minor and major languages on its head. Bellow, an author well situated in a world literary center, is instructed to appeal to an outermost periphery for his oeuvre to have a chance at survival. His literary fate in the long run hinges on his translation into modern Hebrew, the language of a minor literature and a meager million-and-a-half speakers (at the time). Of course, the research on literature and globalization in recent decades paints quite a different picture of the hierarchy of literatures and languages. Writers of "minor" languages and cultures often yearn to be translated into English, whereas the American literary market, which maintains cultural hegemony over the global market, is largely unreceptive to import from foreign cultures.[3] Literature written originally in English, by contrast, has been extensively translated into other languages for decades, as part of the unequal exchange of translations in an unequally stratified cultural world.[4]

A more revealing context for Agnon's remark is not the global literary market but rather the intercultural relations between the two major centers of world Jewry. For Agnon, English is not the world's lingua franca, nor the language of a major global literary center, but rather only the foreign tongue of a Jewish diaspora. Within this framework, the question of literary translation from English into Hebrew becomes a question of internal Jewish translation. This is true despite Agnon's implicit dismissal of the validity of Jewish literature written in a non-Jewish language, founded on a conception of forever-threatened Jewish life in non-Jewish surroundings, not uncharacteristic of Israeli thought at the time. One need not refer to Cynthia Ozick's dubbing English the New Yiddish and suggesting its cultivation as the literary, cultural, and even liturgical language of its Jewish speakers in the United States, Ozick's new Yavneh.[5] Nor need one rely on the recent sociolinguistic claim that American Jews speak a Jewish variation of English that has phonological, lexical, and metalinguistic features that distinguish it from American English.[6] As suggested in the introduction, Jewish American fiction in Hebrew translation should be labeled internal Jewish translation because of the sociocultural context of its production and because of how it was perceived and (re)constructed in Israeli literary discourse. In this respect, the translation largely mirrors the movement of Israeli works in the opposite direction. Not only were all the agents involved in the translation process and in the discourse that evolved around the translated works Jewish, but also, and more important, the prism through which Israeli critics integrated the works into the target culture's discourse was often that of Jewish identity, inasmuch as they formulated the major themes of the works in question as "Jewish" and assumed that these representations of Jewishness should have a bearing on their Israeli readers.

In the absorption of Jewish American literature in Israel, then, just as in literary transfer in the opposite direction explored in the first section of this book, the significance of translation and its critical reception has ranged far beyond pure stylistics. From its inception, the Hebrew literary field served as a central nexus in which fundamental questions of collective identity were articulated and engaged. It was deeply influenced by the national and social experience, and in turn left an important mark on it. Thus it offers us fertile ground to analyze the Israeli relationship to the cultural alternative of the Jewish diaspora. It is true that early Zionist thought that negated the diaspora as a viable framework for Jewish life saw the European Jewish experience as its primary point of reference. Yet by the time the Zionist idea was fulfilled in the foundation of the sovereign State of Israel in the second half of the twentieth century, European Jewish life had been all but destroyed, and the Jewish communities in the Islamic world were already gradually emptying out. The American Jewish community thus became the main diaspora alternative to Jewish life in Israel, and the spiritual revival that the Zionist project offered the Jewish people in its own land faced its primary competition from American Jewish culture and creativity.

This chapter and the next explore Israeli approaches to Jewish American literary expression based on this premise. I begin, in this chapter, by examining literary debates on Jewish American works and authors in major Israeli newspapers and magazines, and domesticating tendencies in the translations themselves, in roughly the same period covered in the first part of the book, from the late 1950s to the 1980s. These decades, arguably the heyday of Jewish American literature and intellectual thought, saw the unprecedented presence and influence of American Jewish writers on the American literary field. The qualities of "Jewish" sensitivity and alienation ascribed to their works were broadly celebrated as an emblem of the modern era. Saul Bellow and Bernard Malamud in the early 1950s, and later Philip Roth, Cynthia Ozick, and others took root at the heart of the American canon; some of their works were adapted to film and theater productions, further infiltrating mainstream culture. Literary scholar Ruth Wisse even called the postwar decades a "Jewish American renaissance" and described *Commentary*, a major arena for contemporary American Jewish writing and thought, as "the most influential Jewish magazine in history."[7]

Although not all major American Jewish writers were translated into Hebrew during this period,[8] the most canonical ones were, and rather regularly, if not always immediately. When their works reached the Israeli audience, they provided local readers with a meaningful opportunity to encounter representations of American Jewishness that were a product of the Jewish American imagination—that is, not external by nature but a glance from within. Indeed, the Israeli encounter with these intimate portrayals of American Jewish life often led to intellectual and emotional responses of high intensity. Reaction in the Israeli literary and journalistic discourse was personal and acute, perhaps more so than in political or diplomatic channels of contact, ranging from empathy and curiosity to rejection and disdain. And although the works of writers such as Bellow, Malamud, and Roth may have described idiosyncratic characters and lives, they were often perceived and constructed as emblematic of the Jewish American community as a whole. Whether implicitly or explicitly, they were treated by Israeli critics as collective testimony to an alternate way of Jewish life. Their reception is thus particularly useful in gauging the Israeli attitude toward diasporic notions of Jewish identity and existence that may have posed a challenge to the predominant Israeli narrative.

Several social and historical trends stand out in the period from the late 1950s through the 1980s that make the case of Israeli reception of Jewish American literature during these years particularly interesting. As Israel turned geopolitically to the West and ties between Israel and the United States tightened, the Israeli cultural field underwent a gradual yet persistent process of Americanization. From the growth of advertising and the integration of the supermarket and private cars in the Israeli market, through the change in modes of production and consumption of radio content, American practices and values took root in the Israeli cultural repertoire.[9] The Israeli Left's ideological critique of American society and culture as materialistic and vulgar did not disappear but gradually subsided. American literature was translated more extensively, slowly shedding its pulpy image and being published by more reputable houses. At the same time, the presence and impact in Israeli public and intellectual discourse of the negation of exile steadily receded.[10] This happened concomitantly with a growing, invigorated spiritual search in Israeli cultural life for Jewish roots, ranging from the educational to the literary fields.[11] Moreover, on the American side of the ocean, these years saw local Jews draw heavily on Israel and Israeli culture as a source of communal identity—including, as evinced in previous chapters, through the appropriation of Hebrew literature in translation—particularly following the Six Day War. The confluence of these historical trends seemed to create favorable circumstances for Israeli culture to open up to American Jewish thought and imagination via the translation of works by American Jewish writers.

In this chapter, I examine literary reviews, editorials, and author interviews that referred to a wide variety of original works, and were taken from varied venues, including major newspapers and literary journals with different ideological orientations. The vast majority of the reviews appeared after publication of the Hebrew translations, and, as was the case with the American reception discussed in previous chapters, relatively few reviewers seem to have read the original text. The mainstream Israeli press—Mapai's semiofficial organ (and most popular Israeli daily of the time) *Davar*, *Yedi'ot aharonot*, *Ma'ariv*, and the liberally oriented *Haaretz*—and, to a lesser degree, established literary venues such as *Moznayim*, the long-standing journal of the Hebrew Writers Association, accounted for the majority of the reviews. Thus, notwithstanding the occasional pieces in organs such as the right-wing *Herut* and left-wing *'Al ha-mishmar*, most references to Jewish American literature appeared in what was the heart of mainstream Israeli discourse in those years. Moreover, in the approach to American Jewish spiritual life, insofar as it was expressed in these discursive settings, internal political differences were not particularly evident. The Israeli encounter with a dominant diasporic Other, represented here by American Jewish cultural creation, seemed *in itself* to smooth out and to an extent equalize some of the ideological differences inherent in Israeli thought. Therefore, though the patterns illustrated here were part of a multifaceted and complex process of cross-cultural reception, which has never been monolithic, these diverse sources nevertheless point to a relatively robust, broad common ground. Across the spectrum of political affiliation and literary criticism, and through three decades from the late 1950s to the 1980s, Israeli discourse on Jewish American works demonstrated some surprisingly persistent trends, which outlasted significant internal changes in Israeli society and culture during these years.[12] The approach to the diaspora embodied in these discursive tendencies, though enduring, was far from uniform. In what follows, I discuss the ambivalence inherent in these trends and in the symbolic boundary work that they represent.

On the one hand, I claim that there existed a tendency to particularize and "Judaize" universal aspects of works by Jewish American authors, to take pride in their literary achievements or to criticize them when they were "too harsh" in their depictions of Jewish life, generally assuming a common Israeli destiny with American Jews and exhibiting an affinity to diaspora Jewish culture. I further demonstrate how shifts in the actual translations, though often part of a broader norm of domestication in Hebrew translation from all languages, coincided with this inclination by accentuating the "Jewishness" of the works at the expense of more "transparent" or "neutral" linguistic features.

On the other hand, I point to a tendency in the Israeli literary discourse to (over)emphasize the difficulty of living as a Jew in a non-Jewish world, from both a spiritual and intellectual standpoint and a physical and social one, in a way that bolstered the conception of Israeli sovereignty as the best and perhaps the only possible solution for contemporary Jewish existence. I further point to appropriating instances in actual translations, as well as an inclination in Israeli reviews to assume a spiritual and cultural hierarchy in the Jewish world that deemed cultural and literary life in Israel more authentically *Jewish* and therefore superior to that of American Jews.

These different trends attest to the dialectical perception, realized in Israeli literary discourse, of the collective boundaries of the Jewish people as a whole. Against the backdrop of the continuous challenge represented by the other major center of Jewish life in the second half of the twentieth century, this Israeli perception of diaspora entailed both inclusivity and dismissal, implied both communal affinity and unequal hierarchy, and may indeed be emblematic of the dual nature of the Israeli approach to diaspora existence in general.

Let me start by presenting one side of the coin, that of the tendency in Israeli reviews to exhibit a sense of connection and common destiny with American Jews. For the sake of clarity, different expressions of affinity to American Jewish culture will be discussed separately. In reality, however, not only were these imbricated in Israeli discourse, they were also entangled with utterances that negated aspects of Jewish life in America, sometimes maintained by the same writer in the same paragraph. I will elaborate on these seemingly contradictory notions later. For now, let us think of the former as a point of departure, a precondition of sorts, for the latter. Were it not for the Israeli charting of boundaries that were inclusive of American Jews, were it not for a basic assumption of affinity to American Jews, one would find not expressions of intense competition and patronization in Israeli literary discourse but rather indifference. American Jewish culture and life would not pose a challenge to Israeli self-perception were they not deemed deeply relevant.

This relevance was indicated in varied ways. A minority of reviews acknowledged in passing the importance of getting to know the American Jewish experience. These voices argued for the necessity of translation as a probe into Jewish life in America, "a subject unfamiliar to the new generation growing in Israel."[13] They believed that "the 'Israeli' protagonist of our native authors should be placed next to the 'Jewish' protagonist of exilic writers, so as to allow the Hebrew reader to get to know both of them, to know them and to be able to compare them to one another."[14] Some reviews went a step further and expressed a forthright sentiment of solidarity with American Jews, framing the encounter with these literary works as holding instructive potential. Works by Jewish American authors were thus depicted as an opportunity for Israeli readers to gain a better understanding of "this mentality of young American Jewishness, with which we have such a hard time of finding a common language."[15] The literary transfer into Hebrew was tied together with a perceived necessity for a more informed acquaintance between the Israeli reader and Jewish American society and life.

Such straightforward expressions, however, were not extremely common. On most occasions, the presupposition of affinity could only be inferred. For instance, critics might make reference to works by Jewish American writers in their commentaries on social and political realities in Israel. Such commentary ranged from the right-wing organ *Herut* invoking Herman Wouk's *The Caine Mutiny* (1951; Hebrew, 1954) and Leon Uris's *Exodus* (1958; Hebrew, 1959) in its lambasting of the ruling Mapai party,[16] to leftist reviews of Bernard Malamud's *The Assistant* (1957; Hebrew, 1962) and *The Fixer* (1966; Hebrew, 1969) by writers Ehud Ben-Ezer and Yoram Kaniuk that juxtaposed Malamud's vision of Judaism with deteriorating moral standards and Israeli disinterest in Palestinian suffering,[17] to reviewers who drew on Jewish themes in works by Saul Bellow and Chaim Potok in their calls for a revival of Jewish discourse and values in Israeli cultural life.[18] These reviews gave expression to very different outlooks yet shared an implicit assumption that American Jewish works were a natural reference point for internal ideological debates in Israel.

It was not only positive reviews, ones that took pride in American Jewish achievements, that presupposed a shared destiny between the two Jewish centers, but also castigating commentaries on Jewish American authors who portrayed Jewish life in a critical way. Echoing the Jewish public reaction to Philip Roth in the United States, though admittedly on a much smaller scale, Israeli critics objected to works such as *Portnoy's Complaint* (1969; Hebrew, 1970) and *Goodbye, Columbus* (1959; Hebrew, 1970). Reviewers regretted Roth's "twisting and distorting the image of American Jews"[19] and expressed fear that "the ignorant, fundamentalists and hate mongers, . . . won't look for Rabelaisian humor in his stories, but for blood: a legitimation for antisemitism and license for xenophobia—and Roth gives them plenty of that."[20] Although some Israeli reviewers disputed and even mocked the institutional American Jewish discourse about Roth, others identified with it openly, describing Roth as a "self-hating Jew," unfair and unrepresentative in his descriptions of American Jewish family life. Famously, Kabbalah scholar Gershom Scholem attacked *Portnoy's Complaint* as "the wet dream of every antisemite, the consequence of which will be worse than that of the infamous *Protocols of the Elders of Zion*," and expressed fear that Roth's work would endanger not only the American Jewish community but Jews as a whole, globally.[21] Such negative reviews by Israeli critics charted an inclusive collective boundary that assumed one large community of world Jews and in effect made little differentiation between Jews of the homeland and Jews of the diaspora.

Perhaps the most important emblem of this trend in Israeli reception of these writers' works had to do with the systematic Jewish *framing* of the literature. Although a few Israeli reviewers described the works first and foremost as American, thus symbolically excluding them from the boundaries of Jewish cultural creation, the majority of Israeli critics tended to downplay the Americanness or universality of this literature. Such Jewish framing, or contextualization, had varied manifestations. First, there were expressions of national pride in personal achievements of Jewish American writers and in American Jewish collective success, as in *Ma'ariv*'s head count of "our brethren, the sons of Israel" that appeared in *Life* magazine's list of forty future American leaders of 1962, which included nineteen Jews, Philip Roth among them.[22] Bellow's Nobel Prize in 1976 was celebrated as a source of collective pride, the acclaimed author as "one of our own."[23] In fact, the literary achievement of American "writers of our race" was appropriated as Jewish in the national sense of the word,[24] even when the authors themselves expressed their doubts or rejected such categorization of their works. Israeli reviewers tended to ignore such doubts or to acknowledge them only to dismiss them. In a 1965 article on Saul Bellow, for instance, reviewer Yosef Raz described Bellow as someone who "declares himself to be a Jewish writer and his worldview to be founded on Judaism,"[25] even though an interview with Bellow cited by Raz in the same article had Bellow claiming that his Jewishness did not concern him. Some early reviews Hebraized Bellow by changing the transcription of his given name (from Saul to *Sha'ul*) or of the names of his protagonists (from Moses to *Moshe*), imposing Hebrew on the Anglicized forms of the names.[26] Such Jewish contextualization was further manifested in reviews by the use of *Jewish* as an adjective for a wide array of (mostly abstract) nouns describing the literary works and their authors, sometimes without a felt need for further explanation: Jewish anxiety, Jewish problematics, Jewish imagination, Jewish morality, Jewish essence, Jewish humor, Jewish soul, Jewish sensitivity, Jewish estrangement, Jewish wit, Jewish casuistry, and so on. This semantic tendency established the works as de facto Jewish without necessarily substantiating this Jewishness.

The insistence of this Israeli approach to American Jewish writers was revealed somewhat amusingly in Saul Bellow's conversation with an Israeli crowd upon his visit to the country in 1970, where the audience "charged on the Jewish issue" and asked Bellow if his works were influenced by writers such as Sholem Aleichem and Y. L. Peretz.[27] Bellow politely replied that he had read these authors as a boy and "rather enjoyed them," yet he enjoyed reading James Fenimore Cooper just as much, and, in fact, it was Cooper who touched him more.[28] The same year, Israeli novelist Hanoch Bartov wrote a column about a meeting he had with Philip Roth in New York, noting that the hours he spent with Roth would remain with him for a long time to come. They spoke about the reception of *Portnoy's Complaint*, about leftist criticism of Israel, and about a new story of Roth's. Bartov, who must have known that Roth was condemned in American Jewish circles for his writings and that Roth had misgivings about his designation as a Jewish writer, concluded his column by stating, defiantly: "I do not know what he [Roth] may think. But I have met with a Jewish man, a Jewish author."[29] In 1976, the same Bartov noted that Saul Bellow was "one of the most important writers of our generation, and even though he is indignant at anyone who attempts to reduce him in such a way, one may still call him at the very least a 'Jewish American' writer, if not simply a Jewish writer."[30]

Interestingly, some tendencies in the actual translations of American Jewish works during these decades coincided perfectly with this trend in Israeli criticism. These shifts in translation were not unique in the literary landscape, and did not target American Jewish works in particular. Nor can they be as easily termed "ideological manipulations" as were the interferences that we have seen in the opposite direction of transfer. Such censoring interferences scarcely occurred in Hebrew translations of Jewish American works, as charged political material was rarer and less explicit in the source texts, and Israeli editorial policies were presumably less sensitive about them.[31] That said, the textual effect of domesticating tendencies in Hebrew translation, which often pertained to more formal features of language, should not be discarded. Although part of a broader stylistic norm of domestication in Hebrew translation from all languages, these translation strategies corresponded with the particular Jewish contextualization of the translated works by the critics—and may have even, to a certain extent, reinforced it. This linguistic-stylistic tendency in translation, whose roots go back to literary norms of the Haskalah period, colored the text with markedly Jewish language.[32]

Perhaps most commonly evident in the preference for an elevated register of language, these stylistic shifts often invoked Hebrew constructs from early Jewish sources and involved earlier strata of Hebrew. A representative example is the use of the biblical suffix *-ah*, as in the 1971 Hebrew translation of Bellow's *Mr. Sammler's Planet* in which *yerushalayim-ah* ("to Jerusalem") was used in rendering Dr. Gruner's entirely mundane remark to Mr. Sammler, "I believe I'll go to Jerusalem."[33] Associated with an archaic-liturgical layer of Hebrew, *yerushalayim-ah* (Chronicles 2 32:9, among others) is much more conspicuous and has stronger Jewish connotations than the commonplace alternative of modern Hebrew *li-yerushalayim*. The preference for elevated language thus subtly transformed the text, making it less transparent and more recognizably Jewish. A similar effect in register could be achieved by lexical rather than grammatical-morphological means. In the 1980 Hebrew translation of Malamud's "The Last Mohican" from the short story collection *The Magic Barrel*, for example, there is a scene in which the Jewish protagonist Fidelman visits a cemetery and imagines "[flowers] dropped stealthily . . . by renegade sons and daughters unable to bear the sight of their dead bereft of flowers, while the crypts of the goyim were lit and in bloom." In the translation, the original modifier "renegade" was substituted with the Talmudic Hebrew idiom for conversion *she-yatz'u li-shmad* [literally: who withdrew into destruction].[34] This obsolete phrase may be tenable here in terms of its formal meaning, but, unlike the English source, or the contemporary Hebrew alternate *she-hemiru et datam* [literally: who changed their religion], the old idiom lends the sentence a much denser Jewish texture, stylistically. Moreover, the Hebrew idiom encompasses the perspective of the collective and carries starkly negative connotations, implying that conversion from Judaism entails both individual and collective destruction (from the root *sh-m-d*).

Preference for a high register with historical Jewish overtones was also manifested in the use of ornate yet anachronistic phrases, as in the translation of Bellow's *Herzog*, which includes the following fragment of dialogue between the novel's protagonist, Herzog, and his psychiatrist, Dr. Edvig: "do you think your wife has a Christian outlook?" "I think she has some home-brewed otherworldly point of view." In the Hebrew translation, "otherworldly" was rendered as *she-lo me-alma ha-din*, a flowery Aramaic idiom that traces back to the Babylonian Talmud (Kiddushin 81).[35] Unlike the noncommittal "otherworldly" of the source text, the Hebrew/Aramaic idiom has unambiguous Jewish connotations that are even further pronounced as they are contrasted with the "Christian outlook" of Dr. Edvig's preceding question. In another dialogue in the novel, Herzog's fellow scholar Shapiro refers to the city of Chicago during their conversation about where it would be most suitable for Mr. and Mrs. Herzog to relocate, while complimenting Herzog's wife on her delicate taste by declaring that "a little woman like Mrs. Herzog is just what the old place needs, too." Whereas the dialogue simply touched on whether it might be a good thing for the couple to move to Chicago, the Hebrew translation uses the obsolete biblical *kiryah* ("city"; Deuteronomy 2:36, Proverbs 11:10, among others) to render "place."[36] Elsewhere in the novel, in a barbed exchange between Herzog and his lawyer, Sandor Himmelstein, the latter threatens to beat up Herzog and warns him that he will "pray for [death]. A coffin will look better to you than a sports car . . . I've done this to guys myself"—the demonstrative pronoun "this" in the last utterance was explicated in Hebrew with the biblical *shfatim*, an antiquated word that is found almost exclusively in Jewish liturgical depictions of the devastating punishment of god (Exodus 12:12, Numbers 33:4, among others).[37] Again, unlike the transparent original text, the language of the Hebrew translation opts for an elevated register that draws from earlier strata of Hebrew and has stronger Jewish connotations.

Finally, there were also more particular interferences in translation that made use of recognizably Jewish language, restricting the denotation of a word or changing its transcription. In Malamud's *The Assistant*, for instance, the name of the major Jewish organ of the first decades of the twentieth century was transcribed in keeping with its Yiddish rather than English inflection. Whereas in the original text, the storekeeper Morris Bober takes the *Forward* from the newsstand, in the 1963 Hebrew translation he picks up the *Forverts*—thus accentuating the paper's Yiddish medium and Jewish readership.[38] In the same novel, Frank, the gentile Italian suitor of Bober's daughter Helen who works in Morris Bober's shop, tries to keep himself occupied as very few customers visit the shop: "To keep from getting nervous he took out a book he was reading. It was the Bible and he sometimes thought there were parts of it he could have written himself." In the Hebrew translation, "Bible" was rendered as *Tanakh* even though this interpretative choice restricts Frank's reading material to the *Jewish* bible, whereas Frank's interests at this point in the novel more plausibly relate to the New Testament.[39]

The final examples notwithstanding, one should not get the impression that "Judaizing" tendencies were more common during these decades in translations of American Jewish works than in translations of other works of world literature. Tracing back to the dominant norm of the enlightenment and revival periods of Hebrew literature to bring foreign works "closer to home," literary translations into Hebrew from all languages displayed domesticating tendencies well into the twentieth century, Judaizing stylistic and even thematic aspects of the original works. That these shifts were not unique does not, however, mean that they should be overlooked in our specific framework. Though not the *cause* of the tendency to contextualize as Jewish the translated American works in Israeli literary debates, these interferences in translation were at least strongly correlated with this kind of contextualization. Despite being mostly general and understated, they may have indirectly contributed to Judaizing discursive tendencies as we have seen here, tendencies that framed Jewish American literature for Israeli eyes.

Such "Jewish" framings were not only evident in norm-governed translation shifts or the rhetoric of reviewers about the authors of the works, as outlined above; they were also manifested in discussions of the characters and themes of the literary works themselves. A 1959 review of Bernard Malamud's *The Magic Barrel* (1958; Hebrew, 1980) in *Moznayim* described the protagonists as "Jewish to the marrow, whether they renounce their Jewishness or accept it."[40] An essay from 1974 in *'Al Ha-mishmar* proclaimed that Bellow, Malamud, and Roth all deal with "Jewish problematics—[Jewish] everyday life, on the one hand, and historical implications, on the other," each of their characters being "Jewish through and through [*ad shorshei nishmatam*], their Jewishness revealed in the minute details of their lives rather than in the so-called bigger picture."[41] The lion's share of the literary discourse assumed that the Jewish element played a major role in determining the topics, themes, and covert meanings of the American works. A majority of Israeli reviewers analyzed the moral preoccupations and vantage points of the protagonists as stemming mainly, if not exclusively, from their Jewish identity. Some critics took such a reading to be self-explanatory, whereas others went to great lengths, in nuanced discussions, to support it. Novelist and literary critic Ruth Almog, who usually belonged to the latter category, may have nonetheless summed up this approach in the Israeli literary discourse most concisely when, upon the death of Bernard Malamud in 1986, she claimed in a tautological manner that "most of Malamud's protagonists are Jews, and even those who are not Jews have the traits of a Jewish character. This means that Malamud's protagonist is always a Jew."[42] Interestingly, such views were expressed not only in literary venues of high symbolic capital but also in local book clubs. One such group, from kibbutzim in the Galilee and Jezreel Valley, declared of Saul Bellow's *Mr. Sammler's Planet* (1970; Hebrew, 1971) that "only a Jew could see the world like that"[43] or, more chauvinistically, that "this degree of intelligence can almost only be found in novels written by Jewish writers."[44]

It should be stressed that this chapter does not attempt to participate, any more than previous chapters did, in the theoretical debate about what Jewish literature is or how one should define a Jewish writer, questions that were central to the aforementioned reviews. Scholars such as Dan Miron and Hana Wirth-Nesher, as noted earlier, have established the reductionist quality of any such set of criteria. Moreover, the features of the literary works are only the means and stimulus, whereas it is the ideological underpinnings of the Israeli public and intellectual discourse, and what they reveal to us about Israeli culture, that are the object of study here. Let me point out briefly, however, that the predominant framework of analysis and classification revealed in Israeli literary discourse was not self-evident. The inclination to contextualize these writers and their works as Jewish, for instance, was less pronounced in the American discourse. An anecdotal illustration of the difference between the two national settings can be found in the Hebrew translation of an article on Saul Bellow that appeared originally in *Newsweek* in 1970. The Hebrew version of the article, which was published in *Davar*, did not retain the original title of the segment about Jewish aspects of Bellow's oeuvre, which read in English "Own Specialty," replacing it with "The Voice of the Jews [*Shofar la-yehudim*]."[45] Along the same lines, the hedge *so-called* was omitted from the sentence "Bellow's own specialty is the so-called Jewish novel," leaving the English source's expressed uneasiness with such broad ethnic/national categorization out of the Hebrew version of the article.[46]

This contrast between national discourses was encapsulated neatly in an Israeli review of the movie adaptation of Chaim Potok's *The Chosen* from 1984. "While this is an American film," critic Aki Shoval began, "it is in fact one of the more 'Jewish' films ever to be seen on the big screen."[47] Later in the review, he quoted from a *Sunday Times* critique that took the opposite path. The *Times* reviewer waxed poetic, writing, "this is not only a movie about conflicts within the Jewish people but rather also a story about the generation gap, cultural differences, and, above all, a unique friendship between young men—and if there are more universal subjects than these, I do not know them."[48] Although a comparative analysis across national literary discourses is beyond the scope of this chapter, these disparate responses to *The Chosen* provide us with revealing insight: the Israeli and American emphases in approaching the same work bordered on antithetical.

This is not to say that American Jewish voices did not attempt to discuss these works through a principally Jewish lens. Such hermeneutic approaches by Jewish critics, in both mainstream and intellectual (Jewish) discourse in the United States, were far from rare. In America, however, the social context and significance of such a Jewish framing were very different than in Israel and chiefly related, in the period under discussion, to ethnic revival and the rise of multiculturalism.[49] As for the more institutional discourse, much of it revolved around the (non)credibility of "unflattering" representations of Jewishness and of the Jewish community and potential damage from the consumption of these images by the general American public. Moreover, that these literary works were also framed as Jewish in Israel should not be taken for granted. After all, American Jews and Israelis have historically *clashed* over the definition of who is a Jew, both culturally and ideologically, and their competing definitions caused much friction between the two Jewish centers.[50] Indeed, a deeper analysis of the literary discourse in Israel reveals that the apparent inclusivity implied by the Jewish contextualization of these American writers, this charting of a collective boundary that includes American Jews in the fold, had further ramifications. The authors and their works may have been approached and discussed as Jewish, yet this was done predominantly on Israeli terms. The other side of this inclusivity implied by Israeli boundary work was implicit dismissal and rejection, buttressing Israeli sovereign identity as the main viable option for Jewish life in a post-Holocaust era.

Accentuating Jewish/non-Jewish Boundaries

One of the dominant themes in works by Jewish American writers in the decades in question was a tension between the universal and the particular as determinants of identity. For Israeli critics, the universal was often equated with Americanness or the Christian West and the particular with Jewishness, two opposite forces pulling the protagonist in different directions. It is in this hermeneutic dichotomy and, more significantly, in the collective social conclusions that accompanied it that the Jewish framing of literary works took on an ideological meaning in Israeli criticism.

The underlying ideology of such interpretations and the function they served in Israeli discourse are perhaps best exemplified in the Israeli approach to works by Saul Bellow and Bernard Malamud. During the decades in question, both authors were translated regularly into Hebrew, discussed at length, and generally very well received. Both were seen as representative of Jewish American literature and cultural creation and as commentators on the major preoccupations of contemporary American Jewish society. The relation (and tension) between the Jewish and the universal as two poles of identity, and between Jews and non-Jews in actual American society, were central to Israeli reviews of their works. Moreover, their protagonists and plots were seen as emblematic of the Jewish situation in America.[51]

As in most good literature, this tension was suggestively left unresolved in Bellow's and Malamud's works, allowing for a wide range of interpretations. Many American readers and critics, for instance, found the identity crisis and emotional confusion embedded in this tension to be not only a truthful depiction of the American postwar condition but also something they could easily relate to—that is, a source of strength.[52] As Terry Cooney noted, the cosmopolitan ideology of New York intellectuals, which informed their literary and cultural preferences (and left its mark on the American reception of authors such as Bellow and Malamud), rejected both particularism and assimilation and assigned value to movement between different forms and sources of identity.[53] The dominant approach of Israeli critics, however, was to resolve such tensions by rejecting the possibility of any common ground or affinity, let alone a fruitful dialectic, between the two poles and drawing a pessimistic social conclusion. A case in point is S. Sagiv's review of *Herzog* (1964; Hebrew, 1965), which assumes that this clear Jewish/non-Jewish dichotomy creates a spiritual impasse:

> [Despite the novel's success, it] gave no solace to the author or his protagonist, who are caught in that international tangle that is so Jewish in Bellow's world. . . . The author may have come to the conclusion that there is no bridge nor any possibility to bridge Jewish identity and an identification with the intellectual sphere of the "other" world, between Jewish transcendental spirituality and the non-Jewish spiritual world. The Herzog case is thus not an isolated incident but rather "Herzogism" per se, and the problem has no solution.[54]

By implying the consequences of such a predicament, Sagiv takes a leap from the idiosyncratic to the representative and from literary interpretation to a collective social observation, typical of Israeli reviews of the time.

Notably, the impenetrable boundary between Jews and non-Jews charted by Sagiv and an ensuing insoluble "Herzogism" for Jews in America are manifested primarily in the intellectual and spiritual sphere. This area of discourse proved to be fertile ground for essentialist commentary. Indeed, other reviewers shared Sagiv's assumption of such a boundary, going a step further to color it with decided moral judgment. Israeli critics equated notions of moral responsibility and social solidarity, humanism and hope with Jewishness or Jewish writing and described the spiritual heritage of the Christian West as characterized by immorality, decay, and despair.[55] In a 1976 essay about Bellow's oeuvre in *Moznayim*, Tzfira Porat described the "ongoing struggle of the human self to retain its humanity in the face of the death drive and inhuman instincts" as "Bellow's Jewish answer to the crisis of murderous-suicidal nihilism that has struck civilization, to some degree at the fault of non-Jewish writers."[56] Porat went on to declare that all of Bellow's protagonists must know that "anyone who yearns to escape the prison of the self and to sacrifice himself would better do so for his brothers, as do Jewish mothers, and not for the sake of death itself, as did the fathers of Christianity."[57] Outlining a boundary between Jews and non-Jews in a particular literary context served to support a trenchant moral critique of Christian thought in general.

More subtly but along the same lines, Malamud's novels *The Assistant* and *A New Life* (1961; Hebrew, 1962) were described in an Israeli review as portraying the "uniqueness of the Jewish soul against the background of gentile environment."[58] Contemporary American critics, by way of comparison, did not necessarily share this conception. This is true of the American Jewish discourse as well. In an essay on Malamud that appeared in the journal *Midstream*, for instance, H. E. Francis asserted that the Jewish and Christian protagonists are constructed as interchangeable: "fundamentally [Frank] has been a Jew throughout, as Morris has been a Christian," and they can be seen as projections of the "universal Everyman."[59] Francis further claims that "the fusion of Hebrew law and Christian love is evident in [*The Assistant* as well as] other works of Malamud" and that, at least in *The Assistant*, Malamud's protagonist (Christian or Jew) "transcends the barriers of theology to answer the demands of his heart."[60] Israeli critic Amnon Hadari had this and similar reviews in mind when he wrote,

> Bellow and Malamud reject in disgust the lustful suggestion of the hosting Christian West to merge with it. . . . [T]here were readers who were taken by [Frank's] conversion [at the end of the novel], and saw it as an

> expression of Malamudian optimism, a utopia of sorts. They associated Malamud with sheer universalism, quoting things he once said in an interview: "every man is a Jew." Nothing, however, could be further from the truth! Reading Malamud's works, I hear the author shout from beyond Bober's grave: "My daughter, know that this is all a lie, a lie, a lie!" That is to say, we have been struck by calamity, by theft and by rape precisely because Western culture declared itself to be enlightened. It was just then that the legal hunting season began and they started stealing the idols [*terafim*] (and girls) of the family business.[61]

Hadari rejects "good-willed" American interpretations of Malamud, supporting this rejection by hinting at palpable instances of antisemitism in Western/American society. The review even likens (gentile) Frank's rape of (Jewish) Helen in Malamud's *The Assistant* to the "lustful suggestion" of Christian America to Jews "to merge with it" (*lehi'ater le-hatsa'ato ha-zimatit ule-hitmazeg betokho*). Such a metaphorical reading of Jewish/non-Jewish relations in America is, no doubt, pessimistically violent in essence; yet it is also reminiscent of a few early Israeli reviews that explicitly protested cases of intermarriage between Jews and Christians in Jewish American novels.[62] Hadari's review is one of many that charted, beside a spiritual boundary between Jews and gentiles, a physical and social one as well. Focusing a great deal on the meaning of living as a Jew in non-Jewish surroundings, Israeli interpretations placed a special emphasis on nonacceptance and demeaning of Jews as a shaping factor of American Jewish identity. Yosef Raz of the daily *Ma'ariv*, for instance, summarized the essence of the Bellovian protagonist as follows:

> Most of Bellow's novels depict a Jew who is forced to live in a hostile environment. The Jew knows that the antisemite and the gentile he lives with side by side in urban society do not perceive him as a [separate] person, but rather see in him only the features he shares with other Jews. He is lonely, unable to converse in earnest with other people, and feels constantly anxious under the gaze of fault-finding and stereotyping eyes. Bellow described things accurately and honestly, and many Americans (not necessarily Jewish) recognized themselves in his descriptions. It is so hard being a Jew—Bellow writes; it is so hard being a man in modern society—many Americans read.[63]

According to Raz, the Bellovian protagonist's Jewish identity is chiefly defined by an unremitting atmosphere of antisemitism in American society.

Any interpretive tension between the universal and the particular is resolved by giving preference to the latter, to the Jewish, in understanding the protagonists' intellectual and emotional hardships. However, considering the fact that this overview of Bellow's career was written in 1965, after *The Adventures of Augie March* (1953), *Seize the Day* (1956), *Henderson the Rain King* (1959), and *Herzog*, such an approach seems far-fetched, perhaps even contrived. American criticism may again prove a useful frame of reference. Quite a few analyses of Bellow's major novels were no less focused than Raz on the more conspicuously Jewish *Herzog* and *Mr. Sammler's Planet*, yet while they traced the oppositional forces at work in the making of the Bellovian protagonist, they made little to no mention of contemporary antisemitism.[64] This is not to say that Jewishness did not figure as a factor, only that, although canonical Jewish American literature of this period excelled in demonstrating how, in Benjamin Schreier's words, "an individual [is] created by multivalent human contexts, an urban operator traversed by diverse influences and allegiances and traditions,"[65] dominant voices in Israeli criticism gave high priority to being (haunted as) Jewish as a hermeneutic key to understanding these works when they appeared in Hebrew translation.[66]

Typical of contemporary Israeli reviewers, Raz also generalized from literary representation to social reality. In addition to the boundary between the Jewish protagonist and his non-Jewish neighbors, Raz's critique assumed a boundary between Bellow, the Jewish author, and his non-Jewish readership. The last sentence in the previous quotation presupposes that the terms *Jews* and *Americans* are mutually exclusive and indirectly implies that any discussion of Bellow's works that probes the source of his characters' malaise differently—that is, with a universalist hermeneutic—would be misconstruing Bellow's true intentions. Moreover, such inaccurate interpretation will inevitably have come from non-Jewish readers, whose misunderstanding stems from their non-Jewishness. Critic Shlomo Grodzenski's general remark on Bernard Malamud's oeuvre in 1968 in *Davar*, that "even today, when the vast majority of U.S. Jews truly belong to that country, complications still exist between a Jewish novelist and an audience that is mostly non-Jewish,"[67] should be read along the same lines, as should journalist and politician Eliezer Livne's much blunter comment in 1965 in *Haaretz* on Bellow's novel *Herzog*: "I am not sure that many American gentiles [*goyim*] who do not specialize in literary criticism have had an easy time reading this book. The six million Jews in North America would in themselves suffice, of course, to make the book a best-seller."[68] Having earlier hinted that the anxiety of Bellow's protagonist has to do with his precarious position in a non-Jewish American capitalist environment, Livne then downplays non-Jewish accessibility to and interest in Bellow's work, and undermines its broad American appeal.

One of the underlying notions that informed the Israeli approach to American Jewish works was that of exile, or *galut*. Like Raz and Livne, literary scholar Mordechai Avishai discussed the source of emotional alienation in Bellow's and Malamud's characters and touched in passing on their cross-national reception. "The gentile reader surely understands their loneliness as an intellectual loneliness per se," he wrote in a 1974 review, "yet we cannot help but understand it as the exilic-Jewish loneliness of our bustling era."[69] Of course, the connotations of exile for Avishai and Raz were very different than, say, those celebrated by the New York intellectuals in the 1940s and 1950s (which dominated American literary discourse for years to come). Israeli critical circles, unlike the New York intellectual scene and its "love affair with alienation," rarely glorified the Jewish writer as a "representative modern figure" for his rootlessness.[70] Quite the opposite: the commentary of Raz, Avishai, and others demonstrates that the affinity for and inclusion of American Jewish literature implied in Israeli reviews—we, Israelis, understand you, our fellow Jews, best—went hand in hand with the imposition of some form of negation of exile. From this perspective, both the psychological instability or malaise of the Jewish protagonists and the American readers' misinterpretation of this state in the Jewish authors' works were primarily rooted in a Jewish existence in exilic, non-Jewish surroundings. Indeed, the more Jewish the protagonists or authors, the more problematic, and ultimately impassable, the boundary portrayed between them and their fellow non-Jews.

The consequences of this exilic condition could occasionally be portrayed in Israeli literary discourse in quite a fatalistic manner. One such example is Y. Koreh's analysis of *Bech: A Book*,[71] John Updike's contentious piece on the life of a self-indulgent, sexist American Jewish writer, which drew accusations of antisemitism against Updike, who was not Jewish himself.[72] In an article titled "The American 'Wandering Jew' Is Back," Koreh rejected these accusations and, though he showed some appreciation for the intellectual achievements of American Jewish writers, suggested the acceptance of what he understood to be one of Updike's implied themes—namely, that Jewish writers did not, and perhaps could not, strike real roots in America. Koreh, who began his article by noting the similarity between the centrality and influence of Jewish writers in early twentieth-century Germany and in contemporary America, concluded it with a chilling remark. "Perhaps some of America's Jewish writers," he wrote, "who know the fate that came upon Jewish writers in Germany from the beginning of the century, should give some thought to the matter."[73] Although such a blatant allusion to the Holocaust in a discussion of the prospects of Jewish life in America was unusual in Israeli literary discourse, it is indicative of the underlying trend we have seen throughout. The inclusion of American Jewish culture reflected in literary debates in Israel, realized in a predominantly Jewish contextualization of the works, was intrinsically tied to charting an impassable boundary or even chasm between Jews and non-Jews. The Israeli assumption of common destiny shared by the two Jewish communities was bound up with a perceived unbridgeable gap between Jewish and non-Jewish spiritual life and an overemphasis on the problem of antisemitism.

Israel as the Winning Alternative to Modern Jewish Collective Identity

What did these discursive trends reflect, and what function did they serve in Israeli culture? The answer to these questions is perhaps best revealed where critics made overt references in their reviews to Israel. Such references are important in that they offer us a means of understanding some of the ideological underpinnings of the Israeli literary discourse. The ways in which Israel was mentioned in the discourse corresponded to the two types of boundaries charted by critics between Jews and non-Jews: a social and physical one, related to issues of personal safety and pride, and a spiritual and cultural one. In both of these areas, Israeli reviewers hinted at, or even openly claimed, the preeminence of Israel over America as a solution for modern Jewish life and identity in a post-Holocaust era.

On the social and physical level, the discourse implied that Israel was safer and offered a more dignified space to live as a Jew compared to the United States. This occasionally coincided with the suggestion that life as a Jewish minority within a non-Jewish majority was unviable. As an anonymous columnist in *Ma'ariv*'s literary supplement suggested in 1970, the bloom of American Jewish literature was only a social illusion, for Jews in America really lived in one big ghetto. The column further assumed that a great outburst of antisemitism might be right around the corner: "Think not with thyself that thou shall escape," it said, quoting Esther 4:13, adding solemnly that these words were delivered from "one of the most ancient Jewish ghettos to the most contemporary one."[74] Most reviewers, however, did not hint at any concrete danger threatening the existence or safety of American Jews. The predicament of Jewish life rooted in a non-Jewish world was rather formulated as an issue of pride, with "[the Jewish soul] fighting a rearguard action to preserve the remnants of its dignity," as one reviewer of Bellow put it, "dispersed as it is among many different peoples."[75] I. M. Neiman's review of the stage adaptation of Herman Wouk's *The Caine Mutiny* conveys this sentiment even more outspokenly.

> The ending rings unconvincing to the Israeli crowd. Herman Wouk, who takes pride in his Zionism and his religiosity, concludes his play with a reconciliation based on good will. The antisemite bursts at the "Jewish kike" but takes his words back after a couple of drinks, and the Jewish spectators find consolation in the illusion that the affliction of antisemitism can be healed with a soft bandage. The author does not have the courage to confront the profundity of the problem. If we accept the clever author's advice, antisemitism in America can be eradicated with but a few glasses of wine. . . . [I]t is [also] strange to hear such defense [of the sadist captain] from a religious Zionist, but apparently even good gentiles do not easily give respect to a good Jew who lives among them—and so he must flatter them, and adjust. Indeed, only an Israeli Jew can take part in the dispute between Jews and gentiles in earnest, as an equal. . . . We wish Herman Wouk to come. Rather than sit in New York, and have his wellspring of creation flow to Israel—it would be better, for him and for us, if he sat in Israel and was allowed full and free expression of his religious Zionism.[76]

Unlike most American Jewish writers, Wouk was repeatedly lauded in the mainstream Israeli press for his frequent visits to Israel, his Zionist views and knowledge of Hebrew, and even his adherence to Orthodox Judaism. He was a guest of the Ministry of Foreign Affairs and visited with presidents Yitzhak Ben-Zvi and Zalman Shazar.[77] His stays in Israel were even mentioned in the gossip columns. But this did not save him from such a review, which doubted his genuineness and decried his literary selections as cowardly.

The ideological (re)framing of Wouk's work in its Israeli setting is further revealed through the lens of its translation. In a critical remark

Wouk made about the Israeli adaptation of his play, which he otherwise praised, the writer questioned the change of an instance of verbal aggression toward Greenwald, the Jewish attorney, at the end of the play. The Hebrew translation deviated from the source's "trickster lawyer" [*peraklit armumi ve-takhsisan*], rendering it "tactics of a kike shyster" [*takhsisei perakliton yehudi*].[78] Wouk told *Davar* that although there is antisemitism in America, naval norms would never allow such a phrase to be uttered in a military court. The addition of this explicitly antisemitic reference in the Israeli adaptation of the play may have triggered, or at least amplified, Neiman's rather patronizing critique of Wouk in the aforementioned review. Both of these forms of mediation, which played a role in framing the play for an Israeli audience, readily coincide with the (over)emphasis on antisemitism we have seen in Israeli readings of Jewish American works.[79] Moreover, they spell out a hard-line Zionist perspective on Jewish life in the United States, and imply its obvious solution to the problem—making aliyah.

But the "predicament" of American Jewry most emphasized by far in Israeli public discourse was the state of its spiritual and cultural life. The Israeli portrayal of collective Jewish life in America inferred from these literary works was largely one of hollowness and dearth, bound with inevitable cultural assimilation. Many reviewers passed implicit or explicit moral judgment on the protagonists' faint Jewish identity and went on to consider this emblematic. As S. Shapira put it in his review of Malamud's *Pictures of Fidelman*, which described Jewish American art student Arthur Fidelman's moral and physical degradation in his failing quest for meaning in Rome and Florence, "this seems almost an allegory of a noble nation being devoured in its goyish environment, having lost its strength and pride the moment it stopped believing in the preeminence of its spirit."[80] Shapira then checked himself and proposed that, "being that Malamud is not Agnon," such a nationalist moral was not the writer's deliberate intention but rather was indicated in his work despite himself, so to speak, on account of his "artistic integrity."[81] Shapira thereby implied that the portrayal of Fidelman was nothing but a faithful depiction of the contemporary Jew in diasporic reality, whence he declared dramatically: "A sad book . . . and any hope is useless."[82]

Along the same lines and with similar emotional intensity, Yaakov Rabi's 1975 survey of contemporary Jewish American literature in *Moznayim* drew the following conclusion about the Jewish community:

> Lacking any real cultural dowry, they [the writers and their protagonists] were bound to clash with the brutal reality of "the land of limitless opportunities." . . . [W]hat is left of the old Jewish home is now only scarce folklore, . . . devoid of any humanistic-cultural merit. No relief and deliverance will come from the "warm parental home"—not for Jewish American literature, nor for Jewish American society.[83]

Rabi's allusion to Esther 4:14 ("relief and deliverance will rise for the Jews from another place") conceptualizes the American Jewish situation as similar to that of the Jewish exiles in Persia under the king Ahasuerus, put in danger of elimination in their non-Jewish host country. Like other Israeli reviews of the time, Rabi's analysis of the works by American Jewish writers was serious and generally appreciative while his projections for American Jewish life were grim. The "tragedy of the American Jew of our times,"[84] as another reviewer put it, was eyed as primarily psychological or spiritual. Critics thus took it upon themselves to assert that Israel was the potential solution to the spiritual and cultural "withering" of the diaspora, much as the assertion that Israel was a safe space for Jewish life appeared as a response to the ostensible social and physical hardships of American Jews in non-Jewish surroundings.[85]

It is worth noting that this assertion of a Jewish hierarchy headed by Israeli culture did not come at the expense of real expressions of affinity and inclusivity toward American Jews. A 1977 article by Pinhas Elad-Lender in the journal *Temurot*, to give one example, genuinely celebrated Bellow's receipt of the Nobel Prize, proclaiming that "today the national Jewish ego beams with satisfaction: one of our own."[86] Elad-Lender then particularized Bellow's literary oeuvre by describing it as "focused in its entirety on the Jewish issue."[87] This, however, did not exclude Bellow from reprimand:

> It is a shame that the Jewish identity of Bellow's Jews had been or is in the process of being swallowed up within American life. It is a shame that their Jewishness bears such fading colors, and that they are destined to cease to belong to a Jewish existence. It is a shame that the state of Israel and the national revival do not infuse substance into the lives of these Jews, the protagonists of Bellow's books. . . . [T]he artist has yet to come to identify with the secret formula for the perpetuity of his people. . . . Jerusalem has not yet won him over.[88]

Tying the paucity of Jewish content in Bellow's characters to their lack of interest in Israel, Elad-Lender implied that a nationalist approach to the question of collective identity might be the only way to fill the characters' lives with Jewish meaning. The dearth of Jewish culture in the diaspora was intrinsically connected to its existence in non-Jewish surroundings[89] and was then developed into an indirect expression of the Zionist negation of exile. In fact, such ideological appropriation of Jewish American works may have been the most pronounced in reviews that both framed the works predominantly as Jewish and were highly enthusiastic about their literary value. In a laudatory 1970 review of *Goodbye, Columbus*, which offered a nuanced discussion of this short-story collection, Yehudit Oryan claimed that Roth dealt with the question of Jewish identity more truthfully and profoundly than most contemporary Israeli writers. She went on to state that although "Roth writes in English and has garnered the *American* National Book Award, he is in fact one of *our* finest writers. And I feel sorry for Hebrew literature that he does not write in its own tongue."[90] Hers was an unabashed, if slightly playful, appropriation: the title of her piece was the wishful "Philip Roth, Come Home!"

As is becoming clear, literary reviews that made unconcealed reference to Israel help us probe the ideological infrastructure of the field of reception. It is here where the critical tendencies toward American Jewish works were most overtly correlated to one another and to the underlying Israeli approach to the diaspora that informed them. Let us conclude this part of the discussion by looking at one evocative example of this, Alexander Barzel's essay about Bellow's *Herzog*, published in 1971—briefly discussed in the beginning of the introduction to this book.[91] In this essay, Barzel went into great depth in describing the humanistic underpinnings of the novel as rooted in Jewish tradition, and Herzog's belief in high ethics and solidarity as founded almost exclusively in his "Jewish consciousness" (and not in anything universal or, rather, individually unique about him). Concomitantly, Barzel drew a stark dichotomy between Jewish and non-Jewish traditions of thought and literature. Although it may seem far-fetched, he argued, such a dichotomy

> is in fact no figment of the imagination. The contrast [between the humanistic Jewish spirit and the apocalyptic spirit of the Christian West] does exist, and it is stronger than any attempt at evasion or denial. . . . The "world" isolates us—the "all too many Rabinovitches" in the East and Herzogs in the West.[92]

The passage demonstrates the charting of two symbolic collective boundaries: an exclusive boundary separating Jews and non-Jews and an inclusive boundary surrounding Israeli Jews and American Jews. The coalescing of these two boundaries indicates an affinity between Israel and the diaspora that is paramount to any affinity the Jews of the diaspora could ever have with their neighbors in their "host" countries. The moral dichotomy that Barzel formulates between Jews and non-Jews not only supports an unambiguous ethical image of Israel, the Jewish state, but also reinforces the spiritual connection between the two Jewish communities.

Entangled with the charting of these symbolic boundaries, however, one also finds an implied *dismissal* of the independent value of diaspora cultural creation, bound with an implication of an inherent preeminence of Israeli culture:

> Just as [Christian] Western culture decided to punish the Jews for keeping alive the very same values it had declared to be dead, the Jewish state was established, with passion and dedication which in and of themselves differentiate it as unique from other nations of the world. . . . [A]t the very same time, Jewish men of letters around the world have begun to speak their mind, and not only as authors, but *as Jews*, with a full consciousness of their uniqueness. There is a growing sense of singularity of the Jewish worldview, of this derided "Jewish heart," both as remnant and seed of *humaneness*; as well as a growing understanding that this truth can and must be told with great volume and in proud stature. The Jewish state is perhaps the "sound box" of the Jewish writer's voice in the world, lending power to his voice.[93]

If some of the aforementioned reviews implied that the Jewish American writer depended on Israeli readership for a true understanding of his or her work, here the reliance of American Jewish cultural creation on Israel is even greater. According to Barzel, diaspora literary achievements, from the motivation of American writers to write a "Jewish" work to the actual effect of their work, are contingent on Israel. They derive from the inspiration of Israel and gain their power from its existence. With such a conception of spiritual life in the diaspora, it is not surprising that Barzel concluded his essay with a familiar Zionist grievance: "a sad thought pierces the heart: why don't *Sha'ul* Bellow and his peers come *home, to the nation's homeland*, to forge the conceptual weaponry and armor of the Jewish soul?"[94] This statement seals the review, suggesting the imprint Barzel might have sought to leave on his readers and lending it greater weight.

Apart from the explicit plea, Barzel appropriates the American novelist by Hebraizing his name and stresses the words denoting where the Jewish home is, signifying emphatically where it is not.

It is also worth mentioning, in this context, that some Israeli critics described, in rhetoric similar to that describing the Zionist imperative of aliyah, the translation of works by diaspora writers into Hebrew. Echoing Agnon's words to Bellow quoted in the beginning of this chapter, the translation of Jewish works from non-Jewish tongues was conceptualized as an act of collective recovery. I will expand on this in the next chapter. For now, let us note that appropriation of American Jewish authors and works in the Israeli literary discourse was principally twofold. It could be realized in an explicit call for aliyah and an ensuing active participation in the spiritual life of Israel. Or it could be manifested implicitly in the description of the literary achievements of the diaspora as dependent on Israel for a substantiation of Jewish meaning. Both approaches gave expression to the same conception of cultural hierarchy in the Jewish world, headed by Israel.

These inclinations were also reflected in subtle shifts in the Hebrew translation of several, albeit not many, passages in Jewish American works. Whether done unwittingly, or conscious and ideological in aim, these changes imposed on segments of the original texts an Israeli frame of reference. In the translation of Malamud's aforementioned "The Last Mohican," for instance, the impoverished European Jewish peddler Susskind explains to Fidelman in practical terms why he cannot find a job in Italy as an Israeli citizen:

> You don't understand, professor. I am an Israeli citizen and this means I can only work for an Israeli company. How many Israeli companies are there here?—maybe two, El Al and Zim, and even if they had a job they wouldn't give it to me because I have lost my passport. I would be better off now if I were ~~stateless~~ [**without a homeland**]. A ~~stateless~~ person [**without a homeland**] shows his laissez passer and sometimes he can find a small job.[95]

In the source text, "stateless" serves as a rather formal-legalistic term and is used primarily to denote Susskind's frustration over practical limitations on working as a noncitizen. In the Hebrew translation, the word is substituted with an emotive expression of a higher register, the ideologically charged *hasar-moledet* [literally: "homeland-less," or "without a homeland"]. This choice may have stemmed from stylistic and grammatical rather than ideological considerations, yet its outcome is that the text has come to reflect an implicit nationalistic standpoint. In a sense, the interference changes the implied focus of the utterance from Susskind's own condition to that of the State—Israel, not Susskind, becomes the sentences' focal point; and the phrase designates the state as a symbolic home rather than as a political entity.

In other shifts in which an Israeli frame of reference was employed, translation choices subdued the linguistic or cultural difference that, from an Israeli perspective, was embedded in the original text. One such instance appears in the translation of the epigraph to Philip Roth's *Goodbye, Columbus*, which originally reads, "The heart is half a prophet—a Yiddish proverb." In the 1970 Hebrew translation, the origin of the proverb was changed from Yiddish to Jewish,[96] even though the differentiation between the two terms—"Yiddish" [*Yiddish*] and "Jewish" [*Yehudi*]—exists in Hebrew, and the translation could have just as easily used "Yiddish." Roth's allusion to his characters' Yiddish cultural and emotional baggage was thus transformed into a broader, less "exilic" Jewish frame of reference that would be more relatable to Israeli readers. A similar example is an exchange in Bellow's *Mr. Sammler's Planet* between Sammler and his young niece Angela, in which Sammler notes that he can still remember her confirmation, and recalls being impressed by her studiousness in learning Hebrew. In the translation, "confirmation," a Reform and Reconstructionist ceremony celebrated on Shavuot exclusively in North America, was substituted with *Bat-Mitzvah*.[97] The translation did not retain nor explicate this American Jewish ritual—largely unknown to Israelis—but rather opted for replacing it in the dialogue with a ritual practiced in both communities. An Israeli frame of reference was also loosely integrated into a scene in which Mr. Sammler's sick, bedridden father-in-law, Elya Gruner, expresses his affection for Israel and his wish to go visit there one more time: "I love ~~it there~~ [**the Land/***Ha-aretz*]."[98] In the translation, Gruner's use of the adverb "there" to refer to Israel was substituted with the ubiquitous Hebrew moniker *ha-aretz* [the Land]. The Hebrew word implies, almost presupposes, a close familiarity with Israel—a sense that is completely absent from the transparent "there" of the source text; it is as though the text's point of vantage was inadvertently changed in translation from "there" to "here." This interference thus joins the shifts discussed earlier, which, though not plentiful and perhaps resulting from a simple preference for accessibility, nevertheless reveal how an Israeli frame of reference was imposed on different contexts in the American Jewish works.

To complete this part of the discussion, it is worth touching on responses in Israeli journalistic discourse to some contentious images and notions of Israel that were charted by American Jewish writers. Here, Israeli culture not only was confronted with a challenging concept of American Jewish identity but also had to face *itself* in the proverbial mirror by encountering its own representations harbored by the Jewish American literary imagination. During the decades in question, most works of fiction by canonical Jewish American writers did not portray Israel or have Israeli characters in them,[99] yet a few works—Roth's *Portnoy's Complaint* and Bellow's *Mr. Sammler's Planet* the most notable of them—had charged images of Israel that drew intense Israeli response. Although Israeli criticism often dismissed these portrayals as "utterly stereotypical and false,"[100] its underlying rhetoric and proposed interpretation of the Israeli episodes in the two novels is most revealing in how it works to frame the American Jewish gaze on Israel.

Discussions of the final chapter in *Portnoy's Complaint*, in which Portnoy visits Israel and suffers from impotence in an embarrassing sexual encounter with a Sabra Israeli woman, echo the ideological undercurrents we have seen all along. Some Israeli critics suggested that Portnoy's sexual complexes not only were rooted in his unsolved complexes with Judaism but also inherently stemmed from his split existence as a Jew living in a gentile milieu. His impotence in Israel was conceived as representing a pathological inability to connect to an "authentic form of Jewishness," symbolized and embodied by the Israeli women he meets.[101] If the Jewish protagonist (and his author) were to live in Israel, it was implied, their sexuality might have been healthier and happier.[102] As Yehudit Oryan concluded in her generally appreciative review, in which she defended the novel before Israeli readers and asked them not to reject it because of its depiction of Israel, "Portnoy's failure [to perform sexually] in Israel does not attest to the flaws of Israel but rather to his own."[103]

Israeli reviews of *Mr. Sammler's Planet* are particularly interesting because of Bellow's unfavorable representation of Eisen, the novel's main Israeli character and Sammler's son-in-law, as uncultivated and excessively violent, and of Sammler's nauseating account (as a war correspondent reporting on the Six Day War) of swollen Egyptian corpses in the Sinai desert. These representations could be seen as emblematic of an American Jewish critique of the ethical implications of Israeli militancy or, in literary scholar Emily Miller Budick's words, as Bellow's attempt at "portraying the Israeli identity that American Jews must . . . resist."[104] Some Israeli reviewers preferred to ignore this portrayal altogether or only to mention Sammler's decision to travel to Israel as the Six Day War broke out, contentedly noting his sudden identification with the fate of the Jewish state without, however, confronting the more challenging images of Israel that followed.[105] Israeli thinker Jacqueline Kahanoff represents this approach by attributing to Sammler a high moral appreciation of Israel (which was never expressed in the novel) and then providing the following reassuring description of Sammler's experience as a witness to the Six Day War:

> There he is, an old, weary journalist, silently facing the dead bodies strewn across the Sinai desert. Although Sammler does not express this in words, Israel symbolizes for him the feat of staying alive, the kind of sanity the world seemed to have forgotten. Individually and collectively, the Jews here continue to nurture their "little flowerbeds" come what may, employing violence when necessary but never glorifying it as a value in itself or using it for the sake of [romantic] "self-liberation."[106]

Earlier in her review, Kahanoff lauded Bellow's novel for conveying the ethical priority of going about one's mundane everyday life and nurturing one's own "little flowerbeds"—that is, families and homes—with persistence and restraint "in the face of the unrestrained anger of the human soul."[107] In the previous excerpt, this ethical imperative is conflated with Israeli society, as Kahanoff seems to project on Sammler her own favorable moral impression of Israel while suppressing evidence to the contrary from the novel. Moreover, Kahanoff does not specify the *Egyptian* identity of the dead whom Sammler sees scattered in the Sinai dunes, despite its obvious significance to Sammler, and refers only in passing to the brutal character of Eisen. She does not mention Eisen by name, nor elaborate on his behavior, nor assign him with any symbolic meaning, despite his centrality to the text.

Critics who did acknowledge Bellow's representation of Israeli forcefulness in the novel often voiced indignation over what they perceived to be a privileged, unfounded moral critique that ignored the perilous constraints of Israeli reality. For Amnon Hadari, in his review of the novel in the magazine *Shadmot* in 1972, "there [was] little doubt that Eisen symbolizes the iron quality of the IDF's various formations," whereas the character of the African American pickpocket who threatens Sammler and is then brutally beaten by Eisen stands for Israel's defeated Arab enemies in the Six Day War.[108] Hadari later wrote, with subdued yet unambiguous irony, "He is uncomfortable, Sammler, with the price he has to pay for our salvage. We [Israelis] appear too tough, too easy to smile—like Eisen."[109] In a book club discussion of the novel documented in the kibbutz literary journal *Alei siah* in 1978, reader Tuvia S. expressed explicit anger: "Our own casualties, as Jews, do not interest him—not to mention the struggle for the country's existence. The only thing that matters to him: do not raise a hand—a kind of one-sided humaneness."[110] Fellow reader Haim Yisraeli protested Bellow's perceived stance in the novel in the same vein, but bolstered his argument by undermining Bellow's Jewish identity:

> Bellow's perspective is similar to that of the New Left. . . . [It is in the portrayal of Eisen that] Bellow is revealed as an assimilated [*mitbolel*] Jew—he sides against Eisen, while ostensibly rooting for the wretched and oppressed—the Egyptians in Sinai, the Negroes in America. He, Sammler, lost an eye. But when the Negro loses an eye, Sammler agonizes! Sammler is, therefore, rootless and estranged from human reality and Jewish reality. The book appeals to reason. But what can one do? Reason is useless when you appeal to a corrupt world—a world of Nazis. Only a detached Jew would think this could be done.[111]

The universal model of morality concretized in Sammler's disgust of Eisen's overbearing attack on the black pickpocket, and his pity for the Egyptian casualties of the war, was dismissed by Israeli reviewers as an offensively unrealistic approach to the contemporary conditions of Jewish/Israeli survival. Moreover, Bellow/Sammler's "false" conception of morality was often framed in Israeli literary debates as a product of his assimilation into non-Jewish American society (note Haim Yisraeli's use of the derogatory *mitbolel*), and his experience as a diaspora Jew as what led him to misunderstand the Israeli condition. Critic Tzfira Porat even designated Bellow's implied moral stance on Israel as non-Jewish in form and essence, and suggested an undesirable impact of Christian notions on his thought:

> Figures of his creative imagination, such as Herzog and his aunt, believe that a good Jew would never carry a gun or clench a fist. And Sammler, who quickly traveled to Israel in the Six Day War, traveled there in order to die in the anticipated slaughter rather than to prevent it, and, as he is disappointed to see napalmed Egyptian carcasses in the desert being eaten by dogs, he hastens back to his home in the United States. . . . It is as if the author was disappointed not to hear the language of Jesus Christ

> of Galilee in the State of Israel. Perhaps violence is not to the author's liking, but Judaism is not as squeamish as he, and does not adhere to his yearning for a "realism that is not brutal." After all, realism without a trace of brutality is, to all intents and purposes, the idealism of Jesus. In his conflicted, undecided attitude to the fighting State of Israel, Bellow proves that he is, unwittingly, still very much a man of Western Christian culture, is unwittingly held captive by the Christian symbols that he wishes to decry, and has himself become a victim of the Christian words he had set out to contest.[112]

Porat's review joins other reviews that dealt with Bellow's uneasiness with Israeli force by faulting the writer with assimilation or diasporic cosmopolitanism, but takes this criticism one step further in accusing Bellow of embracing Christian values.[113] Generally, then, the moral imperative of the novel was not only framed as fanciful (in its relation to Israeli reality), but this fancifulness was also implicitly or explicitly tied to the conditions of Jewish life in a non-Jewish environment.

Israeli novelist A. B. Yehoshua also referred critically to American Jewish depictions of an immoral Israel, a few years after Porat, when he polemically asserted that "the Jewish responsibility of a Jew in the *Golah* is very circumscribed. In a certain sense he stays a 'clean' Jew, for as a Jew he is not responsible for the foreign policy of the country in which he lives, nor for the army, the prisons, social inequalities, the perversions of government, and so forth. He has his books filled with lofty values, few of which are put to the test in actual life."[114] However, unlike Porat, who claimed the precedence of his historical-theological view of Judaism over Bellow's, Yehoshua maintains that living as a Jew without sovereignty in a non-Jewish majority society means that one's moral values are less Jewish *by definition*: "In Israel, on the other hand, every detail of life is tested against Jewish values, beliefs, conduct, and dreams. Whoever is concerned about the continuity of these values must examine them not in theory but in their application. . . . [W]hen soldiers in Israel's army observe the 'purity of arms,' Jewish values are reinforced; and when they commit an atrocity, Jewish values crumble. There is no longer the distinction between a closed spiritual world within which ideas are discussed and reality not at all relevant to that discussion."[115] Only Jewish sovereignty, in other words, allows for meaningful discussion of moral or immoral conduct in Jewish terms and for gauging this conduct according to Jewish criteria. The values of diaspora Jews may be moral, but they are not intrinsically, formally Jewish. To conclude, in line with literary debates on the cultural implications of Jewish existence in America, Israeli critics also highlighted Jewish/non-Jewish boundaries in their response to a perceived critique of Israeli morality and ethics, in another attempt to imply the precedence of the Israeli alternative to American Jewish life.

Between Inclusivity and Dismissal

The multifaceted nature of Israeli discourse on Jewish American literature makes it difficult to outline a common framework and requires uneasy generalization. In addition, the ideological expressions underlying reception of Jewish American works often appeared in passing, intertwined with one another yet without a self-evident or clearly causal relation between them. Nonetheless, the different modes of framing and interpretation outlined in the previous sections were anything but arbitrary; they were, in fact, not only ideologically informed but also deeply correlated. The tendency to contextualize the works as primarily Jewish coincided with the tendency to chart an impenetrable boundary, both spiritual and cultural and social and physical, between Jews and non-Jews, and these two trends corresponded to the forms of Israel-centric appropriation of American Jewish cultural creation. The blueprint for understanding these tendencies may be Israel's competitive relationship to the diaspora version of Jewish life in its American manifestation, which posed both a conceptual and a concrete challenge to Israeli culture and thought.

On the conceptual level, American Jewish culture challenged an Israeli ethos strongly determined by the implications of the Israeli–Arab conflict and the memory of the Holocaust and founded on a nationalist-isolationist perspective on Jewish continuity. In the words of Jackie Feldman, this collective ethos induced the construction of "well-defined, but constantly threatened boundaries" that were maintained with practices of differentiation meant to "reinforce . . . apartness."[116] American Jewish culture presented a challenge to this way of thinking precisely in the fluidity and flexibility of its collective boundaries. The conception of universality and Jewishness as two notions that not only could coexist but also were enmeshed to the degree of being indistinguishable from one another, and the receding importance of the physical and spiritual boundary separating Jews and non-Jews in modern society, were themes embedded in canonical Jewish American works. American Jewish authors may have problematized these notions, but the potential validity of these aspects of identity was nonetheless present in their works. Their pertinence for American Jewish life was clearly entailed by the mental landscape and social reality depicted by the authors and was obvious from the very need to problematize them. This is why the stark framing of these works and authors as Jewish in Israeli discourse, the charting of an impermeable spiritual and social boundary between Jews and non-Jews, and the emphasis of critics on this boundary's ever-harmful implications could be seen, both together and separately, as undermining the viability of the American Jewish nonsovereign solution for modern Jewish life.

On the more concrete level, the insistence in Israeli discourse on the spiritual and social hardships of living in the American diaspora can be readily understood against the background of Israel's own internal doubts. These were decades when the United States proved to be increasingly attractive to Israeli emigrants, or *yoredim* as they were derogatorily called, and when, in the words of Nir Cohen, "out-migration was conceived as a major threat to the existence of both the Jewish state and society."[117] Considering the competitive stance toward the intellectual achievements of diaspora Jews, which was expressed explicitly at times, the unfavorable comparison with a Jewish literary corpus that held the symbolic capital of global recognition may also have triggered a defensive approach. In this respect, it may be no coincidence that the areas of difficulty of American Jewish existence pointed out by Israeli critics were exactly those in which Israeli society had itself historically struggled. Israeli discourse from the late 1950s through the 1980s, perhaps excluding a few years following the Six Day War, commonly expressed skepticism and apprehension about social solidarity, personal safety and national security, the direction in which spiritual and cultural life was headed, and the moral foundation of the collective ethos.[118]

In this frame of reference, representations of American Jewish life challenged Israeli culture by way of an unspoken question that they posed: Where was it better for Jews to live? Of course, accentuating the difficulties of being a Jew in the diaspora, and suggesting the precedence of Jewish life in Israel, could be traced to the major traditions of Zionist thought from their inception. In their relation to the concept of diaspora, most Zionist thinkers presupposed the inherent priority of Jewish life based, in the words of Jacob Klatzkin, on "[the two poles] of a national land and a national language."[119] Moreover, Israeli critics did not create their portrayal of American Jewish life out of thin air; these were real difficulties expressed in the translated literary works that Israeli discourse tapped into. Nonetheless, the encounter with literary representations of an alternate Jewish way of life can also be seen as a way for Israeli thinkers to unburden their own doubts and fears—by accentuating those of others. In the rhetoric of some of its most dominant voices, the Israeli literary discourse on Jewish American literature may be indicative of several of the collective insecurities that have accompanied Israel's existence through most of its first decades.

Finally, it is important to reemphasize that these discursive trends do not repudiate the deep-seated assumption of affinity with American Jews rooted in intellectual debates in Israel. The major approach to American Jewish culture in Israeli discourse was reflected in the seemingly contradictory notions of inclusivity and dismissal—not only in the latter. Previous studies of Israeli perspectives on American Jewry in Israel's first decades seem to have understated the inherent tie between these two notions.[120] The dialectic of inclusivity and exclusivity, however, may be at the heart of the Israeli approach to diasporic Jewish culture and life. If the American diaspora were not deemed deeply relevant, we would not see such energetic Israeli Zionist attempts to grapple with it and appropriate it in the literary discourse. If there were no assumption of true affinity with the diaspora, there would be less competition and conflict with it. At this juncture of competing notions of Jewishness, it did not matter that an Israeli readership may well have been the last thing on the minds of American Jewish authors. It did not matter that these works were written for an American audience and aimed first and foremost at acceptance by an American critical discourse and an American literary tradition. What mattered was that this corpus of work was perceived as germane, that its images of Jewishness were seen as related to concerns at the core of contemporary Israeli identity. For it is by engaging with the challenge of American notions of Jewishness that Israeli thinkers wished to shape the symbolic boundaries of Israeli national identity, and those of the Jewish people as a whole, on their own terms.

5

"Judaism in Translation"

The anecdote about Agnon and Bellow's conversation on the necessity of Bellow's translation into Hebrew, presented at the beginning of the previous chapter, neatly encapsulates the entangled existence of two components in the Israeli appropriation of diaspora cultural expression. The first, elaborated earlier, refers to the meaning and consequence of Jewish spiritual life in a non-Jewish majority society. The long-term survival of Bellow's works was threatened, Agnon implied, because they were dreamed up in, and in their original language belong to, a non-Jewish cultural world. Not unique in literary debates of the time, this position represents an Israeli emphasis on the impermeability of Jewish/non-Jewish boundaries and the ensuing doubtful prospects for American Jewish life. Agnon's quip, however, also obliquely invokes and exploits the notion of authenticity. Underlying his remark on translation from languages of the diaspora—by which, in Bellow's words, Agnon was "sweetly needling" the American author[1]—is subtle skepticism about the authenticity of Jewish literature written in a non-Jewish tongue.

This chapter expands on the rhetoric of authenticity in Israeli thought on American Jewish literature and culture through the prism of language. In what follows, I outline an Israeli tradition of reflection on translation as a spiritual bridge between homeland and diaspora, between Israel and America, and on the meaning of Jewish cultural expression in non-Jewish languages such as English. As we will see, this tradition of thought is quite different from the metatranslational emphases we encountered in the other direction of transfer—translated Hebrew works being primarily framed in

American Jewish discourse as a probe into the Israeli psyche, worthy of translation for their unique truth-telling, moral capacity. Israeli deliberations on intra-Jewish translation between homeland and diaspora assumed a more competitive, hierarchical approach; writing in Hebrew, it implied, carried inherently superior Jewish value and significance. Rooted in a venerable tradition going back to progenitors of the Hebrew cultural revival such as Hayim Nahman Bialik and Ahad Ha'am, this notion indirectly suggests that authentic Jewish works cannot be written in any other tongue. The ideological underpinnings of Israeli engagements with the American diaspora are usefully understood in the context of this metalinguistic and metatranslational discourse: set against the backdrop of the cultural competition between the two Jewish centers, it suggests an Israeli effort to seize pride of place in the Jewish world by implying an intrinsic linguistic hierarchy between the two cultures.

Before I trace expressions of this tradition of thought from the late 1950s to the late 1980s, to provide background I will briefly touch on the intellectual climate of Hebrew culture in the late 1940s and its conception of American Jewish life at the time. Upon the foundation of the state, the years-long limitations on Jewish immigration to Israel were lifted, highlighting the issue of aliyah and inciting friction between the political establishments of the two communities, friction largely rooted in the false expectation of Israeli leaders that American Jews would make aliyah en masse. The negation of exile, still a mainstay of the Israeli ethos and a common feature of public discourse, assumed different shapes and forms.[2] Perhaps its most radical expression was the rise of the Canaanite movement, whose thinkers opposed the concept of Judaism as a religion and rejected Israel's ethnic affinity with diaspora Jews. Some Canaanite figures even called to annul all links between the "Jew" of the diaspora and the "Hebrew" dwelling in the land of Israel. For our purposes, it is important to note that both institutional Zionist perspectives, which did not adhere to this radical position, and the Canaanite thinkers who challenged them saw the Hebrew language as the single most important foundation for national cultural expression. As evidenced in the emotional disputes over linguistic research on Hebrew in the 1950s,[3] the preoccupation with Hebrew instruction in the state educational system,[4] and the institutional approach to Yiddish and other languages in the public sphere, this ideology of language was still prominent in the early poststatehood years.

Intellectual Israeli approaches to American Jewish culture at the time are perhaps best represented in the famous series of satirical poems by national poet Nathan Alterman on American Jews, which were featured in his highly influential column for *Davar* during the late 1940s and early 1950s, *Ha-tur ha-shevi'i* (The Seventh Column). Alterman's poems centered on what he perceived to be American Jewry's aversion to making aliyah, but they also entailed a dismissive stance toward the possibility of authentic Jewish cultural creation in the United States.[5] In his much-publicized "The New Pumbedita," for instance, Alterman derisively described the main thrust of contemporary American Jewish intellectual creativity as focused on justifying and "advocat[ing] why they shouldn't immigrate."[6] Although the poem does not refer explicitly to the issue of language, it hints at it with the mocking Hebrew transcription of English phrases ("pass," "isn't it lovely?")—a linguistic jab at what Alterman conceived of as American Jews' distancing from the national endeavor. In another poem, "Sakanat ha-tsiyoni ha-nitsehi," (The Danger of the Eternal Zionist), Alterman criticized a speech given in Yiddish by American Zionist Nahum Goldmann at the Zionist Congress of 1951 in Jerusalem, particularly belittling the part in which Goldmann argued for the necessity of political and cultural activity in the diaspora.[7] Alterman never expressed appreciation or empathy for American Jewish culture, and his harsh critique of the American Jewish middle class stands out against the sympathetic strains in his poetic oeuvre on the European diasporic past or Jewish communities in Muslim countries.[8]

Alterman's centrality in Israeli public thought notwithstanding, the most comprehensive Hebrew reflection on American Jewish culture at the time was that of writer and literary scholar Shimon Halkin. Employing an ideology similar to Alterman's, Halkin's *Yehudim ve-yahadut be-Amerika* (Jews and Judaism in America) from 1947 anticipated the way Hebrew thought would tend to contextualize Jewish literary and spiritual life in America for decades to come. Halkin immigrated to the United States from Belarus as a teen before World War I and developed in America as a Hebrew writer and scholar, before leaving for Palestine in the late 1940s to head the Department of Hebrew Literature at the Hebrew University. His essay presents American Jewish culture without much appreciation and from a highly pessimistic viewpoint. The Jewish identity of the vast majority of American Jews, he proclaims, is "so vague and depleted that they have but one identifying mark left—having been born to Jewish parents."[9] Halkin bemoans what he considers to be the blindness of contemporary American Jewish intellectual and sociological thought, which dares not acknowledge the dearth of Jewish spiritual life and "has come to behave, in addressing an alarming factual reality, as the ostrich does."[10] The distinctive Zionist underpinnings of Halkin's historiosophy shaped his judgment of the waves of mass immigration of the late nineteenth and early twentieth centuries and the social institutions that Jews established on American shores, as well as their spiritual and cultural life. "It is no revelation," he asserts in his essay, "that leaving the ghetto, unless it led to nationalism, that is, to Zionism, has brought Judaism in every single country to utter paucity and exhaustion. . . . The departure from the ghetto called Americanization has [similarly] brought American Jewry to the spiritual fatigue and scarcity that we witness today."[11] In the few places in which Halkin does note Jewish American cultural achievements of the time, he concentrates on Hebrew education and the activities of Zionist organizations.[12] The short-lived resurgence of Jewish spiritual life in America, which held much promise but eventually faltered, was, in his eyes, that of Yiddish and Hebrew creation alone. Never once does Halkin mention the rich expression of Jewish creativity in the English writings of Abraham Cahan, Henry Roth, Anzia Yezierska, Ben Hecht, and Ludwig Lewisohn, among others, and it is clear that he associates the gradual loss of knowledge of Hebrew and Yiddish, and the depletion of literary creation in these languages, with what he sees as the disintegration of Jewish culture in America. When Halkin bemoans the fact that the American Jewish intelligentsia has failed to spawn a new generation of followers, he mentions only those committed to "secular Jewish culture in its varied forms, whether in Yiddish or Hebrew. Just like the devout orthodox rarely fathered sons who studied Torah, so the disciples of the new Hebrew and Yiddish literatures seldom engendered sons and daughters who read a modern Hebrew or Yiddish book."[13] Jewish language is thus entailed as a precondition for Jewish culture, to such an extent that a work of literature, even if completely secular, is not deemed Jewish unless it is written and read in Hebrew or Yiddish. Halkin lived up to his ideological imperative: he was a lecturer in Hebrew at the Jewish Institute of Religion in New York and chose to write and publish his literary work in America in Hebrew, despite the quixotic implications and the marginalization in literary discourse that such a decision entailed, before ultimately leaving America to live and create in Israel.

From the 1950s onward, the presence in Israeli public and intellectual discourse of the negation of exile steadily receded, along with a growing spiritual search in Israeli cultural life for Jewish roots, ranging from the educational to the literary fields. Still, neither of these trends had a notable effect on the Israeli conception of contemporary American Jewish culture. When it came to the diaspora, Israeli thought tended to be more open to past, not present, spiritual creation, and American Jewish literary production was not treated as a source of inspiration. An early sign of this inclination, at the end of the first decade of statehood, was the Israeli board of education's decision to establish the Committee for Jewish Israeli Consciousness in order to assess school curricula. The Knesset discussion on the committee's suggestions indicates that the infusion of traditional Jewish content into school curricula was seen, among other things, as a means of strengthening feelings of solidarity between Israel and the diaspora. The committee's ostensible goals for the new curriculum were also to "get to know the Jewish people in the present, particularly the Jewish center in the United States."[14] Yet this was not at all manifested in the proposed curriculum itself. In practice, the board responsible for implementing the committee's recommendations almost exclusively incorporated traditional and historical sources of Judaism—and nothing from American Jewish cultural creation and thought.[15] Jewish American writers were also excluded from the Ministry of Education's 1964 program for literature, in which the only American writer was Ernest Hemingway.[16]

The Hebrew literary sphere itself showed a similar tendency: despite growing interest in Jewish themes, Israeli authors scarcely opened up to contemporary diaspora experience. Existentialist novelist Pinchas Sadeh, who had dismissed Judaism in his early work, and writers such as Aharon Appelfeld, Yehuda Amichai, and Yoram Kaniuk began to engage intensely with Jewish themes and to place questions of Jewish (rather than exclusively Israeli Zionist) identity at the heart of their work.[17] Even prominent voices from the older generation that had fought in Israel's War of Independence, such as Matti Megged and Dahn Ben-Amotz and Canaanite author Benjamin Tammuz, veered away from the anti-Jewish ethos that had guided their early work, and sought reconciliation with the notion of diasporic Jewishness.[18] None of these writers, however, showed a genuine interest in contemporary American Jewish creation. They scarcely acknowledged the importance of the burgeoning field of Jewish American literature, and did not relate to its particular modes of expression as a potential source of influence. This is perhaps most revealing in the case of Tammuz, on account of his explicit treatment of the question of diaspora in his literary and publicist writing. Tammuz openly criticized the disinterest of Israelis in diaspora Jewry and identified this breach as a major cause for what he perceived to be the dismal state of contemporary Hebrew literature. Tammuz, however, related the hoped-for resurgence of Hebrew literature to the rejuvenation of national Russian literature and completely ignored the renaissance of Jewish American literature of the 1950s and 1960s. This is particularly striking because Tammuz celebrated exilic alienation not only as fruitful but also as the basic form of human existence, his underlying outlook being that "the Jewish genius is at its very best in the diaspora, among the gentiles."[19] This echoes the predominant discourse of alienation in the writing of Jewish American intellectuals of the time, such as Alfred Kazin and Isaac Rosenfeld, among others. Nonetheless, Tammuz and his estranged protagonists, always wandering in Europe and not in America, never treated American Jewish thought as a source of inspiration.[20]

These tendencies serve as a background to, and are further illuminated by, the tradition of Israeli thought on questions of language and translation between Israel and the diaspora. At the end of the 1950s, translation—to and from Hebrew—was increasingly contemplated as a necessary means for the growth of a thriving Israeli culture, as some critics presented it as a two-way bridge between the latter and diaspora Jewish culture. The hierarchy entailed in this endeavor, however, as a site for the construction of Jewish identity, positioned Israel at the center with diaspora communities—at the very best—as its satellites. As Stanley Lowell, vice president of the American Jewish Congress, protested to Abba Eban a few years later, this reductionist attitude "consider[ed] Judaism synonymous with Israeli nationalism and the existence of Israel."[21] Baruch Karu's introduction to Emil Feuerstein's anthology *Jewish Authors in World Literature* (1959), which introduced Hebrew readers to fifteen Jewish authors writing in other languages, is a case in point. Karu spoke of the translation of these authors into Hebrew as comparable to restoring a lost object to its rightful, original owner, thus appropriating the writers and their translations—existing translations as well as future ones—to the national Israeli project: "In our vision, the day will come when every Jewish author in a foreign tongue will recognize the obligation to translate his works into Hebrew; 'to give back what was stolen,' as Maimonides wrote to his translator."[22] These comments, which implicitly diminish and even annul the value of Jewish texts in languages other than Hebrew, echo Ahad Ha'am and Bialik's view of translation from several decades earlier. In the context of the linguistic war being waged against Yiddish in the *Yishuv*, Ahad Ha'am declared, "Any [Jewish] works whose value merits survival through the ages—will survive in Hebrew translation alone. . . . Everything else will be lost and forgotten as if it had never existed, just as Yiddish will."[23] In a similar vein, in a speech delivered to an American crowd during his 1926 visit to New York, Bialik stated that "our roots, our foundation, lay solely in Hebrew. Any [Jewish literature] created in foreign tongues, is of no existence [to us], unless it is translated into Hebrew."[24]

The particular selection of authors for Feuerstein's anthology reflects the national atmosphere of the period. In his introduction, Karu stated: "The creative [contribution] of Jews to world culture belongs to us—it was conceived by the Jewish genius. Jewish authors in whichever language [they write] are our brothers."[25] As for Jewish American literature, however, these "brother" authors were chosen with extreme care. Among the fifteen authors included in Feuerstein's anthology, most of whom wrote in German, only two were American: Ben Hecht and Herman Wouk. The rationale for choosing Wouk and Hecht in place of more important contemporary and earlier writers such as Saul Bellow, Bernard Malamud, Henry Roth, or Abraham Cahan was clearly based on their affinity to Zionism, an affinity that found expression in their work. An Orthodox Jew with excellent command of Hebrew, Herman Wouk expressed his pro-Zionist sentiments publicly, visited Israel many times, and wrote about it. Ben Hecht was a prominent Zionist activist in the United States in the 1940s and 1950s who raised funds for the *Yishuv* and later for the state. He was affiliated with the revisionist Zionist American League for a Free Palestine and wrote the popular Zionist play *A Flag Is Born*, produced on Broadway in 1946 and openly advocating for Zionist causes. The biographical commentary, interviews, and excerpts included in Feuerstein's anthology emphatically illustrate to the Hebrew reader the writers' commitment to and deep affection for Israel.

Hebrew thought on translation in the other direction—that is, from Hebrew into other tongues used by Jewish diasporas—similarly reflected this hierarchical conception of Israel as culturally superior to diaspora Jewry. In 1957, literary critic and essayist Yisrael Cohen attributed translated Hebrew works with the power to breathe new life into the hearts of Jewish readers in the "withering" diaspora and called for the undertaking of more translations from Hebrew into foreign languages. His words leave no doubt with regard to his viewpoint on the cultural prospects of the diaspora:

> The majority of our people [living in the diaspora] are bound to assimilate into the culture of *am ha'aretz* [literally, "the people of the land";

> the term carries pejorative connotations of boorishness and ignorance]. It is thus necessary to translate the finest Hebrew works that have appeared and continue to appear in high literature, intellectual thought and science for their sake, so that they can relish them, even if it is only in their foreign tongue. Becoming familiar with these works would amplify their self-consciousness and sense of nationhood, even as spiritual elements, forged in the Israeli foundry, are imprinted in their soul. In this fashion, a Jewish fortitude will be infused in them, and they will be able to weather the gusty winds.[26]

Cohen would later act on this claim and go on to cofound the seminal Institute for the Translation of Hebrew Literature, which would indeed have a significant impact on the dissemination of Hebrew literature abroad. In this essay, he not only takes for granted the impossibility of a viable Jewish culture outside of Israel but also assigns the Hebrew language acute importance as a foundation of Jewish identity. This entails a clear hierarchical positioning of Jewish literature written in Hebrew over Jewish literature written in other languages. This stance is further evident in Cohen's expressed hope that "the translated source will awaken many [of its readers] and speed them toward the source itself, [leading them] to imbibe it not with a borrowed vessel but with a Hebrew one."[27] Translation is thus conceived of as a bridge between cultures, but the bridge is not at all level; rather, it is inclined, its slope descending from Israel to the diaspora. The ideologically charged migration concepts *aliyah* and *yeridah* apply to the migration of texts, not only people: the linguistic-cultural bridge of translation descends from Israel to the diaspora or ascends from the diaspora to Israel. Elsewhere in his essay, Cohen's judgmental description of the foreign tongue used by diaspora readers as "a borrowed vessel" comparable to the inferior nourishment of *lechem nekhar* (foreign bread; bread of exile) further highlights his linguistic ideology.

In a speech delivered by S. Y. Agnon in honor of Gershom Sholem in 1958 (subsequently published in *Haaretz*), the renowned author echoed Cohen's stance with regard to the national function of the translation of Hebrew texts. After praising Sholem's German translations of his works, Agnon commented on the need for additional translations of Hebrew literature into foreign languages and expressed hope that these translations would lead to a situation in which "those among the Jewish people who do not know the Hebrew language would strive to know our literature in its own language."[28] Fostering the unmediated familiarity of diaspora Jews with Hebrew literature is presented as an important rationale of translation, a goal unto itself. Agnon’s conversation with Bellow, related in the opening of this and the previous chapter, represents another, if more lighthearted, expression of this linguistic orientation. Agnon hinted that the employment of a foreign tongue by Jewish writers in the diaspora must result, to a certain extent, in a deficiency with regard to the Jewish character of their work—a deficiency whose only remedy could be translation into Hebrew. His words, though tinged with typical irony, echo Hebrew thought at the time. The positions of Bialik and Ahad Ha‘am regarding translation of diaspora Jewish texts into Hebrew, the historical context of which was the war of languages that pitted Hebrew against Yiddish, unfolded here in the Israeli relationship to Jewish writing in English.

Hebrew as the Definitive Yardstick

In the first half of the 1960s, the American Jewish Congress organized a series of dialogues between Jewish intellectuals from the United States and Israel in a variety of Israeli cities. Moshe Shamir and Aharon Megged were among the Israeli authors who participated, Philip Roth and Leslie Fiedler among the Americans. The dialogues took place amid the sense of a widening rift between the two Jewish communities, yet they also evinced a genuine desire on both sides to bridge this gap and to find “ways of collaborating for the mutual reinforcement of Jewish existence throughout the world.”[29] During the first dialogue in Jerusalem, Zionist scholar and thinker Nathan Rotenstreich noted a difference between Israel and American Jewry that was in line with the dominant orientation of literary discourse in Israel. Succinctly summarizing the Zionist negation of the diaspora in its spiritual-cultural context, Rotenstreich distinguished between “the objective of diaspora Jewry, Jewish survival, and the aim of Jewish society in Israel to maintain creative Jewish life.” These remarks aroused strong resentment on the part of the American participants, who felt that this “was underestimating the importance of American Jewry, and they protested that, if these were the views of the Israeli delegation, there was no room for dialogue between the two sides.”[30]

The Americans may have felt so vexed because American Jews had actually seen a decade and a half of exceptional creative flowering alongside comparable improvement in their socioeconomic status. No less important, in contradistinction to the early decades of the twentieth century, this flowering took place in a social climate that did not demand that Jews deny their Jewishness, change their names, or hide their identity. American Jewish literary production especially distinguished itself in these years, becoming one of the most prominent and influential phenomena in postwar American literature.

From the mid-1960s onward, authors such as Bernard Malamud, Saul Bellow, and Philip Roth began to be translated steadily into Hebrew, and their works elicited lively debate in Israeli public discourse. In the previous chapter, I analyzed the ideological ambivalence of Israeli criticism, which approached Jewish American literary production as a litmus test of the capacity of Jewish American culture to survive and flourish while charting the symbolic boundaries of Israeli collectivity vis-à-vis the competing alternative of American Jewish life.

Alongside this critical conversation, yet within the same framework of Israeli grappling with American Jewish culture, the tradition of thought on Hebrew as a foundation for Jewish creativity, and debates regarding translation both into and from Hebrew, continued to receive diverse expression. At times, one finds in such debates the old polemics of negating the diaspora in its classical formulation: Gershon Zack's article from August 1970, for instance, addresses the "large, rich, and confident diaspora, in America the great" and urges its Jews to immigrate to Israel, quoting, as a note of caution for the future, Bialik's early description of western Jewry: "cut by the sharp knife of a foreign culture and strange tongue from the living body, it did not find the way back to the faithful source that nursed it—and dried out."[31] The symbolic capital of Hebrew and its power to confer authentic Jewish identity were, however, often implied in a more oblique manner. For one, the names of authors and their protagonists, as we saw in the previous chapter, were sometimes Hebraized. Not only did Saul Bellow become Sha'ul Bellow and his protagonist Moses Herzog become Moshe Hertzog, but even a writer of Jewish extraction who was never really considered a "Jewish writer," Nathanael West, became Natan Weinstein.[32] The significance of Hebraization here was threefold: to express an affinity with Jewish authors of the diaspora; to appropriate them to the Israeli national project; and to indicate a hierarchy of Jewish cultural creativity in Hebrew and Jewish cultural creativity that was not in Hebrew. Along the same lines, many of the articles on Herman Wouk celebrate his facility with Hebrew, and one even mentions Israeli president Zalman Shazar's request of Wouk to write some of his novels in Hebrew.[33] Shulamith Hareven's July 1974 review of two of Chaim Potok's novels attributes a stylistic strength to his work that she traces to his knowledge of Hebrew. Hareven lauds Potok for writing in a concise manner, in contrast to what she perceives as the excessiveness of most other Jewish American authors (who lack facility in Hebrew), and implies that Potok is perhaps influenced "by historical Hebrew sources and the Hebrew tongue more generally, a tongue that despises rambling and is more succinct than any other."[34] In similar fashion, Hanoch Bartov's August 1976 review of a book by Elie Wiesel that was translated from French through English describes the author's knowledge of Hebrew as one of the reasons that "even though it is a translation of a translation, the language did not create a divide between the source text and me."[35]

During these years, the prominence and meaning of Hebrew were also deliberated in intellectual debates that did not engage directly with translated literature. Continuing the tradition of thought that began with Bialik and Ahad Ha'am, but adapted to this later period, Israeli thinkers considered the tension between Hebrew and English in the context of Israeli relations with the diaspora. In *On Contemporary Jewish Existence* (1972), Nathan Rotenstreich suggested that in spite of the solidarity American Jews express toward Israel, they could not truly *identify* with life in Israel: "first of all, in the most simple and concrete sense, [given the fact that] they do not know Hebrew. . . . Ahad Ha'am assumed that there would be a continuous connection between Eastern European Jews and those who would live and create in the land of the Jews. The most important link here was language . . . and yet, the linguistic connection is absent and does not obtain with the Jews of the West."[36]

A more severe tension between the languages and even deeper significance accorded to the role of Hebrew in modern Jewish life are found in an essay by Yaakov Rabi, published in *Moznayim*, the journal of the Association of Hebrew Writers, in 1973. A translator, critic, and recipient of the esteemed Sokolov Award for journalism, Rabi was also a linguist, and his essay, "To Expand the Domain [*nahala*] of Hebrew," is perhaps the most articulate display of the linguistic ideology at the root of Israeli thought on diaspora Jewish culture. In a section of his essay that relates to the Jewish community in America, Rabi admits that "English is today mastered by the majority of the Jewish people," but warns that "the gravitational force of English essentially pushes toward assimilation, or cosmopolitanism. With regard to Jewish nationhood, it is a *centrifugal* force."[37] Needless to say, notions of cosmopolitanism hold for Rabi little of the merit they were assigned by

Jewish American intellectuals of the time. Rabi bewails the sad state of Hebrew in the United States and devalues the establishment of Jewish Studies departments at American universities, proclaiming that "there isn't much 'meat' in these departments, and, in most, it is doubtful that there is much 'spirit' either. Students learn some 'basic' Judaism second- or thirdhand, and in English."[38] The superficiality of this endeavor is rooted, in his view, in the absence of "a unique linguistic consciousness," and he sees a "most urgent and essential" need to expand the circle of Hebrew speakers in America, for "only study of the Jewish heritage from its source, *in its tongue*, will ensure a deep, robust spiritual identification with the values of our culture; only firsthand learning, without the barrier of translation, will ensure genuine, profound familiarity with these values."[39] The boundaries of collective Jewish culture are therefore primarily linguistic: "our culture," as Rabi formulated it with the intention of comprising Jewish culture generally, cannot include works not written in Hebrew. By rejecting the capacity of translation to afford authentic access to works in Hebrew, however, Rabi essentially rejects the possibility that Jewish culture in America can flourish, even though it has always sought to forge continuity with the Hebrew sources, principally through translation. In an article written a few years later, Rabi even more explicitly denied the value of English, or of any language other than Hebrew for that matter, as a valid platform for Jewish culture. He argued that historically "distinctive values of Jewish civilization have never been created in these languages, but rather only some fraction of Jewish values in a secondary or marginal manner. There was no authentic Jewishness, whether religious or secular, in German, and there is no authentic Jewishness in English. And at any rate, Jewish totality, whether material or spiritual, cannot be realized or expressed in these languages."[40] The prominence of this worldview in Israeli intellectual circles is indicated by the fact that Rabi's "To Expand the Domain of Hebrew" earned him the Reuben Wallenrod Prize for Literature in 1974.

In the same vein, as noted earlier, Israeli critics described the translation of works by diaspora writers into Hebrew in rhetoric similar to that typical of the Zionist ethos of aliyah. Echoing Bialik and Ahad Ha'am, such translation was conceptualized as an act of collective recovery. "Translation into Hebrew sometimes serves as a restoration of sorts whereby the works return to their common, Jewish origin, and are thus granted something of a redemption. It seems to me that only in Hebrew is a kind of [Jewish] literary pantheon being brought into existence," wrote author and literary critic Ehud Ben-Ezer in a review in *Davar* in January 1980.[41] It was the transmission of Jewish American literature to a Hebrew-reading audience, according to Ben-Ezer, that conferred on this literature its (Jewish) significance. Only in Hebrew did the very different Jewish authors living and writing in the diaspora "appear to constitute one literature, and belong to one another perhaps more than to the literature of the language in which [their works] were written (except for Yiddish authors)."[42] Three years later, Ben-Ezer again cast Hebrew translation of Jewish texts in the appropriating framework of the Israeli concept of the ingathering of exiles: "I do not think there is any language in the world today like Hebrew, into which so many works of Jewish authors not originally written in Hebrew have been translated. . . . In this respect, we are the center into which Jewish cultural production in all tongues is gathered."[43] The Hebrew language is portrayed as a medium that can not only provide a home for individual works but also actually create a collective Jewish corpus out of them, a corpus that has not previously existed. This brings to mind Bialik's earlier advocacy for the idea of *kinus* (gathering) of Jewish spiritual treasures in Hebrew translation: "When [Jewish literature in foreign languages] is connected to the Hebrew language, it is once again connected to the living. . . . With the introduction of new 'material,' so too will [Hebrew's] container expand, and we will no longer have separate national and nonnational [Jewish] literatures. The language will 'nationalize' all that comes into it and all that is contained within its borders."[44]

In the context of these remarks, the way in which Israeli American Hillel Halkin, this generation's preeminent translator of Hebrew literature into English, considered the issue of Jewish American literature and culture is particularly interesting. Halkin immigrated to Israel in 1970 and was the first to introduce English readers to translations of classics from leading writers of the first generation of the Hebrew renaissance, such as Yosef Haim Brenner, Mordechai Zeev Fireberg, and Uri Nissan Gnessin, in addition to those of subsequent canonical authors such as Agnon, A. B. Yehoshua, Haim Be'er, and Amos Oz. In 1977, he published the polemical novel *Letters to an American Jewish Friend.* (The book was first written and published in English but was released a year later in Hebrew translation.) The novel is structured as a correspondence between the figure of Halkin, an American Jew who immigrated to Israel and settled there, and a Jew living in America whose letters are presented only in quoted excerpts. In this framework of imagined debate in correspondence, Halkin tries to persuade his interlocutor to immigrate to Israel. The genre of the epistolary novel, and the fact that the narrator bears the name of the author, Hillel, lend a strong sense of authenticity and credibility to the work. In his foreword to the 2013 edition, Halkin admitted that the novel indeed reflected, and to a great extent still does, his life and worldview.

Throughout the novel, even as he does not withhold his social, cultural, and political criticism of the contemporary Israeli reality, the narrator sees life in Israel as the only Jewish life of any value. This perspective is based, among other things, on linguistic ideology: "I tell you, they are still everything. Everything. A land and a language! They are the ground beneath a people's feet and the air it breathes in and out."[45] From Halkin's viewpoint, the flourishing of secular Yiddish culture in America could not have lasted for more than a generation, first because it lacked the territorial footing of a sovereign state and second because, unlike Hebrew, "even the Yiddish language, for all its vibrancy, lacked roots in the greater part of the Jewish past. . . . Like a plant unable to tap the deeper nourishment of the earth, secular Yiddish culture flourished vigorously for a season and died."[46] Hebrew is conceived of as representing roots in the Jewish past and as a necessary basis for a secular Jewish culture in America that will endure; without it, according to Halkin, along with Yiddish, "the one reasonable hope there has ever been for a secular Jewish culture in the diaspora died also."[47]

The narrator's position reaches its most extreme in another passage, in which Halkin casts doubt on the Jewish value of any intellectual work produced by a Jew in the diaspora, asking:

> What good has it done *us*? Have the Heines, the Prousts, the Babels, the Bellows, and the Mandelstams contributed anything to the creation of modern literature we can call our own? . . . It would surprise me if your list of intellectual giants spawned by the Diaspora contains a single figure who has occupied himself with an essentially Jewish sphere of thought. It's all very well to say that we have been affected by our marginality in the Diaspora as an oyster is by an irritant which makes him produce a fine pearl, but once the much praised oyster is pried open, and the pearl extracted from within him, what remains for the oyster?[48]

This hyperbolic approach, which categorically dismisses every Jewish intellectual work ever written outside of Israel, suggests that the common Israeli skepticism regarding the "authenticity" of American Jewish literature was still current in the 1970s. The linguistic dimension of this doubt is explicitly revealed in a more recent essay by Halkin, published in *Commentary* in June 2008, in which he decries the trend of elevating English to the status of the international language of the Jews, "[having] been aided in its displacement of Hebrew by [American] Jewish assimilation, which has deprived millions of Jewish children of the Hebrew they once acquired as part of a religious upbringing."[49] Halkin goes on to imply an unambiguous hierarchy of Jewish identity in Israel and in America—a hierarchy founded on language—as he deplores the lack of a Hebrew ethos in contemporary American Jewry, of "the belief that without Hebrew, Jewish lives are incomplete."[50] Furthermore, echoing Bialik's perception of language, Halkin sees an inherent problem in translation from Hebrew to English because "it dilutes the culture it disseminates, weakens Jewish distinctiveness, puts Jews at a remove from themselves." But then, too, in a different vein, "it makes them vulnerably transparent to the outside world. A people's language is its private home; in it, it can pursue its own business, conduct its own quarrels, make its own jokes, let down its hair; it can be itself without fear of eavesdroppers."[51] The conception of language as a central basis for Jewish authenticity—based on a rhetoric of "full" versus "partial" identity—is bound up here with an additional paradigm in Israeli discourse on American Jewish culture, which as we saw in the previous chapter seeks to maintain and emphasize the existence of boundaries between Jews and non-Jews. These two paradigms, each on its own as well as in consort, serve the structuring of a hierarchical distinction between Israel and the diaspora.

The dominance of this approach in Israel's public discourse is further evidenced in a speech delivered by Saul Bellow in November 1976, on the occasion of his receiving the America's Democratic Legacy Award from the Anti-Defamation League. In his speech, which reflected on the influence of his Jewish identity on his work, Bellow recounted his visit to Israel a year before: "In Israel, I was often and sometimes impatiently asked what sort of Jew I was and how I defined myself and explained my existence."[52] To this, Bellow replied that he was an American, a Jew, a writer by trade. He further said that he was not insensitive to the Jewish question, was painfully conscious of the Holocaust, and longed for peace and security in the Jewish state. However, when he added "that I had lived in America all my life, that American English was my language, and that . . . I was attached to my country and the civilization of which it was a part"—so Bellow describes—"my Israeli questioners or examiners were not satisfied. They were trying to make me justify myself. It was their conviction that the life of a Jew in what they call the Diaspora must inevitably be 'inauthentic.'"[53]

These remarks indeed echo the Israeli approaches to Bellow discussed in the previous chapter, some of which reflected the linguistic dimension. Critic Pinhas Elad-Lender, in an essay otherwise filled with pride and admiration for Bellow and his receipt of the Nobel Prize, passes the following judgment: "the artist has yet to come to identify with the secret formula for the perpetuity of his people. His frequent visits to Israel show that he is aware of its existence, as do his debates on the essence of being a Jewish author whose language and culture are [American] English. . . . The issue remains unsolved. Something must have been revealed to him in his recently published book, *To Jerusalem and Back*. But, as is clear [from the title]: he still comes back from our Jerusalem. Jerusalem has not yet won him over."[54] Implicit in these lines is a patronizing rebuke: Bellow has not yet grasped the real "essence of being a Jewish writer" with regard to his language and spiritual homeland. This is an understanding that, unlike Elad-Lender and the other (Hebrew-speaking) Israelis, Bellow has yet to achieve.

According to Bellow's biographer, Zachary Leader, Bellow's reference to language in his 1976 speech was a continuation of an early line of thought, already revealed in 1963 in his editor's introduction to *Great Jewish Short Stories*. There, Bellow protested the assumption that Hebrew was the only authentic tongue of the Jews and polemically linked this reductive view to German historian Oswald Spengler's notorious contention that Jewish culture would forever belong to the premodern period.[55] According to Leader, with these remarks Bellow defended Jewish authors who did not write in Hebrew against "what he saw as a xenophobic strain in Israeli attitudes to the literature and experience of Diasporan Jews."[56] Bellow's remarks from 1963 and 1976 thus provide "external" confirmation of the persistent connection between Hebrew and the "validity" of Jewish literary creation assumed in 1960s and 1970s Israeli culture.

Israeli thought on Jewish American culture in the 1980s conferred similar significance on the question of language, as canonical authors such as Amos Oz and A. B. Yehoshua and leading literary scholar Gershon Shaked turned to the subject. In contrast to dominant Israeli voices in preceding decades, these figures had increasing symbolic capital not only in Israeli culture but also on the American Jewish scene, where they were often treated as the intellectual representatives of Israeli society. Also worth noting is the lifetime connection all three of them had to Israeli academia, teaching courses in literature departments in Israeli universities. Recipient of the prestigious Israel Prize for his scholarship, Shaked was a professor at the Hebrew University of Jerusalem (and served as head of the Department of Hebrew Literature); winners of the same prize for their oeuvres, Yehoshua has been affiliated with the University of Haifa, Oz with Ben-Gurion University of the Negev. Although the syllabi and notes for their classes during the years in question are unavailable, their perspectives on American Jewish literature and culture may be presumed to have found expression in their teaching—even if only in passing. The ways in which these thinkers conceived American Jewish culture thus not only were an important component of Israeli public thought but also should be weighed in the particular context of the channel of mediation of Israeli academia, and of the representative role increasingly assigned to them as Israeli intellectuals on the American Jewish scene. As it turns out, this representative role did not prevent them from using severe rhetoric to express their doubts about the value and viability of American Jewish cultural life.

Thus, for instance, in his influential collection of essays *Between Right and Right* (1981), A. B. Yehoshua describes diaspora Jewish existence as fundamentally neurotic, "incapacitated and incomplete."[57] "A Jew in the *Golah* undoubtedly feels himself to be whole and complete as a Jew," Yehoshua patronizingly suggests, "but in his reality as a Jew (in terms of the range of possibilities that the Jews and Judaism have themselves posited) he is a limited being, incomplete and obstructed."[58] This formulation of Jewish identity in the diaspora as inherently "partial," compared to the "totalness" or fullness of Jewish identity in Israel, resonates with common understandings of translation as unavoidably partial (and inferior) in relation to the source. The ideological underpinnings of this linguistic metaphor become explicit when Yehoshua claims that "the word *Israeli* is in fact the original and authentic term for a Jew."[59] Yehoshua's conception of the Hebrew language as central, or even a prerequisite, to "full" Jewish existence is indeed in line with the tradition of thought that postulates Israeli culture as the Jewish "source text" of our time. In this, he merely repeats what Bialik laid out in his well-known essay "On Nation and Language," in which the connection between language ideology and translation is manifested explicitly in his typology of Jews—of people, not texts:

> The basic dividing lines in our nation are not, in my eyes, our religious and political parties, but rather the proximity to or distance from the Hebrew language. There are "original" Jews, who are rooted in the very

> foundation of the soul of our nation, and there are "translated" Jews, who live their lives in foreign tongues, rather than in their own.[60]

Yehoshua's understanding of Jewish American culture is not explicitly laid out in his essays from the 1980s, but in later years found decidedly concrete expression. In a lecture delivered in New York in 2003, for instance, Yehoshua asserted that

> in spite of the scholarly and teaching activity in universities and research institutions [in the United States], encouraged by generous grants contributed by wealthy Jews . . . Jewish culture, and especially Jewish art in the diaspora, have been in recent years nursing from an increasingly waning reality of Jewish life.[61]

Yehoshua granted a central place in his remarks to knowledge of Hebrew, asserting that "if the educated and artistic Jews in the diaspora would commit themselves to the acquisition, even of only partial command of Hebrew . . . their contact with Israeli culture would be incomparably more alive, rich, and authentic than it is today in English."[62] In a 2012 lecture, Yehoshua once again described Jews in the United States as "partial" and not "total" Jews, negating the authenticity of Jewish existence outside Israel, and called for American Jews to learn Hebrew.[63]

A similar stance, if slightly more subtle, appears in Amos Oz's 1988 lecture at a conference in San Francisco. Later published in a collection of essays on the writer in the Jewish community, Oz's talk described the Jewish diaspora and Israeli cultures as immersed in a "subterranean struggle," an "uneasy relationship for all the kinship that is involved"—a polemic in which Oz in fact takes part in his lecture.[64] Jewish collectivity in America, in his view, is limited in its ability to produce an authentically living Jewish culture. American Jewry is therefore likened to a museum, as opposed to the "live drama" of Israel. In this museum of American Jewry, culture, religion, values, and the like are "neatly arranged in glass cases and parents take their children to show them those assets and try to inspire them," if only in hopes that the keys to the museum will be handed over to the next generation, so that they in turn will bring more visitors. In such circumstances, there is no chance for change to occur. Jewish life remains as "safe as death itself."[65]

In his lecture, Oz relies on an implicit assumption that territory and language are imperative for modern Jewish identity. A "new Kafka" who will arise on American soil, he argues, will not merit the designation of a Jewish author, despite being of Jewish origin, and could only be described as an American author. Kafka's work indirectly drew on the Eastern European cultural influences of Kabbalah, *hasidism*, and Yiddish theater, among others, whereas this hypothetical American author will lack a dynamic collective Jewish life from which he might draw inspiration, and which he might satirize and work within and against. The individual prospects of this American Kafka as a Jewish writer, according to Oz, are therefore dependent on an uncle who lives in Jerusalem or a cousin on a kibbutz, or some formative experience by the Dead Sea. In short, he will depend on some connection to the "live drama" of Israeli life, without which, Oz concludes, he "may become a new Faulkner, but not a new Kafka."[66]

Drawing on the perceived risk that American Jewish life will turn into a "museum," Oz concluded his talk with two suggestions for American Jews. The first, the best option lying before the American Jew, in his opinion, is to immigrate to Israel—to "mount the stage [and] steal the show" in Israeli religion, politics, literature, and culture. Should American Jews choose to continue living outside Israel, however, Oz suggests that they "at least learn Hebrew, so [they] can follow the drama without earphones."[67] Like Yehoshua, then, Oz reveals an underlying assumption of Israeli Hebrew culture as the Jewish "source text" of our time, to which American Jewish culture has current access merely in translation (with "earphones"). American Jews' ability to absorb this Jewish "source text," he implies, is intrinsically impaired, as it is done through the veil of another language. Oz emphasizes the centrality and primacy of Hebrew elsewhere in the article as well, when he cites the revival of Hebrew as a great collective Jewish creation of our time, engendered by Zionism. Although no one will receive a Nobel Prize for this, Oz writes with irony, it is no less important than the volumes of Saul Bellow's works, "with all due respect to the Nobel Prize committee."[68] Oz's attitude toward American Jewish culture is ultimately revealed in his concluding remark that if American Jews "want to avoid the option or the danger of becoming a spectacularly beautiful museum, but, in the long run, Heaven forbid!, an empty one," they must acknowledge the precedence of Israel and its utmost necessity to their collective future.[69]

"Judaism in Translation"

The most comprehensive Israeli discussion of Jewish American culture and creative expression in the four decades since the publication of Shimon Halkin's *Jews and Judaism in America* is found in Gershon Shaked's

"Alexandria" (1988).[70] The leading scholar of Hebrew literature at the time, Shaked dedicated this essay to the memory of Halkin, who had been his teacher, and began by noting Halkin's own 1947 essay, symbolically delineating Hebrew thought on American Jewish culture in these four decades.

In "Alexandria," Shaked describes his impressions of Jewish cultural life in America after having spent a sabbatical year in New York. He presents Jewish American culture as in constant tension between the preservation of Jewish particularity and the Americanization and assimilation into non-Jewish society, and discusses the role of translation in this tension. Shifting between admiration and skeptical irony, Shaked details local intellectual endeavor, as he likens New York to the Jewish community in Hellenistic Alexandria, whose cultural life relied heavily on the translation of Jewish sources. He admits to having often struggled to determine whether this is "a pseudo-Jewish culture of sorts, or an authentic and thriving culture; if this is a rearguard battle, the end of which will be suicide or self-destruction, or whether there is a glowing coal amid the ashes."[71]

Shaked is careful not to take an unequivocally judgmental position and asserts that "only time will tell if the enormous enterprise of translation underway here will stabilize Jewish American culture and provide American Jews with an identity of their own, or whether it will flatten out their culture and deprive them of their uniqueness."[72] His implicit assumption, however, may not be significantly different from that of the Israeli thinkers discussed earlier with regard to the question of the dependence of Jewish culture on Hebrew. This is particularly evident in his description of American Jewish spiritual life as a culture renewing itself while seeking to create continuity with the Jewish past. Here, Shaked compares contemporary American Jewish culture to the secular culture of the *Yishuv*, which had similarly shed the traditional trappings of Judaism. He emphasizes that we must remember and not forget the "minor" difference between these two incarnations of tradition: the Israeli one draws on Hebrew and is embedded with internal [Jewish] linguistic and cultural sources, whereas the American one draws on English and tries to adapt itself to the social environment of another culture.[73]

Shaked goes on in many other places in his essay to address the near-total dependence of Jewish American culture on translation.[74] In fact, even when Shaked marvels at the earnest effort invested in translation, the considerable attention he devotes to it in the portrayal of American Jewish experience betrays his position on the relation between Jewish identity in

Israel and in America. Such an approach perhaps resonates most with the notion of Jewish translation offered by Bialik, who had asserted in 1917 that

> to employ a foreign tongue, to know Judaism in translation alone, is like kissing one's mother through a veil. Peeking through translation only allows [one] to see through a blurred speculum, and not to sense her flavor or the yearnings of her soul; for only she [Hebrew], is the language of the heart and the soul.[75]

When Shaked's essay appeared five years later in a revised English version, this view was expressed in its new title: "Judaism in Translation." Reflecting the hierarchical approach that has been at the foundation of Western translation theory throughout history and remains dominant today, translation is considered secondary to the source and inferior to it. What is perceived by Shaked as authentic Jewish existence is clearly viewed through this ideologically informed linguistic lens.

The notion of American Judaism as "translation" not only appears in Shaked's title but also is alluded to in his description of the Jewish book fair he attended in New York, which, as Shaked made a point of emphasizing, may have been highly popular, yet presented hardly any Hebrew or Yiddish books. "There are producers of literature who are convinced they are working with Jewish materials for the Jewish reading public, and there are consumers of these products," he notes of the fair with subtle sarcasm. "The society is based on supply and demand, therefore everything is all right, and everyone is pleased, profiting from each other and supporting each other."[76] Later in the essay, Shaked passes more explicit judgment on the immense translation enterprise and the awakening of Jewish cultural identity in America, suggesting that

> they may feel that they no longer need Zion in order to live a Jewish life. Perhaps they only barely remember that part of this renaissance was fomented by the social and cultural challenge presented by the State of Israel, and that they still have not created cultural autonomy with truly intrinsic creative power.[77]

Shaked also relates his doubts regarding the recent surge in scholarship on Jewish history and culture to the issue of language. His skeptical view of Jewish Studies programs "cropping up like mushrooms after the rain" at American universities is rooted in the fact that most of the curricula engage translated texts and not the original sources.[78] Jewish students come to study, Shaked suggests, principally because it offers them a way to identify with their community, but "forgoing the linguistic element hampers prospects for the development of scholarship."[79] Elsewhere in his essay, he criticizes the scholarly work and literary criticism published by university presses because they rely not on sources but on their translations.[80] His harsh conclusion that "the loss of significance of the Hebrew sources is what gives the new chairs in Jewish studies their *raison d'etre*"[81] reduces the entirety of Jewish Studies in American academia to the narrow context of the lack of Hebrew proficiency.

Shaked's ideological orientation is further expressed in the original version of his essay by his omission of any mention of Jewish American writers as contributors to American Jewish identity. The only passage that refers to modern literature as a component of American Jewish identity notes the translation from Hebrew into English of works by Israeli authors such as Oz, Yehoshua, Shabtai, Appelfeld, and Kaniuk. "These books have become part of their Jewish identity," he claims with regard to the American readership, going on to suggest that "just as ancient Hebrew literature is being translated into English to make it part of the cultural heritage of American Jews, so also modern literature is being translated for the same purpose, and even criticism of modern literature (mainly after it has been translated!)."[82] Only in sections added to his revised English version of the essay does Shaked mention Jewish American literature as a source of contribution to Jewish identity, and recognize that its influence on American readers has been greater than that of Hebrew literature.[83] Yet, even here, his comparison of Israeli and Jewish American writers sets up a clear hierarchy in terms of the Jewish significance of their literary expression, manifested in temporal precedence and in measures of quantity and even quality. According to Shaked, what the Israeli writers of the poststatehood generation

> succeeded in communicating, perhaps more successfully than American Jewish writers, is mainly the shared Jewish fate. What Philip Roth has recently done in *The Counterlife*, has been done by Pinchas Sadeh, Yehuda Amichai, Amos Oz, Aharon Appelfeld, Yaakov Shabtai, A. B. Yehoshua, Yoram Kaniuk, and others in all of their works that have reached American Jewish (and non-Jewish) readers, creating a kind of common platform for original Jewish writing from Israel and American Jewish writers.[84]

In spite of his visible efforts to appear impartial, then, Shaked struggles not to cast doubts on the spiritual, intellectual, and literary life of American Jewry, doubts that were at least partially tied to the critic's ideological assumptions about language.

For nearly four decades, beginning with the establishment of the State of Israel, one of the dominant paradigms in Israeli thought on translation and language in the context of homeland–diaspora relations revealed both reservations about and condescension toward Jewish American culture. These reservations, anchored in an early tradition of Zionist thinking embodied by Ahad Ha'am and Bialik, involved critique of the "authenticity" of American Jewish spiritual life and its prospects for the future. Notably, most of this discourse was, from at least the 1970s onward, part of a general Jewish dialogue, either written originally in English or published in English translation and presented at conferences before Jewish American audiences (unlike earlier Israeli debates on the subject). However, even when this discourse engaged in a sort of dialogue with American Jews, the dismissive orientation that assumed the "inferiority" of American Jewish creative expression on the basis of language did not change much. The linguistic argument continued to enable Israeli thinkers to downplay the importance of Jewish American literature, rather than treat it as an independent corpus representing one of two equally important Jewish cultural centers.

As one seeks to situate this rhetoric of Jewish authenticity in a broader context, one must also take into account the Israeli conception of broader American society. American culture and the values of capitalism were largely derided as materialistic and vulgar in Israeli public thought during the decades in question, and sweeping categorizations of American consumerism occasionally colored the Israeli attitude toward American Jews and their culture.[85] Although the impact of this perspective should not be underestimated, it was more prominent in the early poststatehood period and seems not to have been the decisive factor in Israeli approaches to Jewish American culture overall. The greater reason, as discussed in the previous chapter, was the overtone of cultural competition between the two Jewish communities. Seen through the lens of metalinguistic and metatranslation discourse, then, Israeli attitudes toward American Jewish literary creation were far from political philosopher Joseph Agassi's vision of "creative cooperation between Israel and world Jewry . . . with regard to questions of Jewish culture"[86] and closer to sociologist Eliezer Ben-Rafael's description of "[divergent] Jewish populations fighting for status and predominance within the Jewish world as a whole."[87] From an Israeli standpoint, Jewish life in

America in the second half of the twentieth century presented the fiercest competition among its diasporas, not only in terms of personal safety, economic well-being, or even the moral supremacy attributed to diaspora life by some Jewish thinkers—even though these factors surely had an oblique impact on the literary discourse—but also regarding the question of the spiritual and cultural source of Jewish identity.

The assumption of competition between the two Jewish centers over symbolic, cultural, and human capital was sometimes implied between the lines and sometimes pronounced explicitly in metalinguistic discourse. In both cases, as with the tendency to emphasize Jewish/non-Jewish boundaries discussed in the previous chapter, the assumption persisted against the backdrop of the social and political vicissitudes of Israeli reality throughout those decades. This is not to say that the essays of Hillel Halkin, Shaked, Oz, and Yehoshua were not influenced by contemporary events or political change; in fact, they offered significant moral critique of Israeli society, mainly in the context of the Israeli–Palestinian conflict, and expressed the notion that there is much to be learned from the liberal-pluralist ethos of American Judaism. Moreover, as we also saw in the previous chapter, some Israeli critics expressed genuine appreciation for the complexity and artistry of the translated works, and by and large exhibited serious and honest interpretive efforts. A handful of critics even asserted the artistic supremacy of Jewish American literature over Hebrew literature as a corpus of Jewish creation (further demonstrating the implicit competition between the two cultures). However, over the course of these decades, a deep-rooted reservation ran like a thread through much of Israeli writing on intra-Jewish translation between Israel and the diaspora: Israeli thinkers continued to cast doubt on the authenticity of cultural Jewish identity in America and often connected this doubt to the linguistic argument. The dialectical shifting in Hebrew discourse between arrogance and anxiety, between dismissal and apprehension, can be seen as the rhetorical expression of these competitive undertones. And the language occasionally employed by Israeli writers to portray Jewish American culture shows the extent to which the topic was charged: in Amos Oz's work, the image of the empty museum and derivatives of the word *death*, as in *dead end* and *as safe as death itself*;[88] and in Gershon Shaked's writing, through such expressions as the *Masada of culture*, *suicide*, and *self-destruction*, among others.[89] This rhetoric juxtaposed a living Israeli culture (rooted in the Hebrew tongue) with a waning Jewish American culture (built without Hebrew).

Although the collective meaning of Hebrew was central to Israeli thought on Jewish culture in America, most literary debates did not articulate a systematic theory of language, of its function and significance. Nevertheless, it seems that one can isolate three paradigmatic aspects that lay at the heart of commentators' relation to language: the romantic (or essentialist), the symbolic, and the practical. These perspectives were not part of a methodological framework, nor are they mutually exclusive, and indeed they occasionally intermingled in the texts.

The romantic paradigm attributed to Hebrew an essentialist meaning and saw it as intrinsic and imperative to authentic Jewish identity. In Bialik's early articulation, which anticipated views articulated in Israeli intellectual discourse in later decades, "language is what distinguishes one nation from another, it is the thread upon which the myriad permutations of the soul are strung, the 'I' of the nation is woven upon it. Everything forever changes, everything is removed, plundered, taken away; land, too, may be taken away. Everything—but language."[90] In a strict interpretation of this approach, genuine Jewish works cannot be written except in Hebrew.

The symbolic paradigm assigned Hebrew primary importance on account of its representational value as the language of the Jewish nation living in its sovereign state. In Yosef Gorny's personal afterword to *The Quest for Collective Identity*, the historian engages with the ideological debate by attributing symbolic value to the knowledge of Hebrew, asserting that in the context of the "special connection of diaspora Jews to the state . . . in addition [to immigration], study of the Hebrew language should play a central place. The effort invested in the study of a language which is neither fashionable nor useful, is the most important popular expression of the communal will to survive."[91]

Finally, the practical perspective assumed a central role for Hebrew inasmuch as knowing the language would deepen the familiarity of American Jews with Israeli culture and thus bring the two communities closer together. This was, for instance, the rationale behind A. B. Yehoshua's appeal to American Jewish intellectuals and artists to learn Hebrew, so as to ensure that their interaction "with Israeli culture will be incomparably more alive, rich, and genuine than it is now through English."[92]

Because these three perspectives were blended together in a range of texts, occasionally even in the same text itself, it is difficult to determine whether the linguistic argument constituted a genuine ideological foundation, from which reservations regarding Jewish American literature emanated, or whether it was only intended to confer legitimacy on these reservations, which in fact stemmed from different sources. Either way, the most important point is that Hebrew served Israeli thinkers in their efforts to establish cultural primacy in the Jewish world by virtue of its historical symbolic capital. Whether by detracting from the value of American Jewish culture through reference to its past (and its severance from the "original" Jewish tongue) or dismissing its value by relating to the Jewish future (and the assimilation that will inevitably come from linguistic and cultural assimilation into a non-Jewish environment), literary discourse in Israel placed considerable significance on the linguistic dimension. Hebrew was not only the tongue that absorbed and transmitted Jewish American works to the Israeli audience; it also functioned as a conceptual and ideological platform for debating these works as texts bearing Jewish meaning.

Conclusion
Entangled Self-Perceptions

Literary translation, so has been the premise of this book, constitutes a particularly revealing site of encounter and dialogue between homeland and diaspora. This "spiritual bridge" between Israeli and American Jewish cultures, as Gershon Shaked quipped, was not, however, devoid of contention. Each literature was conceived in the target culture as representative of an alternative way of Jewish life, and its works often posed a challenge to local audiences; the images that readers met did not always agree with the self-perception that they had or were looking for. In this intellectual juncture between the two major Jewish cultural centers of the twentieth century, translation agents often assumed the social role of ideological mediators: translation strategies, metatranslational discourse, and the interpretations of translated works were neither transparent nor free of ideology. Undertones of friction were sometimes more intense, sometimes less so, as these mediations of literature could be seen as a cross-cultural negotiation of ideas and images of modern Jewish identity.

It is true that in this literary conversation, it was not the same agents who played an active role in each cultural sphere. It was not the same translators, editors, or critics who introduced and, to a certain extent, transformed the translated works en route to local audiences. It was not even the same literary corpus under discussion, as the two translated corpora revolved around and reflected a different historical experience and social reality. Nevertheless, some themes drew particular interest in both literary discourses and were the focus of mediating trends in both receiving cultures. These common themes, which informed both Israeli approaches to American Jewish experience and American Jewish approaches to Israel, may be instrumental for an integrated understanding of the ideological intersection staged here by translation. But before we attempt such an integrated reading, let us first briefly summarize the main findings presented in the two parts of this book.

The first part of the book was dedicated to the absorption of translated Hebrew literature in American Jewish culture. Against the backdrop of the Zionist transformation of American Jews in the mid-twentieth century, this section presented dominant trends in the mediation of Hebrew literature to American audiences from the 1950s through the 1980s. It argued that, alongside a tendency to attribute a self-critical, humanistic image to Hebrew literature, the translated works were moderated to American readers in ways that, mostly suggestively or implicitly, limited and dulled the challenging traits that were celebrated as expressions of Israeli moral reflection. This choice to provide the American reader with a more palatable depiction of the ambiguous moral reality depicted in Israeli literature was also a choice to defend the ways American Jews are perceived in the society in which they live, as the moral profile of Israel, the Jewish state, reflects on their own. The first part of the book also illustrated how other Israeli representations of Judaism and Jewishness that posed a challenge to Jewish American identity were mediated and adjusted. Literary expressions that accentuated Jewish/non-Jewish boundaries through reference to antisemitic persecution or antagonistic portrayals of the non-Jewish world were sometimes obfuscated. A more progressive, yet not secular, notion of Judaism than that depicted in the translated Hebrew works was commended. At times, American Jewish literary discourse rejected, or at least subdued, a nationalistic, territorially centered understanding of Jewish identity, and downplayed antagonistic portrayals of the diaspora or of diasporic characters. As this part of the book demonstrates, then, the appropriation of Hebrew literature in America helped demarcate the boundaries of Jewish American identity, an identity in which images of Israel fulfilled a central role during these years.

The second part of the book concentrated on the reception and framing of American Jewish works in Israeli culture in roughly the same decades. On the one hand, it demonstrated an Israeli tendency to particularize and "Judaize" universal aspects of works by Jewish American authors, to take pride in their literary achievements or criticize them when they were "too harsh" in their depictions of Jewish life, generally assuming a common destiny with American Jews and exhibiting an affinity with diaspora Jewish culture. It further showed tendencies in the translations of American Jewish works that, though part of a broader stylistic norm of *domestication* in Hebrew translation from all languages, seemed to anticipate, and may have reinforced, the particular Jewish contextualization of the works in their Israeli critical reception. On the other hand, this section argued that Israeli critics tended to (over)emphasize the difficulty of living as a Jew in a non-Jewish world, both from a spiritual and intellectual standpoint and a physical and social one, in a way that bolstered the conception of Israeli sovereignty as the best and perhaps the only true solution for contemporary Jewish existence. Universal notions of morality in Jewish American works that undermined an ethical image of Israel were also portrayed as flawed due to non-Jewish influences. This part of the book also traced a tradition of Israeli thought on American Jewish culture as revealed in metalinguistic and metatranslation discourse. It showed that a primary trend in Israeli reflection on intra-Jewish translation has been doubt regarding the "authenticity" of Jewish American literature. This approach often drew, explicitly or implicitly, on the ideological conception that Jewish creation could not be expressed in any language other than Hebrew. On the basis of this notion, Israeli thinkers formulated a hierarchy in the Jewish world that positioned cultural and literary life in Israel as more authentically *Jewish* and therefore superior to that of American Jews.

In short, although the first part of the book substantiates the general claim that Israel played a central role in Jewish American identity from the 1950s through the 1980s, it also attests to the highly nuanced ideological sieve needed for portrayals of Israel to fulfill their role and serve as a viable source of collective identity for American Jews during these years. The second part of the book in turn casts a new light on the prevalent historiographic assumption regarding the decline of the negation of diaspora in Israeli society from the 1960s onward. Although a certain openness developed in Israel toward the historical diaspora experience, thawing around the idea of contemporary American Jewish culture was far more challenging; Israeli literary discourse remained, for the most part, partial and dismissive toward American Jewish life and cultural expression, as the classical Zionist negation of exile transformed into a culturally oriented negation of contemporary diaspora.

As the two parts of the book demonstrate, trends of mediation in each Jewish culture may have differed, yet common questions of collective significance were represented in both discourses. These common themes raised an interest, if different in intensity, and elicited reaction, if sometimes opposite in nature, from translation agents in both literary spheres. Among these themes, the most prominent were those related to issues of Jewish morality, particularly in the context of the Israeli–Palestinian conflict; those that involved social and cultural boundaries between Jews and non-Jews, mainly against the backdrop of Jewish life in America; and those that represented the underlying cultural competition between homeland and diaspora, between Israeli and American Jewries. How should this commonality in themes, which is far from self-evident, be understood? What does it mean that both receiving cultures were drawn to similar issues, despite the vast differences in experience in each culture and their fictional representation in translated Hebrew and Jewish American works?

The answer, already hinted at earlier, may be that these themes were not only understood as pertinent to Jewish identity *internally*—that is, in each separate culture. Rather, they were also perceived as implied statements about collective Jewry and, as such, as indirect claims about the counterpart community. Thus the intellectual response to the translated literature in each Jewish culture could not but be, at the same time, an expression of self-perception. In other words, the need of each culture to shape its own identity and demarcate its own symbolic boundaries, within its own particular historical circumstances, was part and parcel of the impetus to respond to the translated images of the other Jewish collective as they were given literary shape.

The concrete effect of these acts of symbolic demarcation was the appropriation of translated literature, as demonstrated and discussed throughout the book. Notably, in both cultures these practices of appropriation seem to attest to a certain sense of protectiveness, or insecurity, albeit in different ways. Israeli critics of Bellow, Malamud, and Roth, as we have seen, overemphasized Jewish/non-Jewish boundaries in the translated works so as to indicate the preeminence of Israeli collectivity over the challenging alternative of American Jewish life. American Jewish mediators of works by Oz, Yehoshua, and Kaniuk, in turn, obfuscated critical portrayals of an immoral Israel so as to protect the perceived moral image of American Jewry within broader American society. Of course, defensive responses such as those expressed in each target culture could also be found in each source culture.[1] Yet against the backdrop of relations between the two communities, the mediation of translated literature in each target culture may have had a more acute and significant effect, as this effect was twofold: first, as a result of the mediation, the different Jewish reality portrayed in the original literary works was reframed and skewed; and second, and no less important, the fact that this was how the authors *chose* to describe and imagine this reality was concomitantly obscured. These are two interrelated yet separate matters that characterize a society and culture. By obfuscating literary representation of Israeli wrongdoing, for instance, translation agents withheld from American Jewish readers both a glimpse of actual Israeli reality and the symbolic significance, and implied dissidence, of such critical self-portrayal. In both literary spheres, then, access to a different, often challenging social reality became less intricate, as did the understanding of how the other culture chose, or was able, to imagine itself.

In short, rather than offering an engaged dialogue with a Jewish Other, the juncture of translation often provided a way for each cultural group to chart its own symbolic boundaries, a mediated process in which censorship and self-censorship proved a constituent. As French thinker Paul Ricœur suggested in his hermeneutic approach to translation, identity is defined in opposition to the other, and may often ensue from "mistrustful interaction" and "mutual exclusion."[2] The role of censorship and self-censorship in the relationship and mutual perceptions between the two Jewish cultures in Israel and the US has not been sufficiently acknowledged or studied—yet it may inform and nuance our thoughts on some charged contemporary polemics. Its manifestations, unveiled through translation, may even suggest that Israel–diaspora competition has been, in certain contexts, paramount to particular discussions of Jewish morality as a factor behind tensions in the relationship. In other words, strains over questions of morality could sometimes derive from, or be preceded by, the cultural competition between diaspora and homeland—and not the other way around. Without disregarding the entanglement of these two discourses of Jewish identity, one could see differing ethical views of the Israeli–Palestinian conflict in both directions of cultural exchange also as a means, rather than an end, in the subterranean struggle between homeland and diaspora over competing post-Holocaust alternatives for Jewish existence. This perspective may help to clarify the dialectics of Jewish thought between ideology and social reality, as it resonates with recent positions taken in heated debates on frictions and differences in the relationship.

This obstructed, limited acquaintance with the other Jewish experience raises additional important questions: Is a more genuine encounter, when attempted through the exchange of cultural expression, at all possible?

And what can be learned about the Jewish cultural world as a whole, about collective Jewry, when the findings and general understandings that arise from the two parts of the book are considered together?

First, it is notable that each cultural center wished—indeed sometimes felt an urgent need—to define itself with respect to the values and existence and experience of life in the other Jewish center. Certainly not for the first time in Jewish history, nor presumably for the last, friction with the other Jewish collective served as a means of self-definition. The seemingly dichotomous existence of two separate Jewish cultures, in Israel and America, was in fact merely a point of departure, a premise to understand how each intellectual discourse was not only permeable to but also intermingled with and dependent on the other Jewish culture. Translation, and the discourse it initiated and generated in the target culture, demonstrates that the two communities did not really shape their symbolic boundaries independently but rather reacted to each other, perceived and established their own identity vis-à-vis that of the other community. At least in the case of literary exchange between Israel and the American diaspora, each community's practices of self-definition were inseparable from those of its counterpart.

Second, just as the two discourses interacted and were intermingled through translation, so were expressions of solidarity and conflict, affinity and competition, inextricably bound up in the intellectual dialogue that was staged by translation practices. In fact, expressions of affinity and common destiny, on the one hand, and competition and friction, on the other, not only were entangled but also can in essence be thought of as being borne out of each other. Trends of mediation that expressed cultural competition or even patronization would never have existed had there not been an initial affinity, a deeply felt relevance, between the two Jewish cultures. Then again, feelings of affinity engendered certain expectations of the other Jewish center, which in turn led to intense practices of appropriation. The main source of mutual affinity, and a major point of dispute, was Jewish identity. Both discourses, as we have seen, not only were drawn to but also found it hard to accept another form of Judaism on its own terms: American characteristics of Jewish identity were reframed and contested in Israeli literary debates, and Israeli formulations of Jewish identity were moderated and appropriated in American Jewish discourse. This is why an explanation of the intercultural relations between the two Jewries, instead of proposing two ostensibly competing paradigms of friction and affinity, should instead speak of mutual solidarity and affinity as dialectically bound to friction and struggle, with the two opposing orientations practically stemming from each other. In the charting of symbolic boundaries in each Jewish culture—as expressed in manipulations in translation, metatranslation discourse, and critique of translated works, among others—affinity and appropriation were two sides of the same coin.

In a way, it could not have been otherwise. Both Jewish centers, in Israel and America, represent divergent historical vectors of substantial symbolic and political power: two major alternative trajectories of Jewish collectivity. The relationship between the two communities involved both the centripetal forces of Jewish peoplehood and the centrifugal forces of different Jewish identities of homeland and diaspora. It is true that the feelings of affinity and common destiny in American Jewish culture toward Israel, as expressed in translation and literary discourse from the 1950s through the 1980s, may have been stronger and more palpable than those of friction and competition—whereas in Israeli responses to Jewish American culture in the same years, it was often the other way around, expressions of friction being largely more dominant than those of solidarity. Broadly speaking, however, these two mainstays of the Jewish world continued to exhibit both types of attitudes. Like boxers entangled in a hug at the point of fatigue, disinclined to strike forcefully or to let go, they have hung on to each other; heavyweight in the Jewish world, yet lightweight in the world at large, they continue to circle about in an uneasy hug as if in fear of being left alone.

Against this background, it can be admitted that Philip Roth's description of intimate friendship between (members of) these two communities of "*antithetical* twentieth-century Jewish biographies," quoted in the introduction to this book, does not exactly fit the intellectual dialogue that we have seen here. Roth's vision of Jewish intimacy borne out of deep difference and nourished by an unwavering consciousness of this difference fails to capture the ideological friction in the relationship—at least as it was reflected through the prism of literary translation. Here, however, we may pause to ask: Should this friction be considered as solely harmful? Could it perhaps be thought of not only as testimony of mutual relevance, as suggested earlier, but also as a positively productive force?

Surely, the obstruction of a more open and earnest dialogue between the two Jewish cultures—the inability, manifested and reinforced in the texts' mediations, to accept the other on its own terms—is lamentable. But could the inherent friction between the two competing communities also be seen as a testament to cultural vibrancy in Jewish life? At least some prominent thinkers seem to think so. "We [Israelis and American Jews] need each other to be the other for ourselves," Arnold Eisen suggested in 1993, "with all the guilt and anger and depth of relation that this inevitably involves."[3] In a more recent essay, Michael Walzer spoke of "the ancient and productive dualism of Babylonia and Palestine" against the backdrop of the growing tensions and apparent rift between the communities in recent years. Walzer accepted that there were questions in this competitive constellation that remain, and will likely continue to remain, unanswered. "Where is an authentic Jewish life most possible? "he asks. "Will the Talmud of the Exile once again outshine the Talmud of the Homeland—or will that ancient order be reversed? Will political sovereignty and territorial rootedness produce a glorious efflorescence of Jewish culture? Or, again, will that efflorescence be peculiarly Israeli, with little connection to Jewish tradition and little resonance in the Jewish diaspora?" Effectively mirroring the points of contention in the intellectual dialogue outlined in this book, Walzer goes on to declare that he would not take any bets on the answers to these questions. However, they also do not worry him: "An intellectual/cultural competition between the Jews of Israel and the Jews of the diaspora," he asserts, "can only be a good thing for both."[4] Some sixty years earlier, along similar lines if in a more philosophical vein, Simon Rabidowicz lauded "the eternal union of Babylon-and-Jerusalem" and claimed that "the pairing of Jerusalem and Babylon—before 1948 and after—complicates this paradoxical fact of Israel all the more, this fact full of frustrating yet fruitful perplexity and anguish for every son of Babylon-and-Jerusalem in every Generation."[5] Such a viewpoint may pertain to the nature of the encounter evinced here through translation. The "fruitful perplexity and anguish" in the "pairing of Jerusalem and Babylon," as found in the literary intersection between the two Jewish cultures via translation, though it did not always involve a truly open dialogue, at least pointed to a deeply ingrained, continually productive interdependence of the two cultures' self-definition. Indeed, the friction involved in this interdependence should not be overlooked as one of the main reasons for its inherent, intense liveliness.

Notes

Introduction

1. Compare David Shahar, *Sochen hod malchuto* (Tel Aviv, 2007 [1979]), 279–80, and Shahar, *His Majesty's Agent* (New York, 1980), 264. As I have learned from personal correspondence, Bilu herself was unaware of these alterations, and it was presumably the editor who made the changes while shaping the final draft of the translation. Bilu described her close collaboration with Shahar on the translation, as Shahar was her neighbor at the time, and believed that (the now late) Shahar would have been extremely upset to learn about them. (Dalya Bilu, telephone conversation, June 25, 2015).

2. Alexander Barzel, *Ha-sihah ha-gedola: masot al tarbut ve-sifrut* (Tel Aviv, 1971), 95. Original emphasis. Unless otherwise noted, translations from Hebrew are my own.

3. Barzel, 105. Original emphases.

4. A plethora of scholarly literature has discussed these subjects. Seminal historiographies of Hebrew literature are Gershon Shaked's monumental *Ha-siporet ha-'ivrit 1880–1980*, 5 vols. (Tel Aviv, 1977–1998); and Avner Holtzman, *Ahavot tsiyon: panim ba-sifrut ha-'ivrit ha-hadasha* (Jerusalem, 2006). For histories of Jewish American literature, see Stephen Wade, *Jewish American Literature since 1945: An Introduction* (Edinburgh, 1999); Julian Levinson, *Exiles on Main Street: Jewish American Writers and American Literary Culture* (Bloomington, Ind., 2008); and Hana Wirth-Nesher, ed., *Cambridge History of Jewish American Literature* (Cambridge, Mass., 2016).

5. Rakefet Sela-Sheffy, "The Suspended Potential of Culture Research in Translation Studies," *Target* 12, no. 2 (2000): 348.

6. The seminal work that introduced historical perspectives to translation studies systematically is Jean Delisle and Judith Woodsworth, eds., *Translators through History* (Amsterdam, 1995; then revised and expanded by Woodsworth in 2012). Delisle and Woodsworth provide a captivating overview of the key roles played by translators and translations in transformative historical processes through the ages. For a brilliant study of translation in the context of the charged historical relationship between Jews and Christians, see Naomi Seidman, *Faithful Renderings: Jewish-Christian Difference and the Politics of Translation* (Chicago, 2006). The prism of translation served Seidman as a means of exploring the politics of Jewish–Christian relations, using case studies from antiquity to modern times. For a useful survey of the history of intra-Jewish translation that focuses on Hebrew, see Gideon Toury, "Translation and Reflection on Translation: A Skeletal History

for the Uninitiated," in *Jewish Translation History: A Bibliography of Bibliographies and Studies*, ed., Robert Singerman (Amsterdam, 2002), ix–xxxii.

7. Michaela Wolf, "Introduction: The Emergence of a Sociology of Translation," in *Constructing a Sociology of Translation*, ed. Michaela Wolf and Alexandra Fukari (Amsterdam and Philadelphia, 2007), 3.

8. Gur Alroey, *Ha-mahapecha ha-shkeitah: ha-hagira ha-yehudit me-ha-imperiah ha-russit 1875–1925* (Jerusalem, 2008).

9. See Yosef Gorny, *The State of Israel in Jewish Public Thought: The Quest for Collective Identity* (New York, 1994). See also the collection of essays and articles in Moshe Davis, ed., *World Jewry and the State of Israel* (New York, 1977).

10. Although Jews of Mizrahi origin played an undeniable role in the establishment of Israel and formation of Israeli identity, mainstream and elite Israeli culture, politics, and public discourse were dominated throughout most of the twentieth century by leading figures of Eastern European origin, who largely marginalized Mizrahi cultural production. This was evident in the hegemonic literary discourse and major trends of mediation discussed in this book. The perpetuation of the misrepresentation of Mizrahim in Hebrew literature for American Jewish eyes will be touched on in chapter 1.

11. Ranen Omer-Sherman, *Diaspora and Zionism in Jewish American Literature: Lazarus, Syrkin, Reznikoff, and Roth* (Hanover, N.H., 2002), 4.

12. On conflicts that transpired early on between Zionist thinkers on the relative significance of language (or culture more broadly) and territory (and the political activity pertaining to it), see, for instance, Avner Holtzman, "Ha-sifrut ha-'ivrit ve-pulmus ha-tarbut ha-tsiyonit be-reshita," in *'Idan ha-tsiyonut*, ed. Anita Shapira, Jehuda Reinharz, and Jacob Harris (Jerusalem, 2000), 145–65.

13. Jakob Klatzkin, "A Nation Must Have Its Own Land and Language," in *The Zionist Idea*, ed. Arthur Hertzberg (New York, 1966), 318.

14. Hillel Halkin, *Letters to an American Jewish Friend: A Zionist Polemic* (Philadelphia, 1977), 182.

15. For a discussion of the ways in which representative Israeli works undermined the Zionist ethos by undercutting the linguistic-Hebraic affinity with, or command over, the Land, see Yaron Peleg, "Writing the Land: Language and Territory in Modern Hebrew Literature," *Journal of Modern Jewish Studies* 12, no. 2 (2013): 297–312.

16. Hasia R. Diner, *Lower East Side Memories: A Jewish Place in America* (Princeton, 2002).

17. Sarah Phillips Casteel, "Landscapes: American and the Americas," in Wirth-Nesher, *History of Jewish American Literature*, 416.

18. Irving Howe likened Cahan, in his demands that immigrants learn English, to "a father thrusting a child into the water in the hope it will be forced to swim." Irving Howe, *World of Our Fathers* (New York, 1976), 229.

19. Mary Antin, *The Promised Land* (New York, 1997), 164.

20. Cynthia Ozick, "America: Toward Yavneh," *Judaism* 19, no. 3 (1970): 264–82.

21. Sarah Bunin Benor, "Do American Jews Speak a 'Jewish Language'? A Model of Jewish Linguistic Distinctiveness," *Jewish Quarterly Review* 99, no. 2 (2009): 230–69.

22. As Hana Wirth-Nesher shows, the creative encounter of Jewish American writers with English was characterized by highly meaningful traces and ruptures of Hebrew and Yiddish. This multilingual negotiation of belonging was not without struggle and sentiments of loss. Such engagement, however, does not detract from the dominance of English in Jewish American literary identity but rather demonstrates it. Hana Wirth-Nesher, *Call It English: The Languages of Jewish American Literature* (Princeton, 2006).

23. See, for instance, Amos Oz, "Imagining the Other," in *The Writer in the Jewish Community: An Israeli–North American Dialogue*, ed. Richard Siegel and Tamar Sofer (Rutherford, 1993), 122.

24. See, for example, Mordecai Kaplan's seminal *A New Zionism* (New York, 1959).

25. David Roskies, "Tsiyonut, makom, ve-hadimyon ha-sifruti ha-yehudi," in Shapira, Reinharz, and Harris, *'Idan ha-tsiyonut*, 174. In the mid-1960s, some American intellectuals suggested the lack of territoriality of diaspora life as a positive determinant of Jewish identity (Gorny, *State of Israel*, 97–101). This approach attests, by way of negation, to the centrality of geographical space as a frame of reference in American intellectual thought on Jewish collectivity during these years. This diasporist position was reignited in the 1990s.

26. Zachary Leader, *The Life of Saul Bellow: To Fame and Fortune 1915–1964* (New York, 2015), 575.

27. Yosef Gorny, *Bein Auschwitz ve-Yerushalayim* (Tel Aviv, 1998), 15. The English version of this book from 2003 included some omissions; unless noted otherwise, quotations are translated from the Hebrew source.

28. Amos Oz and Fania Oz-Salzberger, *Yehudim ve-milim* (Jerusalem, 2014), 202. The Hebrew version of this book was published after the English one, and the authors incorporated some changes and new commentary into the text; unless mentioned otherwise, quotations are translated by me from the Hebrew version. An approach similar to the Ozs' is presented in Victoria Aarons, *The New Diaspora: The Changing Landscape of American Jewish Fiction* (Detroit, 2015), 11–13.

29. Jeremy Shere, "Collective Portraits: The Anthological Imagination of Leo W. Schwarz," *Shofar: An Interdisciplinary Journal of Jewish Studies* 23, no. 3 (2005): 39.

30. Hayim Nahman Bialik, "Agudat ha-sofrim ve-'itona," in *Devarim she-be'al peh* (Tel Aviv, 1935), 143.

31. Jonathan D. Sarna, "Two Ambitious Goals: Jewish Publishing in the United States," in *A History of the Book in America*, ed. Carl F. Kaestle and Janice A. Radway, vol. 4, *Print in Motion: The Expansion of Publishing and Reading in the United States 1880–1940* (Chapel Hill, 2009), 377. Sarna explains why a comprehensive unification of the Jewish community in the United States did not succeed despite the achievements of Jewish publishing and the centrality of the written text for various factions of American Jewry.

32. Benjamin Schreier, "Making It into the Mainstream: 1945–1970," in Wirth-Nesher, *History of Jewish American Literature*, 124–43. Representations of "Jewishness" in this body of works were extremely varied, and it would be disadvantageous to oversimplify the meanings and literary significance of this corpus into reductive categories. This point notwithstanding, the construct "Jewish American literature" was largely perceived as emblematic of

(American) Jewishness at least in some cultural and academic discourse, and its centrality in American letters has been undeniable. I will return to this in chapter 4. See also Ruth R. Wisse, "Jewish American Renaissance," in *The Cambridge Companion to Jewish American Literature*, ed. Hana Wirth-Nesher and Michael Kramer (Cambridge, 2003), 190–211.

33. Omer-Sherman, *Diaspora and Zionism*, 4.

34. Ezra Cappell, *American Talmud: The Cultural Work of Jewish American Fiction* (Albany, N.Y., 2007), 5.

35. Aarons, *The New Diaspora*, 17.

36. Oz and Oz-Salzberger, *Yehudim ve-milim*, 26.

37. Gorny, *Bein Auschwitz*, 15.

38. Oz and Oz-Salzberger, *Yehudim ve-milim*, 71.

39. The Tarbut Ivrit movement, active in the first decades of the twentieth century, sought to revive Hebrew art and culture and the study of Hebrew on American land. The movement briefly prospered during the 1910s, but later gradually vanished from the cultural landscape. For a useful overview of the Tarbut Ivrit movement in the United States, see Alan Mintz, ed., *Hebrew in America: Perspectives and Prospects* (Detroit, 1993). For a personal, somewhat suggestive essay that assigns translation a paradoxical role in the loss of Hebrew in American Jewish culture, see Hillel Halkin, "The Translator's Paradox," *Commentary* 125 (June 2008): 38–43.

40. For Goethe, "world literature" consisted of nothing other than European literature. For a discussion of his conception of world literature in the framework of comparative literature, see Hendrik Birus, "The Goethean Concept of World Literature and Comparative Literature," *Comparative Literature and Comparative Cultural Studies* 2 (2003): 11.

41. Kathy Mezei, "A Bridge of Sorts: The Translation of Quebec Literature into English," *Yearbook of English Studies* 15 (1985): 201–26; Yeshayahu Leibowitz, in Yebi, *Gesher bein hofim* (Tel Aviv, 1973).

42. Toury, "Translation and Reflection," xiv.

43. Julia Phillips Cohen and Sarah Abrevaya Stein, "Sephardic Scholarly Worlds: Toward a Novel Geography of Modern Jewish History," *Jewish Quarterly Review* 100, no. 3 (2010): 349–84; Dov HaCohen, *Aron ha-sefarim be-Ladino: mechkar ve-mipuy* (PhD diss., Bar-Ilan University, 2010). See also Benjamin H. Hary, *Translating Religion: Linguistic Analysis of Judeo-Arabic Sacred Texts from Egypt* (Boston, 2009).

44. Yosef Tobi and Tsivia Tobi, *Judeo-Arabic Literature in Tunisia, 1850–1950* (Detroit, 2014), 7–8.

45. Gershon Shaked, "Judaism in Translation: Thoughts on the Alexandria Hypothesis," in Mintz, *Hebrew in America*, 294.

46. Charles Liebman and Steven Bayme, "Foreword," in Olga Zambrowsky, *American Jewish Literature and the Israeli Reader* (New York, 1994), iii.

47. Oz and Oz-Salzberger, *Yehudim ve-milim*, 206.

48. Lawrence Venuti, *The Translator's Invisibility: A History of Translation* (London and New York, 1995), 308. See also Wolf, "Sociology of Translation," 1–36. This recent development in translation studies is greatly indebted to the seminal works of Gideon Toury and Itamar Even-Zohar in the 1970s and 1980s.

49. Christina Schäffner, "Third Ways and New Centres: Ideological Unity or Difference?" in *Apropos of Ideology*, ed. Maria Calzada-Pérez (Manchester, 2003), 23.

50. Johan Heilbron and Gisèle Sapiro, "Outline for a Sociology of Translation: Current Issues and Future Prospects," in *Constructing a Sociology of Translation*, ed. Michaela Wolf and Alexandra Fukari (Amsterdam and Philadelphia, 2007), 103, 104. See also David Damrosch, *What Is World Literature?* (Princeton, N.J., 2003).

51. Postcolonial thought was significant to the emergence of these new understandings of translation. For an overview of influential studies in the field, see Douglas Robinson, *Translation and Empire: Postcolonial Theories Explained* (New York, 2014).

52. On Hebrew-to-English translation, see, for instance, David Aberbach, "Hebrew Poetry in Translation," in *Modern Hebrew Literature in English Translation: Papers, Selected Syllabi and Bibliographies*, ed. Leon I. Yudkin (New York, 1987), 65–76; William Cutter, "Rendering Galicia for America: On Hillel Halkin's Translation of *Sipur Pashut*," *Prooftexts* 7 (1987): 73–88; Menachem B. Dagut, *Hebrew-English Translation: A Linguistic Analysis of Some Semantic Problems* (Haifa, 1978); and Michal Zellermayer, "Shifting along the Oral/Literate Continuum: The Case of the Translated Text," *Poetics* 19 (1990): 341–57.

53. Alan Mintz, "Israeli Literature in the Minds of American Readers," in Mintz, *Translating Israel* (Syracuse, N.Y., 2001), 1–43.

54. Yuval Amit, *Yitsu shel tarbut yisraelit: pe'ulatam shel mosadot rishmiyim be-tirgum sifrut me-'Ivrit le-Anglit* (PhD diss., Tel Aviv University, 2008). Amit's work outlined the diachronic structural trends in the publishing field within a cultural studies framework, focusing on institutional trends of Hebrew-to-English translation. His compiled bibliographical database of Hebrew works in English translation includes the names of translators and publishers, and year and place of publishing. This database is the most exhaustive available, drawing from complementary sources such as library catalogues, bibliographical projects (e.g., the database of the Institute for the Translation of Hebrew Literature), the Amazon catalogue, and more; my book draws on the data Amit has established. Amit details the sources for the database, and explains the reasons why his bibliography cannot be complete (12–14). For a highly useful survey of Hebrew literature's global transmission and reception, see Yael Halevi-Wise and Madeleine Gottesman, "Hebrew Literature in the 'World Republic of Letters': Translation and Reception, 1918–2018," *Israel Studies Review* 33, no. 2 (2018): 1–25. See also American poet Chana Bloch's personal account of her translation of Dalia Ravikovitch's protest poems, "The Politics of Translation: Amichai and Rabikovitch in English," in Siegel and Sofer, *Writer in the Jewish Community*, 130–39; and Israeli American translator Jeffery M. Green's reflections on his translations from Hebrew "as an unashamed, but not belligerent, Zionist," in his *Thinking through Translation* (Athens, Ga., 2001), 83–93.

55. See, for instance, Nitsa Ben-Ari, *Suppression of the Erotic in Modern Hebrew Literature* (Ottawa, 2006); Ben-Ari, "The Double Conversion of Ben-Hur: A Case of Manipulative Translation," *Target* 14, no. 2 (2002): 263–302; and Rachel Weissbrod, "Coping with Racism in Hebrew Literary Translation," *Babel* 54, no. 2 (2008): 171–86.

56. Zambrowsky, *American Jewish Literature* (this overview, published by the American Jewish Committee's Institute on American Jewish–Israeli Relations and the Argov Center for the Study of Israel and the Jewish People at Bar-Ilan University, runs fifteen pages);

Olga Zambrowsky and Malka Or-Chen, "American Jewry as Reflected in the Secondary School Curriculum in Israel," in *Beyond Survival and Philanthropy: American Jewry and Israel*, ed. Allon Gal and Alfred Gottschalk (Cincinnati, 2000), 131–49.

57. Wolf, "Sociology of Translation," 1.

58. The theoretical and methodological advantages of this approach are further discussed here: Omri Asscher, "A Case for an Integrated Approach to the Mediation of National Literature: Translated Hebrew Literature in the United States in the 1970s and 2000s," *Translation and Interpreting Studies* 12, no. 1 (2017): 24–48. Because of the scope and nature of this book, which involves a very large number of agents, my focus is on the acts of mediation themselves, not on the habitus of the reviewers, which in most cases appeared self-evident.

59. For a debate between translation scholars on the disciplinary tension between translation studies and historiographical research, see the forum "Translation and History" in *Translation Studies* 5, no. 2 (2012): 232–48. My work follows the position, advanced by forum participants Dirk Delabastita and Theo Hermans, that the contribution of historical research of translation should not be restricted to specified research fields, but rather that "the insights gained may benefit more than one community" (Hermans, 245), as they contribute not only to our knowledge about translation as a unique contact zone between cultures but also to specific histories and historical contexts.

60. The most influential proponent of research focused on translation norms in the target culture is Gideon Toury, *Descriptive Translation Studies and Beyond* (Amsterdam and Philadelphia, 1995).

61. Anita Norich, "Poetics and Politics of Translation," in Wirth-Nesher, *History of Jewish American Literature*, 492.

62. Mintz, *Translating Israel*, 60. A similar approach can be found in Amit, *Yitsu shel tarbut yisraelit*, 19–20; Shaked, "Judaism in Translation," 293; and Robert Alter, "The Rise and the Rise in the United States," *Modern Hebrew Literature* 7 (1991): 6.

63. The so-called Jewishness or non-Jewishness of a language is, of course, a socially contingent, discursive construct. In the context of this book, these designations are mainly useful in terms of their cultural and ideological functions. For a survey of sociolinguistic approaches to Jewish language varieties, see Sarah Bunin Benor, "Towards a New Understanding of Jewish Language in the Twenty-First Century," *Religion Compass* 2, no. 6 (2008): 1062–80. For an interesting discussion of English as a Jewish language variety, see Benor, "Do American Jews Speak a 'Jewish Language'? A Model of Jewish Linguistic Distinctiveness," *Jewish Quarterly Review* 99, no. 2 (2009): 230–69.

64. Thomas Franssen and Giselinde Kuipers, "Sociology of Literature and Publishing in the Early 21st Century: Away from the Centre," *Cultural Sociology* 9, no. 3 (2015): 291–95.

65. The 1990s may have marked a new period in the respective literary fields, according to Victoria Aarons, as Israeli and American writers began crossing linguistic boundaries and living comfortably in Hebrew and English, Israel and the United States. This loosening of boundaries could be thought of as a challenge to the definition of national literature as "national" literature. See Aarons, *The New Diaspora*, 15.

66. For instance, Mintz, *Translating Israel*, 25–27.

67. Mintz, *Translating Israel*, 19.

68. Toury, *Descriptive Translation Studies*, 17–35, esp. 23.

69. It may be self-evident but still worth noting that patterns of appropriation in both directions did not always accumulate into a neatly linear history in and of themselves. This is mainly because the source literary works that raised the most interest and "invited" ideological mediation in the target culture did not appear in a neatly linear fashion. In other words, the literary imagination was a rather irregular source of "stimulus," more sporadic than systematic in its political implications, with relevant works not only coming out intermittently but also being quite different from one another in their representations of Jewishness. This does not mean that the tendencies of mediation did not closely resonate with cultural and historical trends of the Israeli–American Jewish relationship, only that they could not be expected to do so in a linear, chronological, step-by-step manner.

70. David Biale, "Preface: Toward a Cultural History of the Jews," in *Cultures of the Jews: A New History* (New York, 2002), 1148.

71. Mark A. Raider, *The Emergence of American Zionism* (New York, 1998); Ehud Manor, "'Hem kemo ha-bund': temichat forvertz be-tsiyonut mishenot ha-esrim," *Iyunim Bitkumat Yisrael* 16 (2006): 499–531.

72. Ofer Shiff, *Survival through Integration: American Reform Jewish Universalism and the Holocaust* (Boston, 2005); Thomas Kolsky, *Jews against Zionism: The American Council for Judaism, 1942–1948* (Philadelphia, 1992).

73. Howard M. Sachar, *A History of the Jews in America* (New York, 1992), 595–619.

74. On the omnipresence of Israel in 1950s and 1960s American synagogues, see Marc Lee Raphael, *Judaism in America* (New York, 2003), 129–32.

75. Emily Alice Katz, *Bringing Zion Home: Israel in American Jewish Culture* (Albany, N.Y., 2015).

76. Arthur Hertzberg, *Being Jewish in America: The Modern Experience* (New York, 1979), 220–27. See also Charles S. Liebman, *Pressure without Sanctions: The Influence of World Jewry on Israeli Policy* (Rutherford, N.J., 1977), 197–200.

77. Peter Novick, *The Holocaust in American Life* (New York, 2000), 172–84.

78. Steven T. Rosenthal, *Irreconcilable Differences? The Waning of the American Jewish Love Affair with Israel* (Hanover and London, 2001).

79. Andrew Furman, *Israel through the Jewish-American Imagination: A Survey of Jewish-American Literature on Israel, 1928–1995* (Albany, N.Y., 2012), 11–12.

80. Michael N. Barnett, *The Star and the Stripes: A History of the Foreign Policies of American Jews* (Princeton, 2016), 195–242. Social scientist Theodore Sasson offers an alternative view of this trend of "disengagement," describing the prevailing approach toward Israel among American Jews pre-1990 as "mobilization," and the approach from the 1980s on as one of "engagement," encompassing occasional criticism. Theodore Sasson, *The New American Zionism* (New York, 2013).

81. Along the same lines, Israeli historiography has largely ignored the waves of Eastern European immigration to the United States at the end of the nineteenth century and beginning of the twentieth century, exhibiting a highly Palestino-centric approach to this

historical period. Gur Alroey, "Two Historiographies: The Israeli Historiography and the Mass Jewish Migration to the United States, 1881–1914," *Jewish Quarterly Review* 105, no. 1 (2015): 99–129; Alroey, "Israeli Historiography on American Jewry," *American Jewish History* 101, no. 4 (2017): 501–16. On the ideological underpinnings of major trajectories in Israeli historiography, see David N. Myers, *Re-Inventing the Jewish Past: European Jewish Intellectuals and the Zionist Return to History* (New York, 1995); Myers "Is There Still a 'Jerusalem School?' Reflections on the State of Jewish Historical Scholarship in Israel." *Jewish History* 23 (2009): 389–406.

82. Allon Gal, "Ha-yahasim bein Yisrael le-yehadut Artzot Habrit—ha-perspektiva ha-yisraelit," *Iyunim Bitkumat Yisrael* 8 (1998): 14. The Ahdut ha-ʻavoda and Ha-kibbutz ha-me'uhad publishing houses published a plethora of anti-American literature during the 1950s.

83. Hemi Sheinblat, *Litpos et Amerika: tahalichey americanisatsiah ba-hevra ha-yisraelit, 1958–1967* (PhD diss., Tel Aviv University, 2017).

84. See Anita Shapira, "Le-an halekhah 'shelilat ha-galut'?" *Alpayim* 25 (2003): 9–54; the English version of the article was published as "Whatever Became of Negating Exile?" in *Israeli Identity in Transition*, ed. Shapira (Westport, Conn. and London, 2004), 69–108; Gideon Shimoni, "Behina me-hadash shel 'shelilat ha-galut' ke-raʻayon ve-maʻaseh," in Shapira, Reinharz, and Harris, *'Idan ha-tsiyonut*, 60–63.

85. Shapira, "Whatever Became," 99–100; Ruth Yardeni, *She'arim le-gan naʻul: Binyamin Tammuz—temurot be-yetsirato* (Tel Aviv, 2012), 23–57.

86. Eliezer Don-Yehiya, "'Galut' in Zionist Ideology and in Israeli Society," in *Israel and Diaspora Jews*, ed. Don-Yehiya (Ramat Gan, 1991), 253.

87. Charles S. Liebman, "Diaspora Influence on Israel Policy," in Davis, *World Jewry*, 313–28.

88. Gal, "Ha-yahasim bein Yisrael le-yehadut Artzot Habrit,"17.

89. Gal, 24.

90. Research in the field has largely favored the diplomatic, military, and political aspects of the relationship between the two Jewish centers. Among the few exceptions to this, notable works include Andrew Furman's *Israel through the Jewish American Imagination* and Ranen Omer-Sherman's *Diaspora and Zionism in Jewish American Literature*, on the portrayals of Israel and Zionism in Jewish American literature, already mentioned earlier; and *Our Exodus* by Matthew Mark Silver, which describes the immense influence of Leon Uris's *Exodus* on American perceptions of Israel in the early post–World War II years: Matthew Mark Silver, *Our Exodus: Leon Uris and the Americanization of Israel's Founding Story* (Detroit, 2010). See also Deborah Dash Moore's discussion of Hollywood-made conceptions of Israel that served the self-perception of Jewish American society at the time, in her *To the Golden Cities: Pursuing the American Jewish Dream in Miami and L.A.* (Cambridge, Mass., 1994), 227–62; and Jonathan D. Sarna, "A Projection of Zion as It Ought to Be: Israel in the Mind's Eye of American Jews," in *Envisioning Israel: The Changing Ideals and Images of North American Jews*, ed. Allon Gal (Jerusalem, 1996), 41–59. A recent pioneering work is Shaul Mitelpunkt's exploration of cultural-political mechanisms that shaped Israel's place in the American imagination from 1958

to 1988. Mitelpunkt deals primarily with the images of Israel constructed by American commentators in policy circles, in media, and in the academic elite, yet he also touches on Israeli attempts to promote desirable images for American consumption. Mitelpunkt does not, however, focus on the Jewish American public as his primary point of reference. Shaul Mitelpunkt, *Israel in the American Mind: The Cultural Politics of US–Israeli Relations, 1958–1988* (Cambridge, UK, 2018). Another useful work that focused on constructed images of Israel in American culture in general is Michelle Mart's analysis of the representation of Israel in American media and film: Michelle Mart, *Eye on Israel: How America Came to View Israel as an Ally* (Albany, N.Y., 2006).

91. Katz, *Bringing Zion Home.*

92. Notably, Gorny, *State of Israel*; Gorny, *Bein Auschwitz*; Gal, "Ha-yahasim bein Yisrael le-yehadut Artzot Habrit"; and Alroey, "Israeli Historiography."

93. Philip Roth, *Operation Shylock: A Confession* (New York, 1993), 200–201.

94. Roth, 200–201.

Chapter 1

1. Robert Alter, "The Rise and the Rise in the United States," *Modern Hebrew Literature* 7 (1991): 7.

2. Alter, 7.

3. See http://www.unesco.org/xtrans/bsstatexp.aspx. The data does not refer only to the translation of fiction. Some of the translated books, if not a majority of them, were biblical and other sacred texts of Judaism.

4. Israel Meir Lask, "Translator's Foreword," in S. Y. Agnon, *The Bridal Canopy* (New York, 1937), vii.

5. The data is derived from Yuval Amit, *Yitsu shel tarbut yisraelit: pe'ulatam shel mosadot rishmiyim be-tirgum sifrut me-'Ivrit le-Anglit* (PhD diss., Tel Aviv University, 2008), 192–96, 221–91, and diagram no. 10 on page 64. Unlike Amit's dissertation, this book deals with literary translation from Hebrew in the United States, and therefore my calculations do not include English translations published in Israel or England. These translations were not distributed in America in the same way as works published by American presses, did not receive the same kind of newspaper coverage, and were not accessible to the American reading audience to the extent that the works published in America were.

6. Alan Mintz, *Translating Israel* (Syracuse, N.Y., 2001), 60; Alter, "Rise and the Rise," 6.

7. Sidney Goldstein, "American Jewry, 1970: A Demographic Profile," *American Jewish Yearbook* (New York, 1971), 11.

8. Jonathan D. Sarna, "Two Ambitious Goals: Jewish Publishing in the United States," in *A History of the Book in America*, ed. Carl F. Kaestle and Janice A. Radway, vol. 4, *Print in Motion: The Expansion of Publishing and Reading in the United States 1880–1940* (Chapel Hill, 2009), 377.

9. Johan Heilbron, "Towards a Sociology of Translation: Book Translation as a Cultural World-System," *European Journal of Social Theory* 2 (1999): 430.

10. Gideon Toury, *Descriptive Translation Studies and Beyond* (Amsterdam and Philadelphia, 1995), 23–39.

11. Benno Weiser Varon, "The Haunting of Meyer Levin," *Midstream* 22 (August/September 1976): 13.

12. Andrew Furman, *Israel through the Jewish-American Imagination: A Survey of Jewish-American Literature on Israel, 1928–1995* (Albany, N.Y., 2012), 24.

13. Quoted and discussed in Jeremy Shere, "Collective Portraits: The Anthological Imagination of Leo W. Schwarz," *Shofar: An Interdisciplinary Journal of Jewish Studies* 23, no. 3 (2005): 39.

14. Michael Lerner, "The Editor: A Personal Note," in *Tikkun: An Anthology*, ed. Lerner (Oakland, Ca., 1992), xxiv.

15. For a comprehensive review of Hebrew literature of the period, see Gershon Shaked, *Ha-siporet ha-'ivrit 1880–1980*, vol. 2 (Tel Aviv, 1983), 15–154. According to Avner Holtzman, the struggle between these two opposite orientations "took place within the soul of each author rather than between two rival groups of authors"; Avner Holtzman, *Ahavot tsiyon: panim ba-sifrut ha-'ivrit ha-hadasha* (Jerusalem, 2006), 178. It should be noted that I am referring here to translated works of fiction published by commercial and Jewish publishers, and not to nonfiction published by Zionist organizations. Among translated works of fiction, topics unrelated to Jewish life in Palestine were prevalent at least until the late 1930s, and even the mid-1940s.

16. Irving Howe, *World of Our Fathers* (New York, 1976), 417–554.

17. This cultural gap was also reflected in the rather indifferent American Jewish attitude to the quixotic efforts of the Tarbut Ivrit movement, which strived to sustain a vibrant Hebraist culture on the American scene. The movement briefly flourished during World War I, when several leaders of the *Yishuv* moved temporarily to New York, as evident mainly in its Hebrew periodicals, yet it did not secure a real readership or following, and gradually dwindled and disappeared from the cultural scene. See Alan Mintz, ed., *Hebrew in America: Perspectives and Prospects* (Detroit, 1993), 13–27, as well as Michael Weingrad, *American Hebrew Literature: Writing Jewish National Identity in the United States* (Syracuse, N.Y., 2011). It is indicative that at its height, the major Hebraist organ in America, the cultural monthly *Ha-toren*, had a circulation of thirteen thousand, whereas the Yiddish daily *Forward* had several hundreds of thousands.

The scarcity of Yiddish translations of Hebrew literature in America also attests to a lack of interest in Hebrew letters. Although one finds bibliographies of translation from Yiddish to Hebrew, English, Polish, Russian, and Ukrainian, and from English and Polish to Hebrew, there is no bibliography of Hebrew-to-Yiddish translations. A few stories by Hebrew modernists of the revival period, Y. H. Brenner and U. N. Gnessin, were published in Yiddish translation in the early decades of the twentieth century, but only in Warsaw. Some works by *Haskalah* writers, such as *'Ayit tsavu'a* by Mapu, appeared in American Yiddish journals, but only in 1941 did a collection of modern Hebrew prose (by Brenner) appear in Yiddish in America. Yiddish literary critic Yudel Mark's 1949 overview of recent translations from Hebrew is indicative, as he devotes his lengthy discussion to the Hebrew bible, Talmud, Mishna, and medieval poetry, among others, yet touches on translation from modern Hebrew fiction in a single sentence that refers to Brenner's 1941 translation. See Yudel Mark, "The Return to Traditional Sources: On Translations from Hebrew to Yiddish," *Jewish Book Annual* 7 (1949): 73–82.

18. Jonathan D. Sarna, *The Americanization of Jewish Culture: A Centennial History of the Jewish Publication Society, 1888–1988* (Philadelphia, 1989), 192–95.

19. Sarna, *Americanization*, 192. The poems in this selection were written in English; many of Sampter's other poems were written in Hebrew.

20. Sarna, 193.

21. Joseph Cooper Levine, ed., *Echoes of the Jewish Soul: Gleanings from Modern Hebrew Literature* (New York, 1931).

22. A. D. Gordon, *Mivhar ktavim* (Jerusalem, 1982), 175–76.

23. Compare Levine, *Echoes of the Jewish Soul*, 23, and Gordon, *Mivhar ktavim*, 175–76.

24. Moshe Kleinman, *Demuyot ve-komot: reshimot le-toldot ve-hitpathut ha-sifrut ha-'ivrit ha-hadasha* (Paris, 1928), 60.

25. "Historical Romance of the Days of Isaiah," *New York Times*, April 1, 1923, BR13.

26. Quoted in Shmuel Verses, *Ha-tirgumim le-yiddish shel ahavat tsiyon le-Avraham Mapu* (Jerusalem, 1989), 30.

27. "Historical Romance."

28. Harold S. Wechsler and Paul Ritterband, "Jewish Learning in American Universities: The Literature of a Field," *Modern Judaism* 3, no. 3 (1983): 253–89; Arnold J. Band, "From Sacred Tongue to Foreign Language: Hebrew in the American University," in Mintz, *Hebrew in America*, 171–86.

29. Shalom Spiegel, "Preface," *Hebrew Reborn* (New York, 1962 [1930]), ix.

30. As Weingrad argues, this maskilic tendency had more to do with an ideology of style and aesthetics, a "literary-cultural conservatism," than with a different politics of Zionism, even though he, too, admits that Palestine, as a destination for Hebrew writers, "appealed to a more ideologically radical temperament" (Weingrad, *American Hebrew Literature*, 33–34). In any case, the indirect effect of this conservatism seemed to be a less contemporary, less nationalist framing of Hebrew literature in America during these early decades.

On the cultural differences between American Hebraists and Hebrew writing in Palestine in the interwar period, see Nurit Govrin, "Bein 'olim le-mehagrim: kivunim menugadim be-hitpathut ha-merkazim ha-sifrutiyim be-Eretz-Yisrael uva-Arhav," *Bitsaron* 8, no. 31–32 (1987): 26–33.

31. Harold Strauss, "In Old Galicia," *New York Times*, February 21, 1937, 86.

32. *New York Times*, March 7, 1937, 107.

33. Peter Grose, *Israel in the Mind of America* (New York, 1981).

34. Emily Alice Katz, *Bringing Zion Home: Israel in American Jewish Culture* (Albany, N.Y., 2015); Deborah Dash Moore, *To the Golden Cities: Pursuing the American Jewish Dream in Miami and L.A.* (Cambridge, Mass., 1994). Feelings of national pride went hand in hand with the social underpinnings of the Jewish religious revival of the 1950s.

35. Harold U. Ribalow, "Zion in Contemporary Fiction," in *Mid-Century: An Anthology of Jewish Life and Culture in Our Time*, ed. Ribalow (New York, 1955), 591.

36. Matthew Mark Silver, *Our Exodus: Leon Uris and the Americanization of Israel's Founding Story* (Detroit, 2010), 111.

37. Katz, *Bringing Zion Home*, 19–47.

38. Sarna, *Americanization*, 277.

39. S. Y. Agnon, *In the Heart of the Seas* (New York, 1948). On the poetics and reception of the novella, see Shmuel Verses, *Shay Agnon ki-fshuto* (Jerusalem, 2000): 153–80.

40. Yitzhak Shenhar, *Under the Fig Tree: Palestinian Stories* (New York, 1948).

41. Alter, "Rise and the Rise," 5. Alan Mintz explained that exact sales figures are unattainable, as they are regarded as proprietary information, and publishers are not willing to disclose them for various reasons. Mintz, *Translating Israel*, 249.

42. The data is based on the table in Amit, *Yitsu shel tarbut yisraelit*, 62. My count includes prose and poetry anthologies, and does not include books for children and teens, or nonfiction works. The prominence of literary translation among all translated works was evident as early as the late 1930s and early 1940s. In ensuing decades, its absolute numbers continued to grow, though its proportionate rate fluctuated (while generally constituting about half the translated titles). For slightly different numbers, see Ezra Spicehandler, "Hebrew, Modern: Literary Translation into English," in *The Encyclopedia of Literary Translation into English*, ed. O. Classe (Chicago, 2000), 628; Yohai Goell, *Bibliography of Modern Hebrew Literature in English Translation* (Jerusalem, 1975).

43. This is to say that institutional Zionist and Jewish publishing houses translated more books each decade, but gradually accounted for a smaller relative proportion of all publications of translations from Hebrew to English. Broadly speaking, the books published by privately owned commercial publishing houses were not different from those published by institutional publishers in terms of their topics, genres, or their stylistic accessibility, even as commercial publishers tended to publish authors of higher regard in the source culture. Amos Oz, A. B. Yehoshua, Aharon Appelfeld, and David Grossman, for example, have always been published in America by commercial publishing houses.

44. Alter, "Rise and the Rise," 6.

45. Derived from Amit, *Yitsu shel tarbut yisraelit*.

46. Chaim Potok, "Foreword," in *Firstfruits: A Harvest of 25 Years of Israeli Writing*, ed. James A. Michener (Philadelphia, 1973), viii.

47. Philip Rubin, "The Jewish Storytellers," *New York Times*, December 28, 1952, BR6.

48. "In a Nutshell," *Washington Post*, June 18, 1953, B7.

49. Glendy Dawedeit, "Tale Tellers Again in Good Voice," *Washington Post*, July 1, 1956, E6. In similar fashion, Milton Himmelfarb's article on David Maletz's *Circles* expresses admiration for the novel and, when comparing it to Arthur Koestler's *Thieves in the Night*, lauds it for "[giving] the reader a truer and more deeply felt sense of the lives of men and women than Koestler's gaudy tract," even though Maletz "lacks Koestler's cleverness, and is not a particularly good novelist." Milton Himmelfarb, "Israel Omnibus," *Commentary* 10, no. 6 (December 1950): 608. A similar attitude can be found in the novel's review by Hal Lehrman, "Love in Israel," *New York Times*, May 21, 1950, BR14.

50. Philip Rubin, "Treasures of Israel," *New York Times*, June 10, 1956, BR18.

51. In his review of the book in *Commentary*, New York intellectual Isaac Rosenfeld expressed genuine surprise at the melancholic sense that pervades the stories. He suggested that the implied critique of the new national life was even greater than what was explicitly

expressed: "Self-disappointment is basic; it is the source of much of the feeling toward Palestine, and probably the reason, through guilt, that [Shenhar] does not criticize the country directly." Isaac Rosenfeld, "Unease in Zion," *Commentary* 7, no. 4 (April 1949), 403.

52. Moshe Shamir, "The First Kiss," in *Tehilla and Other Israeli Tales*, ed. Yitzhak Shenhar (New York, 1956), 159–88.

53. Leah Goldberg, "Growing Up," in *Feast of Leviathan*, ed. Leo W. Schwarz (New York, 1956), 263–65.

54. Gideon Tikotzky, *Ke-'or be-shuley he-'anan: hekerut mehudeshet 'im yetsirata ve-hayeha shel Leah Goldberg* (Tel Aviv, 2011).

55. Katz, *Bringing Zion Home*, 19–24.

56. Alexander Ramati, "A Literary Letter from Israel," *New York Times*, May 27, 1951, BR15.

57. Ramati, BR15.

58. Holtzman, *Ahavot tsiyon*, 320–21.

59. Michelle Mart, *Eye on Israel: How America Came to View Israel as an Ally* (Albany, N.Y., 2006), 65.

60. Shaul Mitelpunkt, *Israel in the American Mind: The Cultural Politics of US–Israeli Relations, 1958–1988* (Cambridge, UK, 2018).

61. Moses Zebi Frank, "The Trumpet Has Many Sounds," in *Sound the Great Trumpet: The Story of Israel through the Eyes of Those Who Built It*, ed. Frank (New York, 1955), 15.

62. Silver, *Our Exodus*, 129, 130.

63. Ramati, "A Literary Letter," 183.

64. Shaked, *Ha-siporet ha-'ivrit 1880–1980*, vol. 2 (Tel Aviv, 1983), 237–44.

65. Shaked, *Ha-siporet ha-'ivrit 1880–1980*, vol. 3 (Tel Aviv, 1988), 11–108.

66. Louis Schwartzman, "Creative Hebrew Literature Today," *Southern Israelite*, April 14, 1950, 61.

67. Leo W. Schwarz, "A Word to the Reader," in *Feast of Leviathan*, ed. Schwarz, x. Schwarz's anthology seems to be more one-dimensional than anthologies edited by Israeli editors.

68. Katz, *Bringing Zion Home*, 23.

69. For a comparative transnational discussion of the Israeli and American frontiers as myths and realities, see Ilan Troen, "Frontier Myths and Their Applications in America and Israel: A Transnational Perspective," *Journal of American History* 86, no. 3 (1999): 1209–30.

70. Schwarz, "Word to the Reader," x.

71. Louis Binstock, "A Ripe and Rich Harvest from Jewish Literature," *Chicago Tribune*, July 8, 1956, C2.

72. Mart, *Eye on Israel*, 157.

73. Hal Lehrman, "With Unlimited Joy of the Lord," *New York Times*, April 22, 1956, BR4. Lehrman was a correspondent in Israel, writing for venues such as the *New York Times* and *Commentary*.

74. During the first decades following the establishment of the state, representations of (the generally more traditionally observant) Mizrahi Jews in Hebrew literature tended to be negative and one-dimensional. English translations largely reflected this tendency, and did

not offer the American readership a much different picture. In Sholom Kahn's anthology *A Whole Loaf*, for instance, stories by Moshe Shamir and Haim Hazaz portray Yemenites as backward and pitiful, and as morally and culturally inferior to Ashkenazi Jews. See Sholom Kahn, ed., *A Whole Loaf: Stories from Israel* (New York, 1957). Revealing as well is that the only Hebrew-language anthology of Hebrew literature published in America in the 1950s had but one story with a character of a Mizrahi Jew, "A Guest for Pesach" by Sholem Aleichem. In this story, a Mizrahi Jew, whose clothes and accent are ridiculed, is hospitably invited by a generous Ashkenazi family to stay for Passover; during the night, he steals their money, jewelry, and silverware. See Simha Rubinstein and Benjamin Benari, eds., *Reader in Modern Hebrew Literature* (New York, 1956).

75. Mart, *Eye on Israel*, 90–91; Furman, *Israel through the Jewish-American Imagination.*

76. Alexander Holmes, "Literary Renaissance Nurtured in Israel," *Los Angeles Times*, December 16, 1958, B4.

77. Holmes, B4.

78. Holmes, B4.

79. Holmes, B4.

80. Edmund Fuller, "Ambitious Jewish Historical Novel," *New York Times*, December 21, 1958, B8.

81. Compare David Maletz, *Young Hearts: A Novel of Modern Israel* (New York, 1950), and Maletz, *Ma'agalot* (Tel Aviv, 1945).

82. Compare Maletz, *Young Hearts*, 189, and Maletz, *Ma'agalot*, 198.

83. Arthur A. Goren, "Spiritual Zionists and Jewish Sovereignty," in *The Americanization of the Jews*, ed. Robert M. Seltzer and Norman J. Cohen (New York, 1995), 165–92.

84. Goren, 170.

Chapter 2

1. Milton Hindus, "Israel in the Words of the Storyteller," *New York Times*, January 14, 1962, BR13.

2. Robert Alter, "Introduction," in *Israeli Stories*, ed. Joel Blocker (New York, 1962), 15.

3. David Myers, *Between Jew and Arab* (Waltham, Mass., 2006), 11; Jonathan Jeremy Goldberg, *Jewish Power: Inside the American Jewish Establishment* (Reading, Mass., 1996), 347.

4. Gershon Shaked, "Judaism in Translation: Thoughts on the Alexandria Hypothesis," in *Hebrew in America: Perspectives and Prospects*, ed. Alan Mintz (Detroit, 1993), 292.

5. Nicholas De Lange, "Hebrew," in *The Oxford Guide to Literature in English Translation*, ed. Peter France (Oxford, 2000), 399.

6. Alan Mintz, *Translating Israel* (Syracuse, N.Y., 2001), 10; Robert Alter, *Hebrew and Modernity* (Bloomington, Ind., 1994), 89–90.

7. Robert Alter, "The Rise and the Rise in the United States," *Modern Hebrew Literature* 7 (1991): 6.

8. Mintz, *Translating Israel*, 2.

9. While acknowledging the relatively high visibility of translated Hebrew literature in the American literary field, Alan Mintz was rather skeptical about a truly meaningful

integration of this literature into Jewish American discourse. Mintz attributed this, among other things, to the fact that "the difficult and problematic knowledge of Israel provided by reading Israeli literature . . . is the kind of demystifying knowledge that many American Jews would prefer not to have" (*Translating Israel*, 61). Later in this chapter, I suggest an explanation for trends of mediation of Hebrew literature in America that coincide with and support this viewpoint.

10. Joel Blocker, "Preface," in *Israeli Stories*, ed. Blocker (New York, 1962), 7.

11. Blocker, 7.

12. Alter, "Introduction," 15.

13. Sholom J. Kahn, "Introduction," in *A Whole Loaf: Stories from Israel*, ed. Kahn (New York, 1957), 12.

14. Kahn, 12.

15. Henry W. Levy, "Victory—and Vengeance," *Baltimore Sun*, January 28, 1968, D5.

16. Robert Alter, ed., *Modern Hebrew Literature* (New York, 1975), 293.

17. Thomas Lask, "Books of the Times," *New York Times*, January 26, 1962, 29.

18. Rinna Samuel, "Avram, Erella and All," *New York Times*, December 8, 1963, 408.

19. Morris Dickstein, "In the Beginning," *New York Times*, May 28, 1978, BR2.

20. Macha Louis Rosenthal, "Israel of the Poets," *The Nation*, December 14, 1970, 631.

21. Meyer Levin, "Before and After Statehood," *New York Times*, August 7, 1977, BR6.

22. Amnon Rubinstein, "And Now in Israel, a Fluttering of Doves," *New York Times*, July 26, 1970, 159.

23. Rubinstein, 159.

24. Amos Elon, "The Mood: Self-Confidence and a Subdued Sadness," *New York Times*, May 6, 1973, 315. For further discussion of Elon and Rubinstein as promoters, in the American press, of a favorably liberal image of Israeli society, successfully balancing military activity and civilian life, see Shaul Mitelpunkt, *Israel in the American Mind: The Cultural Politics of US–Israeli Relations, 1958–1988* (Cambridge, UK, 2018), 172–76.

25. Bernard Avishai, "The Arts in Israel: Rebirth," *Vogue* 169, no. 5 (May 1979): 291.

26. Dickstein, "In the Beginning."

27. Naomi Shepherd, "It Is Distorted by a Bitter Past and a Segregated Present," *New York Times*, January 13, 1974, 3.

28. Arthur A. Cohen, "Firstfruits," *New York Times*, September 30, 1973, G46.

29. Eli Oboler, "The New Israeli Writers," *Library Journal* 94 (November 1969): 4026.

30. Myers, *Between Jew and Arab*, 11–12.

31. Emily Alice Katz, *Bringing Zion Home: Israel in American Jewish Culture* (Albany, N.Y., 2015), 22. Mitelpunkt, *Israel in the American Mind*, 119–20.

32. Chaim Potok, "Foreword," in *Firstfruits: A Harvest of 25 Years of Israeli Writing*, ed. James A. Michener (Philadelphia, 1973), viii.

33. Michener, "Introduction," *Firstfruits*, xiv. As Mitelpunkt shows, Israel as a shining example of a citizen-soldier society was actually the *main* prism on Israel in American policy circles and mainstream media.

34. Michener, xiv.

35. Yonatan Sagiv, "The Place Could Not Bear Me: Expulsion and Exile in Khirbet Khizeh," *Hebrew Studies* 52 (2011): 221–234.

36. S. Yizhar, *Midnight Convoy and Other Stories* (Jerusalem, 1969). Since its inception in 1961, the remit of the state-affiliated Institute for the Translation of Hebrew Literature was to disseminate and promote Hebrew literature throughout the world. In practice, the bulk of its activity centered on the representation of writers and their promotion, and not the actual publishing of books. The English translation of Yizhar's collection was distributed in the United States and clearly intended for American readers. This remained Yizhar's only title in English until 2007. The noninclusion of "Khirbet Khizeh" in the 1969 *Midnight Convoy* anthology demonstrates, in this special case in which the publisher was an Israeli institution, how Israeli agents may exhibit a protective stance similar to that of American agents of Hebrew literature in translation.

37. See Anita Shapira, "Hirbet Hizah: Between Remembrance and Forgetting," *Jewish Social Studies* 7, no. 1 (2000): 1–62; David Myers, "She'elat ha-pelitim: mabat hadash 'al zikaron u-shicheha," in *Tarbut, zikaron ve-historia: be-hokara le-Anita Shapira*, ed. Meir Hazan and Uri Cohen (Tel-Aviv, 2012), 655–70.

The years following the War of Independence in Israel saw the publication of several lesser-known protest stories than Yizhar's "Khirbet Khizeh," which nonetheless criticized the Israeli conduct during the war with similar intensity. These works showed awareness of, and empathy toward, the Palestinian woes. Aharon Amir's "Boker hadash" and Shraga Gafni's "Ha-shevach la-el" depicted the occupation of a Palestinian village by Israeli soldiers who treat its residents with pointless violence; "Ha-matmon" by Aharon Megged assumes the viewpoint of a Palestinian refugee who was forced out of his home, articulating Arab longing, rage, and a desire to avenge being expelled; and "Sipur 'al ha-gamal ve-hanitzahon" by Dahn Ben-Amotz describes the meaningless killing of a refugee's camel by an Israeli soldier who just yearns to feel part of the war experience. Although these stories attracted some interest and polemic in Israel, they were never translated into English. This may reflect something of the need to defend Israel's moral image, but one should be careful not to ascribe too much significance to this factor. Unlike Yizhar's stories, the stories by Amir, Gafni, Megged and Ben Amotz came to occupy a rather marginal position in the Israeli literary discourse. Not one of them became engraved in the collective memory as "Khirbet Khizeh" did. Their marginality in Israeli culture thus renders their nontranslation into English less significant from a sociopolitical perspective.

38. See, for instance, *New York Times*, February 8, 1978, A7; *Washington Post*, February 9, 1978, A19; *Washington Post*, February 13, 1978, A15; and *Chicago Tribune*, February 14, 1978, 5.

39. Levi Gertned, "The New Israeli Writer," *Jewish Advocate*, April 25, 1957, A20.

40. Ibis Editions, "About Us," http://ibiseditions.com/home/about.htm.

41. Compare S. Yizhar, *Sipur Khirbet Khizeh* (Tel Aviv, 2010 [1949]), 91, and Yizhar, *Khirbet Khizeh* (Jerusalem, 2008), 104–5.

42. See, for instance, David N. Myers, "Victory and Sorrow," *New Republic*, October 22, 2008, 44. And upon the novella's reissuing in 2015 by Farrar, Straus and Giroux, which in itself attests to its American appeal: David K. Shipler, "One Morning in a Palestinian Vil-

lage, 1948," *Moment* (May–June 2015), 75, 78; Leah Falk, "1949 Israeli Novel *Khirbet Khizeh* Reissued by FSG," *JSTOR Daily*, November 7, 2015.

43. Yizhar, *Khirbet Khizeh*, 131.

44. This translation is part of a more widespread trend regarding Yizhar's story in recent years, which reflects increasing interest in the Israeli–Palestinian conflict, and critical attitudes by European countries toward Israel. "Khirbet Khizeh" was translated and published in Germany in book form (together with "The Prisoner") in 1998, in Italy (also with "The Prisoner") in 2005, in Spain in 2009, in France in 2010, in Norway in 2011, in the Netherlands in 2013, and in Denmark in 2016. It was also purchased for translation by Greek and Swedish publishing houses.

45. According to Yochai Oppenheimer, the objective of popular nonfiction accounts of the war, such as those by Yael Dayan and Shabtai Tevet, was to represent the Israeli combat soldier as sensitive, decent, and spiritually superior to the Arabs, while the novels about the British Mandate era by Shulamit Hareven and David Shahar swayed attention from the present reality of the occupied territories to the multiculturalism in Jerusalem of the 1930s, and "represented its Arab subjects from a Western or colonialist point of view, as dissident and heated mobs incited by religious leaders, or as individuals willing to embrace their ruler's culture and become part of it." Yochai Oppenheimer, *Me'ever la-gader: yitsug ha-'Aravim ba-siporet ha-'ivrit ve-ha-yisraelit, 1906–2005* (Tel Aviv, 2008), 247.

46. Nathan Shaham, "The Seven," in *A Whole Loaf*, ed. Kahn; and "Seven of Them," in *The New Israeli Writers*, ed. Dahlia Ravikovitch (New York, 1969).

47. Aharon Megged, *Fortunes of a Fool* (New York, 1962).

48. Shemuel Yeshayahu Penueli and Azriel Ukhmani, eds., *Hebrew Short Stories: An Anthology* (Tel Aviv, 1965).

49. Yoram Kaniuk, *The Acrophile* (New York, 1961).

50. Abraham B. Yehoshua, "Facing the Forests," in *Three Days and a Child* (Garden City, N.J., 1970); Amos Oz, "Nomad and Viper," in *Where the Jackals Howl and Other Stories* (New York, 1981); Oz, *My Michael* (New York, 1970).

51. Avner Holtzman, *Ahavot tsiyon: panim ba-sifrut ha-'ivrit ha-hadasha* (Jerusalem, 2006), 504.

52. Not all scholars of Hebrew literature agree on the degree of subversion of these works. Some postcolonial critics debate the extent to which Israeli authors expressed a tangible opposition to the hegemonic atmosphere of their era, and further doubt the moral daring of the "generation of the state" in Hebrew literature. These perspectives, however, do not affect the major claim of this chapter, which focuses on the *changes* that occurred in politically charged representations—largely perceived as oppositional in the mainstream Israeli discourse—as they were mediated to American audiences. Whether canonical works of Hebrew literature did in fact undermine the Zionist metanarrative and commit to unveiling aspects of historical violence involved in the Zionist project, or whether they were less humanistic, accepting of the Other, and skeptical of the national story than it seems—the mediation of Hebrew literature to American Jewish audiences generated a less oppositional version of the works than that which was presented in the Hebrew sources.

53. Some of the textual interferences presented in this and the next chapter appeared in

Omri Asscher, "The Ideological Manipulation of Hebrew Literature in English Translation in the 1970s and 1980s," *Journal of Modern Jewish Studies* 15, no. 3 (2016): 384–401, https://doi.org/10.1080/14725886.2016.1151196; reprinted with permission. Copyright © by Taylor & Francis.

54. Compare Nathan Shaham, "Shiv'ah me-hem," in *Hasipur ha-'ivri: antologia*, ed. Yosef Lichtenbaum (Tel Aviv, 1960), 533, and Kahn, *A Whole Loaf*, 91.

55. Compare Shaham, "Shiv'ah me-hem," 533, and Ravikovitch, *New Israeli Writers*, 83.

56. Aharon Megged, *Ha-hai 'al ha-met* (Tel Aviv, 1965), and Megged, *The Living on the Dead* (New York, 1971).

57. Compare Megged, *Ha-hai 'al ha-met*, 173, and Megged, *Living on the Dead*, 158.

58. Amos Oz, *Elsewhere, Perhaps* (New York, 1973).

59. Compare Amos Oz, *Makom acher* (Tel Aviv, 1966), 385–86, and Oz, *Elsewhere, Perhaps*, 302.

60. Compare Oz, *Makom acher*, 359–60, and Oz, *Elsewhere, Perhaps*, 279. Note also the subdual of tone in the translation of Oren's aggressive zeal as he watches a battle between fighter jets in the skies (*Makom acher*, 209; *Elsewhere, Perhaps*, 164).

61. Yoram Kaniuk, *Rockinghorse* (New York, 1977).

62. Compare Yoram Kaniuk, *Sussetz* (Tel Aviv, 1973), 128–29, and Kaniuk, *Rockinghorse*, 152.

63. Compare Amos Oz, *Menuha nechona* (Tel Aviv, 1982), 138, and Oz, *A Perfect Peace* (New York, 1985), 127.

64. Compare Oz, *Menuha nechona*, 139, and Oz, *Perfect Peace*, 127.

65. Compare Oz, *Menuha nechona*, 147–48, and Oz, *Perfect Peace*, 134.

66. Hillel Halkin, Nicholas de Lange, Dalya Bilu, Yehuda Safran, and Mildred Budny described working in close collaboration with the authors in the translation process (Halkin and de Lange with Amos Oz, Bilu with David Shahar, Safran and Budny with Benjamin Tammuz). Dorothea Shefer described rather little interaction with Amnon Jackont and Yitzhak Ben-Ner, and added that, as far as she remembered, there was no editor involved in the work on Jackont's novel. Philip Simpson could not be reached. Misha Louvish was no longer alive.

67. Gideon Toury, *Descriptive Translation Studies and Beyond* (Amsterdam and Philadelphia, 1995), 183.

68. Yitzhak Ben-Ner, Aharon Megged, and A. B. Yehoshua told me that they were unaware of the changes made to their works, and were displeased by them. Amos Oz wrote me that he remembered nothing of the changes, done so long ago, but that in any case his considerations were never political. Amnon Jackont could not be reached. David Shahar, Yoram Kaniuk, and Benjamin Tammuz were no longer alive.

69. Annual conference of the Israel Translators Association, ZOA House, Tel Aviv, February 5, 2017.

70. Gill Paul, *Translation in Practice: A Symposium* (Champaign and London, 2009), 59. I thank Erez Volk for calling my attention to this source.

71. Paul, *Translation in Practice*, 63.

72. Pierre Bourdieu, "La critique du discours lettré," *Actes de la recherche en sciences sociales* 1, no. 5 (1975): 4.

73. Rollene Sall, "All Roads Led to Nightmare," *New York Times*, March 5, 1961, BR40.

74. Jane Hayman, "The Futile and the Uncertain," *Commentary* 36 (June 1961): 550–52, esp. 552.

75. "The Acrophile," *Booklist* 58 (June 1961): 635.

76. Levi Gertned, "The New Israeli Writer," *Jewish Advocate*, April 25, 1957, A20; Sylvia Rotschild, "The Bookshelf," *Jewish Advocate*, July 25, 1963, 20.

77. Robert Alter, "An Apolitical Israeli," *New York Times*, May 21, 1972, BR5.

78. David C. Jacobson, "Intimate Relations between Israelis and Palestinians in Fiction by Israeli Women Writers," *Shofar* 25, no. 3 (2007): 32. According to Robert Alter, the deep moral crisis suffered by the protagonist in the novel stems first and foremost from his trauma depicted in the "White City" chapter (in Blocker, *Israeli Stories*, 18). In his recap of the novel in "Israeli Writers and Their Problems," *Commentary* 34 (July 1962), however, Alter does not mention the occurrences depicted in the chapter at all.

79. Thomas L. Jones, "Fortunes of a Fool," *Washington Post*, September 9, 1962, G7; Rinna Samuel, "Procession of Defeats," *New York Times*, September 23, 1962, BR45. Jones's short review may have ignored the "White City" chapter due to length considerations; Samuel's review, however, is quite long. In a similar vein, George Adelman's review in *Library Journal* describes the novel as an allegory that points up moral, philosophical, and religious issues, but the review does not detail what these issues are.

80. Samuel, "Procession of Defeats," BR45..

81. Challenging representations of the Israeli army were also moderated, as in the anonymous review in *Booklist* from March 1977 of A. B. Yehoshua's collection *Early in the Summer of 1970*, in order to frame the book in more simplified, accessible, commercially effective terms. Although the three stories in Yehoshua's collection demystify and complicate Israeli discourses of war, the review ignored their complexities and dramatized their military themes. The consequence of downplaying the national context and the subversively absurd underpinnings of the stories was the softening of their subtle criticism of the role of the military ethos in Israeli society. "Early in the Summer of 1970," *Booklist*, March 1, 1977, 993.

82. Rosenthal, "Israel of the Poets," 631.

83. Rosenthal, 631.

84. Curt Leviant, "The New Israeli Writers," *Saturday Review*, December 6, 1969, 57.

85. Yizhar's "The Prisoner," which carries a humanistic message despite its difficult themes, and in which the portrayed military unit is not yet part of what would later become the Israeli army, does elicit a positive response from Leviant. Leviant's objection to the other stories in the anthology may stem from the fact that the army—particularly in routine situations such as those portrayed in these works—is perceived as an institutionalized organ, and thus more inherently representative of the state's moral failings. Such a reading is supported by the prevailing idealized American perception of Israel as a well-balanced, harmonious *civilian*-soldier society, as shown by Shaul Mitelpunkt in *Israel in the American Mind*.

86. Alter, *Modern Hebrew Literature*, 293.

87. Alter, 293.

88. Alter, 293.

89. Robert Alter, *America and Israel: Literary and Intellectual Trends* (New York, 1970).

90. Pierre Bourdieu, "The Political Field, the Social Science Field, and the Journalistic Field," in *Bourdieu and the Journalistic Field*, eds. Rodney Benson and Erik Neveu (Cambridge, 2005), 36.

91. Alon Gan, *Ha-siah she-gava?* (PhD diss., Tel Aviv University, 2002), 104–27.

92. Alter, *America and Israel*, 38.

93. Alter, *America and Israel*, 39.

94. Alter, 40.

95. Alter, 42–43.

96. Compare Amnon Jackont, *Pesek-zman* (Tel Aviv, 1982), 52, and Jackont, *Borrowed Time* (London, 1986 [New York, 1987]), 37.

97. An interesting counterexample, in itself ideologically determined, is found in Vivian Eden's 1988 English translation of the autobiographical novel *Arabesques* by Anton Shammas. The translation from Hebrew was done in collaboration with the author. Shammas, a Palestinian Israeli, and his translator perhaps felt more at ease giving voice to the Palestinian narrative of the conflict with an English-reading audience in mind. See, for instance, the following sentences that relate to Shammas's family history in 1948:

"Now they had decided to continue northward to see the rest of their relatives who have ~~departed from~~ [**been driven out of**] Ja'ooneh in 1948 and come to Tarsheeha [**as refugees**]." Compare Anton Shammas, *Arabeskot* (Tel Aviv, 1986), 31, and Shammas, *Arabesques* (New York, 1988), 32.

"Two weeks earlier Israeli planes had dropped bombs on Tarsheeha, just to the south of Fassuta, to which Al-Asbah's relatives had ~~come~~ [**fled**] from their conquered village of Ja'ooneh." Compare Shammas, *Arabeskot*, 105, and Shammas, *Arabesques*, 116.

"That was on the morning of Friday, April 23, 1948. Haifa~~, as the Arabs would say,~~ had already fallen." Compare Shammas, *Arabeskot*, 169, and Shammas, *Arabesques*, 187.

98. Compare Jackont, *Pesek-zman*, 36, and Jackont, *Borrowed Time*, 23; Jackont, *Pesek-zman*, 296, and Jackont, *Borrowed Time*, 224; Jackont, *Pesek-zman*, 136, and Jackont, *Borrowed Time*, 103.

99. Compare Yoram Kaniuk, *Aravi tov* (Tel Aviv, 1984), 87, and Kaniuk, *Confessions of a Good Arab* (London, 1987 [New York, 1988]), 123.

100. Compare Kaniuk, *Aravi tov*, 89, and Kaniuk, *Confessions of a Good Arab*, 126.

101. Compare A. B. Yehoshua, *Ha-me'ahev* (Jerusalem, 1977), 155–56, and Yehoshua, *The Lover* (Garden City, N.J., 1978), 123.

102. For a discussion of "minor language" words that are incorporated into (original or translated) postcolonial literary works as a form of resistance, see Maria Tymozcko, "Post-Colonial Writing and Literary Translation," in *Post-Colonial Translation: Theory and Practice*, ed. Susan Bassnett and Harish Trivedi (London, 1999), 19–40. We find similar cases in which the presence of Arabic was diminished in the text in Dalya Bilu's 1980 translation of David Shahar's *His Majesty's Agent*, Philip Simpson's 1985 translation of Rachel Eitan's *The Fifth Heaven*, and Dorothea Shefer-Vanson's 1986 translation of Amnon Jackont's *Borrowed Time*.

103. In personal correspondence, Halkin described his close collaboration with Oz on the translation's final draft, as Oz came to stay at his house for a week of intense work. Oz not only played an integral role in the translation process, according to Halkin, but also later introduced further changes to the text, together with the editor of his American publisher, most of which Halkin does not approve of.

104. Ranen Omer-Sherman, "Zionism and the Disenchanted: The Plight of the Citizen-Soldier in Amos Oz's *A Perfect Peace*," *Middle Eastern Literatures* 8, no. 1 (2005): 53.

105. Omissions and moderations can be found in several places. Compare Oz, *Menuha nechona*, 21, and Oz, *Perfect Peace*, 16; Oz, *Menuha nechona*, 188, and Oz, *Perfect Peace*, 176; Oz, *Menuha nechona*, 223, and Oz, *Perfect Peace*, 212.

106. Compare Oz, *Menuha nechona*, 133, and Oz, *Perfect Peace*, 122.

107. Compare Oz, *Menuha nechona*, 155, and Oz, *Perfect Peace*, 140.

108. Compare Oz, *Menuha nechona*, 234–35, and Oz, *Perfect Peace*, 225.

109. Omer-Sherman, "Zionism and the Disenchanted," 64.

110. Hugh Nissenson, "Evil, Muted, but Omnipresent," *New York Times*, October 25, 1970, BR29.

111. Gilead Morahg, "Shading the Truth: A. B. Yehoshua's 'Facing the Forests,'" in *History and Literature: New Readings of Jewish Texts in Honor of Arnold J. Band*, ed. William Cutter and David C. Jacobson (Providence, R.I., 2002), 412. For an overview that focuses on Israeli responses that present the fate of the Arab village as marginal to the story, see Amir Banjabi, "Yehoshua' be-re'i ha-sifrut ha-'ivrit," in *Mabatim mitstalvim: 'Iyunim bi-yetsirat A. B. Yehoshua*, ed. Amir Banbaji, Nitsah Ben-Dov, and Zivah Shamir (Tel Aviv, 2010), 14–29.

112. Alter, *Modern Hebrew Literature*, 354.

113. A year before Amos Oz and A. B. Yehoshua were first published in English, Robert Alter offered an insightful introduction to these authors' early work for American audiences ("New Israeli Fiction," *Commentary* 47, no. 6 [1969]: 59–66). In his reference to Yehoshua's "Against the Forests," Alter mentioned the political application of the story and described it broadly as an "unflinching exploration of the shadowy underside of ambivalence in Israeli consciousness within the state of siege." Alter's need to reassure his readers that Yehoshua was "unswervingly committed to Israel's survival and to the constructive development of Israeli society" may have anticipated a lack of readiness in American Jewish discourse for such poignant Israeli self-criticism. Generally speaking, the article coincides with Alter's call for interpretive emphasis on the nonpolitical in the reading of these two writers. A polemic stance against political readings of the two authors is evident in Alter's review of Oz's *My Michael* following its English publication, and of Yehoshua's *The Lover*.

114. Michener, "Introduction," x.

115. Michener, xii.

116. Michener, xxii.

117. James A. Michener, "What to Do about the Palestinian Refugees?" *New York Times*, September 27, 1970, SM12.

118. James A. Michener, "Israel and the Arabs," *New York Review of Books* 9, no. 5 (September 28, 1967), 35–37.

119. Sylvia Barack-Fishman, "Homelands of the Heart: Israel and Jewish Identity in American Jewish Fiction," in *Envisioning Israel: The Changing Ideals and Images of North American Jews*, ed. Allon Gal (Jerusalem, 1996), 278.

120. This perception has also been prevalent in the scholarly discourse on topics ranging from Jewish American social history to Jews in American popular culture.

121. Arthur Hertzberg, *Being Jewish in America: The Modern Experience* (New York, 1979), 223; Leonard Fein, *Where Are We? The Inner Life of America's Jews* (New York, 1988), 19.

122. Yael Feldman, "Contemporary Hebrew Literature on the American Campus," in *Teaching Jewish Civilization: A Global Approach to Higher Education*, ed. Moshe Davis (New York, 1995), 88.

Chapter 3

1. Yosef Gorny, personal conversation (Tel Aviv University, January 2, 2016). Compare Gorny, *Quest for Collective Identity* (New York, 1994), and Gorny, *Ha-hipus ahar ha-zehut ha-le'umit* (Tel Aviv, 1990).

2. Gershon Shaked, "Judaism in Translation: Thoughts on the Alexandria Hypothesis," in Alan Mintz, ed., *Hebrew in America: Perspectives and Prospects* (Detroit, 1993), 285.

3. Shaked, 285.

4. When reviewed in the *Library Journal*, Yoram Kaniuk's *Adam Resurrected* was recommended "for larger college libraries and public libraries, especially where there are many Jewish readers" (Dorothy Nyren, "Adam Resurrected," *Library Journal* 96 [June 1, 1971]: 2009). The reviewer of Dahn Ben-Amotz's *To Remember, to Forget*, also in the *Library Journal*, would not have remarked that "Orthodox Jewish readers may be offended by the central theme of inter-marriage" if she had not presupposed the existence of a chiefly Jewish readership (Greta Haas, "To Remember, to Forget," *Library Journal* 99 [October 1, 1974]: 2498).

5. In Robert Alter's afterword to Elliott Anderson and Robert Friend's anthology *Contemporary Israeli Literature*, the implication of a Jewish readership is clear from the protective stance Alter takes behind novelists identified with the Israeli Left. Alter makes a case against "some observers outside Israel" who may consider Israeli writers "to be covert Anti-Zionists," alluding to American Jewish right-wing voices that denounced Israeli self-criticism—thus participating in what had been a largely *internal* Jewish debate. See Elliott Anderson and Robert Friend, eds., *Contemporary Israeli Literature: An Anthology* (Philadelphia, 1977), 327.

6. In his review of Yehuda Amichai's *Not of This Time, Not of This Place*, Amos Elon described the novel as a "profoundly 'Jewish' novel, in the modern (American) sense of this word. The book takes as its theme the problem of identity . . . offer[ing] a synoptic view of modern Jewish existence" ("Israeli and Jewish," *New York Times*, August 4, 1968, BR4). While discussing Amos Oz's *The Hill of Evil Counsel*, literary critic John Bayley remarked that "unlike much ethnic writing his does not seek to masquerade as *weltliteratur*," referring to Oz's collection explicitly as a particular form of "Jewish literature" ("Pioneers and Phantoms," *New York Review of Books*, July 20, 1978, 35).

7. Writer and critic Alfred Kazin's review of Amoz Oz's *Touch the Water, Touch the Wind* is a case in point. Kazin compared Oz to Saul Bellow and Philip Roth only to say how extremely different these writers are, yet the underlying need he felt for the comparison in itself attests to a postulation of a common premise, a basic assumption of affinity and potential parallelism, among them ("Beyond the Promised Land," *Saturday Review*, November 2, 1974, 38).

8. Whether by defining an Amoz Oz character as "a good Jewish boy," equating the protagonists in a Yoram Kaniuk novel with figures in a Jewish joke, or describing a novel by Benjamin Tammuz as abundant with "Semitism," critics connoted that the intuitive way to make sense of the works was by placing them in a Jewish context. See Milton Rugoff, "My Michael," *Saturday Review*, June 24, 1972, 60; Thomas Edwards, "Troubling Comedian," *New York Review of Books*, February 9, 1978, 38; Ralph E. Hone, "Semitic Love Story," *Los Angeles Times*, August 26, 1973, 58.

9. This is evident, for instance, in writer Milton Rugoff's ironical suggestion that Amos Oz's portraying Jerusalem in *My Michael* as "oppressive" is "heresy of heresies" (Rugoff, "My Michael," 60). John Weisman, by contrast, wholly identified with a nostalgic, mythologized portrait of Jerusalem, in his review of Shulamith Hareven's *City of Many Days*, proclaiming that the protagonist's "ecstasy [about her city] is easily comprehensible for those of us who have 'gone up' to Jerusalem"—indeed signing the review as a "recent visitor" to the city (John Weisman, "Poetic License for Journey to Jerusalem," *Los Angeles Times*, April 24, 1977, V15). Both Rugoff's and Weisman's reviews, if different in the extent of their reverence (or lack thereof) to this emblem of Judaism, implied an assumption that readers of the translated novels were somewhat acquainted and associated with the Jewish world.

10. Admittedly, American critics tended to present translated Hebrew works primarily as probes into *Israeli*, rather than *Jewish*, life and mentality. Although explicit classification or typology of Hebrew works as *Jewish* did exist, it was less pronounced than in the parallel reception of Jewish American literature, in both Israeli and American literary discourses. I elaborate on this in chapter 5.

11. Chaim Potok, "Foreword," in *Firstfruits: A Harvest of 25 Years of Israeli Writing*, ed. James A. Michener (Philadelphia, 1973), viii.

12. Robert Alter, ed., *Modern Hebrew Literature* (New York, 1975), ix–x.

13. Dan Miron, *From Continuity to Contiguity: Toward a New Jewish Literary Thinking* (Palo Alto, Ca., 2010); Hana Wirth-Nesher, "Defining the Undefinable: What Is Jewish Literature?" in *What Is Jewish Literature?* ed. Wirth-Nesher (Philadelphia, 1994), 3–19. It should be restressed that I do not assume the terms *Israeli* and *Jewish*, as employed in literary (or other) discourse, to refer to any stable, essentialist, or mutually exclusive meanings.

14. Itamar Even-Zohar, *Papers in Culture Research* (Tel Aviv, 2010), 52–76.

15. Gideon Toury, *Descriptive Translation Studies and Beyond* (Amsterdam and Philadelphia, 1995), 17–35, esp. 23.

16. Naomi Seidman, *Faithful Renderings: Jewish–Christian Difference and the Politics of Translation* (Chicago, 2006), 243–276. See also Hana Wirth-Nesher, "Language as Homeland in Jewish-American Literature," in *Insider/Outsider: American Jews and Multiculturalism*, ed. David Biale, Michael Galchinsky, and Susannah Heschel (Berkeley, 1998), 216–218.

17. Compare Haim Hazaz, *Ha-yoshevet ba-ganim* (Tel Aviv, 1944), 36, and Hazaz, *Mori Sa'id* (New York, 1956), 36.

18. Compare Hazaz, *Ha-yoshevet ba-ganim*, 39–40, and Hazaz, *Mori Sa'id*, 36.

19. Compare Benjamin Tammuz, *Rekviyem le-Na'aman* (Tel Aviv, 1978), 170–71, and Tammuz, *Requiem for Na'aman* (New York, 1982), 212.

20. As Katherine and Gold take revenge on ex-Mossad agent Arik, they have the following dialogue:

> The sickening smell of scorched flesh spread through the air.
>
> "Let's get away now," she said.
>
> "Someone might come."
>
> "Don't worry. He's not the first Jew to ~~go up in flames~~ [**be buried**] here . . . "
>
> She gave me an agonized look. "Won't you ever finish with that?"
>
> ~~"Not before you stop mentioning Jaffa and Ramle," I answered.~~
>
> ~~"Jaffa and Ramle exist; it's over . . . "~~
>
> I held her hand. Together we climbed up the bank of earth to the road.
>
> (Compare Jackont, *Pesek-zman*, 296, and Jackont, *Borrowed Time*, 224.)

The reference to the crematorium seems even more blunt and defying because of its incidental nature. Note also the reference to the Palestinian *Nakba* (here, the expulsion of Palestinians from Jaffa and Ramle in 1948), omitted from the translation similarly to the interferences discussed in the previous chapter.

21. As in the case of the British journalists who defend their criticism of Israeli policy in the West Bank as follows: "don't think that we are anti-Semitic or anything like that." (Compare Amnon Jackont, *Pesek-zman* (Tel Aviv, 1982), 37, and Jackont, *Borrowed Time* (London, 1986 [New York, 1987]), 24.) This sentence was edited out of the translation, leaving the rest of the polemic dialogue on Israeli politics intact.

22. In earlier decades, such a novel may have been deemed too religiously charged, and declined for publication, at least by Jewish publishers. Such, for instance, was the case with the Jewish Publication Society's decision in the mid-1940s to refrain from publishing Aharon Kabak's novel on the life of Jesus, *The Narrow Path*. (The book was eventually published in 1968 by the Israeli Massada Press.) In 1944, as Jonathan Sarna shows, JPS editor Solomon Grayzel expressed his appreciation for Kabak's book, and added that "the translation is excellent, I really enjoyed reading it. Still, it is Jesus, and I have an ineradicable feeling that it is a subject which is best left alone" (quoted in Jonathan D. Sarna, *JPS, The Americanization of Jewish Culture: A Centennial History of the Jewish Publication Society, 1888–1988* (Philadelphia, 1989), 214).

23. Compare Yigal Mossinsohn, *Yehuda ish krayot* (Tel Aviv, 1963), 8, and Mossinsohn, *Judas* (New York, 1963), 11.

24. Compare Mossinsohn, *Yehuda*, 11, and Mossinsohn, *Judas*, 13.

25. Compare Mossinsohn, *Yehuda*, 136, and Mossinsohn, *Judas*, 103.

26. Compare Jackont, *Pesek-zman*, 34, and Jackont, *Borrowed Time*, 21.

27. Compare Yehuda Amichai, *Lo me-'achshav, lo me-kan* (Jerusalem, 1963), 106, and Amichai, *Not of This Time, Not of This Place* (New York, 1968), 70; as well as Amichai, *Lo me-achshav*, 283, and Amichai, *Not of This Time*, 170. In the first ex-

ample, Amichai writes that all American girls would really prefer to be men, and their psychology leads them to sew buttons on their pants so as "to unlace their complexes." In the second example, Amichai writes that "every American woman" feels the need to repress sexual intercourse she had just had and that that is why she always carry napkins.

28. Compare Amos Oz, *Makom aher* (Tel Aviv, 1966), 163, and Oz, *Elsewhere, Perhaps* (New York, 1973), 130. For other omissions of racial language, compare, for instance, Amichai, *Lo me-'achshav*, 328, and Amichai, *Not of This Time*, 202.

29. Michael Meyers, "Black/Jewish Splits," *Society* 31, no. 6 (1994): 23–27.

30. Ephraim Lisitzky, *At the Grip of Cross-Currents* (New York, 1959); Reuben Wallenrod, *Dusk in the Catskills* (New York, 1957). The name of the translator of Wallenrod's novel is not mentioned in the book, which may imply that it was Wallenrod himself. Israel is not mentioned in Wallenrod's novel at all; it is referred to briefly at the very end of Lisitzky's novel, as the protagonist expresses his commitment to Zionism.

31. Compare Reuben Wallenrod, *Ki panah yom* (New York, 1946), 37, and Wallenrod, *Dusk in the Catskills*, 35.

32. Compare Wallenrod, *Ki panah yom*, 94, and Wallenrod, *Dusk in the Catskills*, 95.

33. Compare Wallenrod, *Ki panah yom*, 94, and Wallenrod, *Dusk in the Catskills*, 95.

34. Compare Wallenrod, *Ki panah yom*, 47–49, and Wallenrod, *Dusk in the Catskills*, 112. The dialogue was moved from chapter 7 to the end of chapter 16, shortened and moderated. For further discussion of this scene, see Michael Weingrad, *American Hebrew Literature: Writing Jewish National Identity in the United States* (Syracuse, N.Y., 2011), 129.

35. Compare Wallenrod, *Ki panah yom*, 47–49, and Wallenrod, *Dusk in the Catskills*, 112.

36. Compare Ephraim Lisitzky, *Eleh toldot adam* (Jerusalem, 1949), 180, and Lisitzky, *At the Grip*, 181.

37. Compare Lisitzky, *Eleh toldot*, 89, and Lisitzky, *At the Grip*, 89.

38. Compare Lisitzky, *Eleh toldot*, 193, and Lisitzky, *At the Grip*, 195.

39. Compare Lisitzky, *Eleh toldot*, 203, and Lisitzky, *At the Grip*, 204.

40. Anita Norich, *Writing in Tongues: Translating Yiddish in the Twentieth Century* (Seattle, Wa., 2014), 51.

41. Matthew Mark Silver, *Our Exodus: Leon Uris and the Americanization of Israel's Founding Story* (Detroit, 2010), 126.

42. Arnold M. Eisen, *The Chosen People in America: A Study in Jewish Religious Ideology* (Bloomington, Ind., 1983), 50.

43. Arthur Gilbert, *A Jew in Christian America* (New York, 1966), 196.

44. Jacob Neusner, *American Judaism: Adventure in Modernity* (New York, 1978).

45. See Howard Singer, *Bring Forth the Mighty Men: On Violence and the Jewish Character* (New York, 1969), 227–32; Arthur A. Cohen, "Between Two Traditions," *Midstream* 12, no. 6 (1966): 31–34.

46. Arthur Hertzberg, "The American Jew and His Religion," in *The American Jew: A Reappraisal*, ed. Oscar I. Janowsky (Philadelphia, 1964), 101–3, 115–17.

47. Earlier iterations of the arguments presented in this chapter appeared in Omri Ascher, "Israel for American Eyes: Literature on the Move, and the Mediated Repertoire of

Jewish-American Identity" *AJS Review* 42, no. 1 (2018), 21–38; reprinted with permission. Copyright © by Cambridge University Press.

48. Robert Alter, "The Rise and the Rise in the United States," *Modern Hebrew Literature* 7 (1991): 6.

49. See selected syllabi in Leon I. Yudkin, ed., *Modern Hebrew Literature in English Translation: Papers, Selected Syllabi and Bibliographies* (New York, 1987).

50. Sylvia Barack Fishman, "Homelands of the Heart: Israel and Jewish Identity in American Jewish Fiction," in *Envisioning Israel: The Changing Ideals and Images of North American Jews*, ed. Allon Gal (Jerusalem, 1996), 271–92, esp. 278.

51. Richard Elman, "With Faith in the Lord," *New York Times*, May 28, 1967, BR2.

52. Elman, BR2.

53. Elman, BR2.

54. Laurence Lafore, "Short Turns and Encores," *New York Times*, December 10, 1967, 388.

55. Lafore, 388.

56. Henry W. Levy, "Two Novels by Agnon, Nobel Laureate," *Baltimore Sun*, May 21, 1967, D5.

57. Neusner, *American Judaism*, 148.

58. Curt Leviant, "Nobel Laureate of Hebrew Literature," *The Nation*, December 12, 1966, 645.

59. Leviant, 645.

60. Curt Leviant, "The New Israeli Writers," *Saturday Review*, December 6, 1969, 57.

61. Perhaps the most influential American Jewish thinker to propose such criticism of Israel was the Reform rabbi and Zionist leader Abba Hillel Silver. "[The Jews of the State of Israel] need Judaism quite as much as we do," Silver stated in a well-known sermon. "A political state cannot be counted upon to preserve our spiritual heritage." Rabbi Abba Hillel Silver, "Living Judaism," in *American Jewish History: A Primary Source Reader*, ed. Gary Phillip Zola and Marc Dollinger (Waltham, Mass., 2014), 291.

62. Richard Elman, "Parable and Commentary," *New York Times*, April 28, 1968, BR5.

63. Mintz, *Translating Israel*, 35–36.

64. Mintz, 244–45.

65. Mintz, 244–45

66. Anita Shapira, "Le-an halekhah 'shelilat ha-galut'?" *Alpayim* 25 (2003): 9–54.

67. Zvi Ganin, *An Uneasy Relationship: American Jewish Leadership and Israel, 1948–1957* (Syracuse, N.Y., 2005), 81–104. Following recurring, bluntly phrased demands made by David Ben-Gurion in the wake of the establishment of Israel that American Jews make aliyah, head of the American Jewish Committee Jacob Blaustein pressed Ben-Gurion to clarify the relations between the two Jewish centers by providing public assurances that American Jews owed no political allegiance to Israel.

68. This is demonstrated in works by Cynthia Ozick and Philip Roth, as shown in Ursula Zeller, "Between *Goldene Medine* and Promised Land: Legitimizing the American Jewish Diaspora," *Cross Cultures* 66 (2003): 1–44.

69. Arnold J. Band, "From Sacred Tongue to Foreign Language: Hebrew in the American University," in Mintz, *Hebrew in America*, 171–86.

70. Eisig Silberschlag, *Hebrew Literature: An Evaluation* (New York, 1959).

71. Silberschlag,61.

72. As in Mordecai Kaplan, *A New Zionism* (New York, 1959).

73. Eliezer Schweid, *Shalosh 'ashmorot* (Tel Aviv, 1964), 202–24. The resistance to themes and modes of expression associated with the exilic European past would later gradually diminish, but preconceptions of cultural supremacy still characterized Israeli thought on contemporary American Jewish life for years to come, as I show in chapters 4 and 5.

74. Yisrael Cohen, "Yafyuto shel shem be-'oholey yefet," in *Sha'ar ha-hav hanot* (Tel Aviv, 1962 [1957]), 132–41, esp. 136.

75. David Stern, "Morality Tale," *Commentary* 58 (July 1974), 100–101.

76. As already noted in Mintz, *Translating Israel*, 34.

77. Along the same lines, empathic portrayals of the diaspora were sometimes celebrated as such. An essay by Jacob Tzur, for instance, lauds S. Y. Agnon as a writer who "built a bridge between Jewish past and present, diaspora and Israel" and as the literary voice that revealed to Israeli readers "who had been accustomed to looking at the 'Galut' through the cruel, satirical barbs of Mendele . . . the 'old world' in its beauty and purity" ("The Two Worlds of Shai Agnon," *Southern Israelite*, May 1, 1970, 2, 3).

78. Dvir Tzur, "Whose Holocaust Is It Anyway?" forthcoming.

79. Compare Shahar, *Sokhen hod malkhuto*, 278–79, and Shahar, *His Majesty's Agent*, 264.

80. Compare Shahar, 289, and Shahar, 273.

81. Compare Shahar, 289, and Shahar, 273.

82. Compare Shahar, 310–11, and Shahar, 292. The only passage from the unfavorable episode retained in the translation was that in which Lilly, Driesel's American assistant, explains why Driesel looks so tired the next morning: "The last to emerge from his room was Jules, crumpled and blinking with sleep. He got into the long Plymouth that fell into line behind us, and dozed off the moment we hit the road. . . . 'All night long he didn't sleep a wink,' Deborah explained to the director. 'He spent the whole night working on the last chapter of his book.' (Shahar, *His Majesty's Agent*, 292–93). Of course, the irony of the passage is now lost, and the reason for Driesel's fatigue is very different in the Hebrew source and the English translation.

83. Compare Jackont, *Pesek-zman*, 166, and Jackont, *Borrowed Time*, 123.

84. Compare Jackont, *Pesek-zman*, 54, and Jackont, *Borrowed Time*, 39.

85. Compare Jackont, *Pesek-zman*, 135–36, and Jackont, *Borrowed Time*, 102–3.

86. Alter, "Rise and the Rise," 6.

87. Zeller, "Between *Goldene Medine* and Promised Land," 9.

88. Kaplan, *A New Zionism*; Yosef Gorny, *The State of Israel in Jewish Public Thought: The Quest for Collective Identity* (New York, 1994), 79–91.

89. Eliezer Ben-Rafael, Judit Bokser Liwerant, and Yosef Gorny, "Introduction," in *Reconsidering Israel–Diaspora Relations*, ed. Ben-Rafael, Liwerant, and Gorny (Boston, 2014), 1–22, esp. 4–6.

90. Emily Alice Katz, *Bringing Zion Home: Israel in American Jewish Culture* (Albany, N.Y., 2015), 137.

91. Mintz, *Translating Israel*, 24–25, 227–42.

Chapter 4

1. Saul Bellow, ed., *Great Jewish Short Stories* (New York, 1963), 14. This chapter is a revised, expanded version of Omri Asscher, "Jewish-American Literature Makes Aliyah? Jewish/non-Jewish Boundary Maintenance, and the Israeli Approach to the Diaspora," *Jewish Social Studies* 23, no. 3 (2018): 128–59; reprinted with permission. Copyright © by Indiana University Press.

2. Bellow, *Great Jewish Short Stories*, 15. For an insightful discussion of approaches in Hebrew literary discourse to Heinrich Heine, see Na'ama Rokem, *Prosaic Conditions: Heinrich Heine and the Space of Zionist Literature* (Evanston, Ill., 2014). For an analysis of Agnon's ideological conception of modern Hebrew as it arises from his novel *Only Yesterday*, see Todd Hasak-Lowy, *Here and Now: History, Nationalism, and Realism in Modern Hebrew Fiction* (Syracuse, N.Y., 2008), 68–100.

3. Kirsten Silva Gruesz, "Translation: A Key(word) into the Language of America(nists)," *American Literary History* 16, no. 1 (2004): 85–92, esp. 88–89.

4. Abram de Swaan, "The Emergent World Language System: An Introduction," *International Political Science Review* 14, no. 3 (1993): 219–26. For a recent discussion of the genealogy of the term *world literature* and its contemporary political implications, see Aamir R. Mufti, *Forget English! Orientalisms and World Literatures* (Cambridge, Mass., 2016).

5. Cynthia Ozick, "America: Toward Yavneh," *Judaism* 19, no. 3 (1970): 264–82.

6. Sarah Bunin Benor, "Do American Jews Speak a 'Jewish Language'? A Model of Jewish Linguistic Distinctiveness," *Jewish Quarterly Review* 99, no. 2 (2009): 230–69.

7. Ruth R. Wisse, "Jewish American Renaissance," in *The Cambridge Companion to Jewish American Literature*, ed. Hana Wirth-Nesher and Michael Kramer (Cambridge, 2003), 206.

8. Olga Zambrowsky, *American Jewish Literature and the Israeli Reader* (New York, 1994). As noted earlier, Zambrowsky's overview runs fifteen pages, and focuses on publishers' decisions in Israel. Zambrowsky argues that ideological considerations have governed the selection of titles for translation, and she broadly surmises that Israeli publishers have been reluctant to publish affirmative portrayals of Jewish spiritual life in America; this claim, however, remains largely unsubstantiated, as Zambrowsky does not analyze the reception of the works. The gender bias noted in the introduction to this book, largely evident in Israeli discourse on Jewish American works outlined in this chapter, is corroborated by Zambrowsky's list of translated American Jewish writers, which shows that male authors had a much more visible presence in Hebrew translation than women authors during these decades (see p. 6).

9. Hemi Sheinblat, *Litpos et Amerika: Tahalikhei amerikanizatsiah ba-hevrah ha-yisraelit, 1958–1967* (PhD diss., Tel Aviv University, 2017).

10. Anita Shapira, "Le-an halekhah 'shelilat ha-galut'?" *Alpayim* 25 (2003): 9–54; Gideon

Shimoni, "Behina me-hadash shel 'shelilat ha-galut' ke-ra'ayon ve-ma'aseh," in *'Idan ha-tsiyonut*, ed. Anita Shapira, Jehuda Reinharz, and Jacob Harris (Jerusalem, 2000), 45–63.

For the differences between the secular and religious sectors of Israeli society in this respect, see Eliezer Don-Yehiya, "'Galut' in Zionist Ideology and in Israeli Society," in *Israel and Diaspora Jewry*, ed. Don-Yehiya (Ramat Gan, 1991), 219–57.

11. Shapira, "Le-an halekhah," 27; Gideon Katz, "Shivato shel Pinchas Sadeh el ha-yahadut," *Israel* no. 17 (2010): 191–209; Gershon Shaked, *Ha-siporet ha-'ivrit 1880–1980*, vol. 5 (Tel Aviv, 1998), 97–102.

12. As noted earlier, another reason why I could not trace a linear and coherent evolution in Israeli approaches to American Jewish cultural creation in these years may have been the contingency of literary debates in Israel on a rather irregular "stimulus"—the publication of challenging translated works. One of the features of this ongoing encounter was that Jewish American works that raised the most interest in Israeli discourse not only appeared in Hebrew translation intermittently over the span of decades but also were acutely different from one another in their representations of Jewishness.

13. A. Hava, "Ha-'ozer," *Moznayim* 5–6 (November 1957): 426. (This is a review of Malamud's *The Assistant.*)

14. Hava, "Ha-'ozer," 426.

15. Yigal Shenkman, "Ma me'ik al Dr. Spielvogel?" *Haaretz*, January 9, 1970, 22. See also Eliezer Livne, "Te'uda yehudit 'aguma," *Haaretz*, October 29, 1965, 10.

16. Yirmiyahu Halpern, "Paranoya," *Herut*, July 26, 1955, 3; Benjamin Z. Ben-Hayim, "Rav ha-mecher, *Exodus*," *Herut*, January 1, 1960, 5.

17. Ehud Ben-Ezer, "Ha-'ozer: ha-het ve-'onsho," *Moznayim* 29 (August–September 1969): 247–53, esp. 253; Yoram Kaniuk, "Lishtok be-milim," *Davar*, April 13, 1973, 39.

18. Alexander Barzel, *Ha-sihah ha-gedolah: masot 'al tarbut ve-sifrut* (Tel Aviv, 1971), 101; Hanoch Bartov, "Dim'at kin'ah," *Ma'ariv*, February 14, 1984, 8.

19. Yisrael Gur, "Min ve-hamin," *Ha-umah* 8, no. 30 (1970): 258.

20. Henry Unger, "Likro et 'atzmi ve-'et ha-'aherim," *Yedi'ot aharonot*, January 4, 1991, 22. See also Eliyahu Slepter, "Portnoy ke-semel yehudi," *Haaretz*, January 5, 1973, 14.

21. Eli Shai, "Kovlanat ha-sod ha-mushtak (ve-kilelato): likro me-hadash et Scholem kore et Agnon ve-et Roth," *Mehekarei Yerushalayim be-mahshevet Yisrael* 20–21 (2007): 548.

22. "Ha-Abramovitchim ha-lalu," *Ma'ariv*, October 17, 1962, 4.

23. Pinhas Elad-Lender, "'Al meshorer 'ivri ve-sofer yehudi," *Temurot* 1–2 (1977): 54.

24. A. Tag, "Kehal ha-kor'im ha-amerikai mit'anyen be-tematika yehudit," *Herut*, March 6, 1959, 5.

25. Yosef Raz, "Saul Bellow mehapes 'olam she-kulo ahava," *Davar*, October 22, 1965, 24.

26. See, for instance, Yeshurun Keshet, "Bernard Malamud be-'Ivrit," *Molad* 21 (1963): 679–82; Hillel Barzel, "Herzog, yetsirat mofet shel Sha'ul Bellow," *Ha-po'el ha-tsa'ir* 36, no. 17 (1966): 18–20; and Livne, "Te'uda yehudit," 10. It is worth noting the irony that Bellow's given name was Solomon, which was shortened to Sol and then changed to Saul, meaning that his "original" Hebrew name should have been Shlomo.

27. Eli Mohar, "Sofer gadol ve-adam hakham," *Davar*, June 30, 1970, 10.

28. Mohar, 10.

29. Hanoch Bartov, "'Im Philip Roth be-Algonquin," *Ma'ariv*, July 3, 1970, 50.

30. Hanoch Bartov, "Ehad midrash, ve-'ehad Elie Wiesel," *Ma'ariv*, August 27, 1976, 35.

31. This is not to say that the Israeli publishing field did not exhibit censorial tendencies in other areas; several Israeli publishers used strategies of omission and moderation to mediate to their readers varied Christian themes and images, or forms of eroticism. See Nitsa Ben-Ari, "The Double Conversion of Ben-Hur: A Case of Manipulative Translation," *Target* 14, no. 2 (2002): 263–302, and Nitsa Ben-Ari, *Suppression of the Erotic in Modern Hebrew Literature* (Ottawa, 2006). On interferences in Hebrew translations of political philosophy, see Neve Gordon, "Zionism, Translation, and the Politics of Erasure," *Political Studies* 50, no. 4 (2002): 818–28.

32. Overviews of this translation norm and its effects can be found in Gideon Toury, *Descriptive Translation Studies and Beyond* (Amsterdam and Philadelphia, 1995), 102–12; Rachel Weissbrod, "Mock-Epic as a Byproduct of the Norm of Elevated Language," *Target* 11, no. 2 (1999): 245–62; Nitsa Ben-Ari, "'Tirgumit 'o—'Ivrit shel tirgumim" in *Aderet le-Binyamin*, ed. Barbara Harshav and Ziva Ben-Porat (Tel Aviv, 1999), 293–304.

33. Compare Saul Bellow, *Mr. Sammler's Planet* (New York, 2004), 66, and Bellow, *Kochav ha-lechet shel mar Sammler* (Tel-Aviv, 1971), 61.

34. Compare Bernard Malamud, *The Magic Barrel* (New York, 2003 [1958]), 176; Bernard Malamud, *Havit ha-kesamim* (Tel-Aviv, 1980), 123.

35. Compare Saul Bellow, *Herzog* (New York, 1964), 54, and Bellow, *Herzog* (Tel-Aviv, 1965), 61.

36. Compare Bellow, *Herzog*, 74 [English], and Bellow, *Herzog*, 82 [Hebrew].

37. Compare Bellow, *Herzog*, 88 [English], and Bellow, *Herzog*, 97 [Hebrew].

38. Compare Bernard Malamud, *The Assistant* (New York, 1957), 18, and Malamud, *Ha-'ozer* (Tel-Aviv, 1963), 19.

39. Compare Malamud, *The Assistant*, 192, and Malamud, *Ha-'ozer*, 234.

40. A. Hava, "Havit ha-kesamim," *Moznayim* 8 (April–May 1959): 454.

41. Mordechai Avishai, "Ha-tsayar me-Bruklin," *'Al ha-mishmar*, November 29, 1974, 7.

42. Ruth Almog, "Ha-yehudi ke-anti gibor," *Haaretz*, March 21, 1986, 18.

43. Rivka Durkevitch, "Ha-'enoshi she-ba'adam," *'Alei siah* 6 (1978): 225.

44. David Zonenfeld, "Arachim humaniyim," *'Alei siah* 6 (1978): 228.

45. Compare Wade Green, "How to Please the Highbrows and Still Make the Best Seller Lists," *Pottstown Mercury*, February 19, 1970, 29 (originally published in *Newsweek*), and Green, "Saul Bellow: ha-kohen ha-gadol shel ha-sifrut ha-amerika'it aharai milhemet ha-'olam ha-2," *Davar*, February 18, 1970, 5.

46. Green, "How to Please," 29, and Green, "Saul Bellow," 5.

47. Aki Shoval, "Tse'irim me-'olam she-haya—ve-'adayin kayam," *Ma'ariv*, February 20, 1984, 25.

48. Shoval, 25.

49. Benjamin Schreier, "Making It into the Mainstream, 1945–1970," in *Cambridge History of Jewish American Literature*, ed. Hana Wirth-Nesher (Cambridge, Mass., 2016),

137. Schreier himself criticizes the assumptions of such "ethnic" scholarship and criticism as nationalistic.

50. See Yosef Gorny, *The State of Israel in Jewish Public Thought: The Quest for Collective Identity* (New York, 1994).

51. These attributes all largely apply to Philip Roth's Israeli reception as well, particularly of *Goodbye, Columbus* and *Portnoy's Complaint*. Nonetheless, I have chosen not to focus on the dynamics of the Israeli understanding of these works because of Roth's overt exploration of Jewish/non-Jewish difference as key to Jewish American identity. The boundary between Jews and non-Jews was portrayed much less suggestively in Roth's writing, and was much more prevalent in his American critical reception, than in Bellow's or Malamud's. Whereas the Israeli approach to Roth's work thus corresponds with the main claims of this chapter, I believe that it is less revealing with regard to the ideological underpinnings of the Israeli literary discourse or the social significance of representations of American Jewishness constructed by Israeli critics.

52. See, for instance, Ben Siegel, "Bellow as Jew and Jewish Writer," in *A Political Companion to Saul Bellow*, ed. Lee Trepanier and Gloria L. Cronin (Lexington, Ky., 2013), 36.

53. Terry A. Cooney, "New York Intellectuals and the Question of Jewish Identity," *American Jewish History* 80, no. 3 (1991): 344–60, esp. 355.

54. S. Sagiv, "Herzog le-Sha'ul Bellow," *Davar*, August 27, 1965, 7. Sagiv also makes a point of differentiating Bellow from modernist Hebrew writer Y. H. Brenner, whose characters' tragedy, unlike Herzog's, is born out of a "fountain of deep-seated and profound love for their people." Sagiv implies a Zionist critique of Herzog/Bellow's lack of national identification.

55. See, for instance, Alexander Barzel, *Ha-sihah ha-gedolah*; Hillel Barzel, "Herzog"; Shlomo Bader, "Roman 'al hanut makolet: *ha-'ozer* shel Bernard Malamud," *Ma'ariv*, April 30, 1959, 7; A. H. Elhanani, "Kohan shel milim," *Davar*, January 13, 1976, 12; and Amos Oz, "Mar Sammler ve-ha-banaliyut shel Hannah Arendt," *Prose* 99 (1987): 15–16.

56. Tzfira Porat, "Ha-aryeh ha-met ve-ha-kelev ha-hai: 'al mekoma shel ha-yahadut be-kitvei Saul Bellow," *Moznayim* 42 (January 1976): 106.

57. Porat, 107.

58. Keshet, "Bernard Malamud be-'Ivrit," 679.

59. H. E. Francis, "Bernard Malamud's Everyman," *Midstream* 7, no. 1 (1961): 95; Hebrew translation, Francis, "Bernard Malamud," *Moznayim* 15 (July–August 1962): 178.

60. Francis, "Bernard Malamud's Everyman," 95.

61. Amnon Hadari, "Pehadav shel Bernard Malamud," *Yedi'ot aharonot*, March 28, 1986, 20.

62. See, for instance, Haya Lazar, "*Mila 18 le*-Leon Uris: hilul zichram shel mordei geto Varsha," *Herut*, September 10, 1961, 5.

63. Raz, "Saul Bellow mehapes," 24.

64. See, for instance, Jan Bakker, "Saul Bellow: A Writer's Despair," in *Essays on English and American Literature, and a Sheaf of Poems: Offered to David Wilkinson on the Occasion of His Retirement from the Chair of English Literature in the University of Groningen*, ed. Jan Bakker, J. A. Verlen, and J. v.d. Vriesenaerde (Amsterdam, 1987), 177–91. The extensive in-

terview conducted with Bellow in his prime and published in 1975 in the Skidmore College magazine, *Salmagundi*, is similarly indicative in this respect. The interview covered most parts of Bellow's creative work and touched on major themes such as morality and ethics, but never referred to Jewishness, Jews, or antisemitism. See "Literature and Culture: An Interview with Saul Bellow," *Salmagundi* 30 (1975): 6–23. Interviewing Saul Bellow were Robert Boyers, Robert Orrill, Ralph Ciancio, and Edwin Mosely. Such examples abound.

65. Schreier, "Making It into the Mainstream," 127.

66. Stemming from an adherence to formal equivalence in translation, a shift in the Hebrew translations that may have contributed to these readings was the literal translation of the expletive interjection "Jesus" or "Jesus Christ." This stylistic choice changed the resonance and implication of the interjection, which in most original contexts carried little to no religious coloring. Consider the translation of the following fragment of dialogue between the young, self-indulgent Brenda Patimkin and her mother in Roth's novella *Goodbye, Columbus*: "'When's the last time you washed the dishes!' 'Jesus Christ!' Brenda flared, 'Carlota washes the dishes.' 'Don't Jesus Christ me!' 'Oh, mother!' And Brenda was crying." In the Hebrew translation, the exclamative "Jesus Christ" was translated literally as *Yeshu ha-notzri* [Jesus the Christian], and Mrs. Patimkin's scolding reaction "Don't Jesus Christ me" was rendered with the forced Hebrew wordplay *al tenatzreri li be-Yeshu*—a vague, awkward construct that may be translated back roughly as "do not talk in Christian/Jesus terms." (Compare Philip Roth, *Goodbye, Columbus* [Boston, 1989 (1959)], 65, and Roth, *Heye shalom Columbus* [Jerusalem, 1970], 57.) Whereas the bickering revolved around Brenda's sidestepping household chores and being self-indulgent, the translation implies that Mrs. Patimkin takes issue with her daughter's "un-Jewish" ways of expression. The Hebrew version thus imposes an interreligious frame of reference for understanding the mother-daughter dynamics even though this seems irrelevant to the original context. The expletive interjection "Jesus Christ" was translated literally elsewhere in Roth's collection, as well as in other authors' works, thus transforming a rather transparent exclamative into conspicuous constructs that were explicitly tied to, even as they themselves represented, Jewish/non-Jewish difference.

67. Shlomo Grodzenski, "Siha ʿal Bernard Malamud," *Davar*, April 12, 1968, 9.

68. Livne, "Teʿuda yehudit," 10.

69. Avishai, "Ha-tsayar me-Bruklin," 7.

70. Cooney, "New York Intellectuals," 349, 356.

71. Y. Koreh, "'Ha-yehudi ha-noded' ha-amerikai hozer," *Davar*, March 18, 1983, 21.

72. See, for instance, Cynthia Ozick, "Ethnic Joke," *Commentary* 50 (November 1970): 106–14.

73. Koreh, "Ha-yehudi ha-noded," 21.

74. "Ha-ghetto ha-gadol she-shmo Artsot Ha-brit," *Maʿariv*, June 26, 1970, 31.

75. Elad-Lender, "Al meshorer ʿivri," 54.

76. I. M. Neiman, "Misha Asherov nilham le-maʿan ha-tsedek be-ha-mered ʿal ha-Kein," *Davar*, November 5, 1954, 27.

77. "Kol yom daf gemara," *Maʿariv*, October 27, 1978, 89. Wouk said that Shazar entreated him to write some of his novels in Hebrew.

78. "Herman Wouk meshabe'ah et hatsagat 'ha-mered al ha-Kein be-Ha-bima,'" *Davar*, May 15, 1955, 2.

79. See also Yaakov Rabi, "Parashat ha-Rozenbergim be-masve ha-dimyon," *'Al ha-mishmar*, July 29, 1977, 6.

80. S. Shapira, "Ha-mashal he-'atzuv be-sipurei Fidelman le-Bernard Malamud," *Ma'ariv*, January 30, 1970, 19, 31.

81. Shapira, 31.

82. Shapira, 31.

83. Yaakov Rabi, "Ha-meri she-lo nistaye'a," *Moznayim* 40 (March 1975): 303.

84. R. Rabinovitch, "Ha-yehudi ha-amerika'i 'al sapat psychiater," *Ma'ariv*, June 27, 1969, 27.

85. These Israeli assumptions, it is worth noting, were not unknown to American Jewish writers, as is evident in the latter's varied responses to them through parody, intellectual polemics, or warm humor—for example, in the closing chapter of Roth's *Portnoy's Complaint*; Bellow's remarks on language ideology in his introduction to *Great Jewish Short Stories* (1963); and Malamud's bemused comments at a symposium in Israel, in Grodzenski, "Siha al," 9.

86. Elad-Lender, "Al meshorer 'ivri," 53.

87. Elad-Lender, 53.

88. Elad-Lender, 53.

89. Elad-Lender, 54. In this respect, Israeli reviewers seemed to differ from nationalistically oriented Jewish critics in America such as Meyer Levin and Marie Syrkin, who often charged the canonical Jewish American writers with emphasizing assimilation and omitting references to "the inner continuation as well as the creative and identifying activities in Jewish life," thus implying that the writers' depictions of American Jewish existence were in fact not credible, or at least were more excessively and demonstratively negative than American Jewish reality (Meyer Levin and Charles Angoff, eds., *The Rise of American Jewish Literature* [New York, 1970], 14). Israeli critics, however, tended not only to accept the portrayal of the difficulties of Jewish existence in non-Jewish surroundings as reliable but also to overaccentuate them while presenting them as proof of the dearth of American Jewish cultural life in general.

90. Yehudit Oryan, "Philip Roth, bo ha-bayta!" *Yedi'ot aharonot*, May 15, 1970 (the reviewer's emphasis).

91. Alexander Barzel, *Ha-sihah ha-gedolah*, 92–108.

92. Barzel, 105.

93. Barzel, 95.

94. Barzel, 105 (the reviewer's emphasis).

95. Compare Malamud, *Magic Barrel*, 164; Malamud, *Havit ha-kesamim*, 115.

96. Compare Roth, *Goodbye, Columbus*, vii, and Roth, *Heye shalom Columbus*, 6.

97. Compare Bellow, *Mr. Sammler's Planet*, 125, and Bellow, *Kochav ha-lechet*, 112.

98. Compare Bellow, *Mr. Sammler's Planet*, 67, and Bellow, *Kochav ha-lechet*, 61.

99. This absence could in itself elicit a troubled Israeli reaction. As Eliezer Livne re-

marked in his otherwise appreciative review of Bellow's *Herzog* (Livne, "Te'uda yehudit," 10):

> Few problems of modernity are left uncontemplated in Moshe Herzog's frantic reflections. . . . One subject, however, is *entirely* missing from the book: missing as a problem and as a vision, as an intellectual challenge, even as a dwelling place of people who pertain to the novel's characters and their lives: Israel! I believe its name is not even mentioned in the book's 341 pages. That a novel expressing the sensibilities of the intellectual strata of the American [Jewish] ghetto can ignore Israel and its Jewish collective to such an extent—this should be heeded as a serious warning.

Perhaps the scarce treatment of Israel in the Jewish American literary imagination, so distressing for Livne, worked to intensify the Israeli reaction to Jewish American portrayals of Israel that *did* appear on the literary scene.

100. Aharon Megged, "Me-tasbichei ha-smol ha-yehudi," *Davar*, October 20, 1972, 15.

In the late 1950s, the critical reception of Leon Uris's *Exodus* abounded in critique of the melodramatic flavor and unfaithfulness of the novel to the reality of Israeli life. See, for instance: Aliza Levenberg, "Exodus," *Davar*, August 21, 1959, 6.

101. Yaakov Rabi, "'Akarut ha-ratson u-meha'a le-vatala," *Moznaim* 29, no. 1 (June 1969), 62.

102. Gur, "Min ve-hamin," 264; S. Shariya, "Rav ha-mecher be-Amerika: al yehudi ha-soneh et 'atzmo," *Ma'ariv*, February 28, 1969, 27.

103. Yehudit Oryan, "Min ve-yiddishkeit, o': mi mefahed me-Philip Roth?" *Yedi'ot aharonot*, January 16, 1970, 18.

104. Emily Miller Budick, *Blacks and Jews in Literary Conversation* (Cambridge, Mass., 1998), 154.

105. See, for instance, Uri Milshtein, "Dagesh al ha-iratsionali," *Davar*, July 9, 1971, 13; Mordechai Avishai, "Olam be-hitdarderuto be-einei Saul Bellow," *Ma'ariv*, March 12, 1971, 31.

106. Jacqueline Kahanoff, "Hazarah el ha-tevunah," *Haaretz*, February 19, 1971, 14.

107. Kahanoff, 14.

108. Reprinted as "Ha-professor eino me'uban" in his book-length study, see Amnon Hadari, *Revah beli hatzala: ha-roman ha-yehudi be-america* (Tel Aviv, 1972), 113.

109. Hadari, 113. More acerbically and indignantly, critic Ehud Ben-Ezer complained that Sammler sees Israel's "grand message" to the world as nothing but "Napalm and Eisen"—a crazed violence that constitutes "a new way to ruin that fragile, delicate culture in which exquisite Artur Sammler is trying to live." Later in the review, Ben-Ezer proclaimed rather emotionally, "not only does Israel insist to reject George Steiner's ideal of sheep mentality, the excessive cultivation, the cosmopolitanism that relinquishes any physical power, but it also dares to demonstrate to American Jews how they can protect their lives by means of violence—and for that Sammler/Bellow surely cannot forgive it!" (Ehud Ben Ezer, "Ha-kochav shel Mar Sammler," *'Al ha-mishmar*, February 19, 1971).

110. Tuvia S., "Saul Bellow ke-yehudi uke-tsiyoni," *Alei siah* 6 (1978): 225.

111. Haim Yisraeli, "Tlishut me-ha-metziut ha-enoshit veha-yehudit," *Alei siah* 6 (1978): 227.

112. Porat, "Ha-aryeh ha-met," 107.

113. Bellow, and American Jews in general, are also faulted with assuming Christian

values and thus being in the wrong on issues of Jewish morality, in Eliezer Livne's review of *Herzog* in *Haaretz* (1965). The backdrop to Livne's comments is his impression of the worrisome, increasing role of psychiatry in American Jewish life. Whereas Freud's psychoanalysis was "Hebraic and dissenting" in nature and demanded that one assumed moral responsibility for one's choice between contradictory desires, so Livne suggests, the contemporary American psychiatrist absolves the Jewish patient all too easily of moral responsibility and the burden of choice, in ways similar to the Christian priest hearing confession. Here too, then, American Jewish morals were framed as corrupted by Christian influences, even as Freud, who represents a higher moral ground for Livne, was attributed with a "Hebraic" quality and implicitly associated with Israeli culture. See Livne, "Te'uda yehudit," 10.

114. A. B. Yehoshua, *Between Right and Right* (New York, 1981), 139.

115. Yehoshua, 139.

116. Jackie Feldman, "Marking the Boundaries of the Enclave: Defining the Israeli Collective through the Poland 'Experience,'" *Israel Studies* 7, no. 2 (2002): 91.

117. Nir Cohen, "From Overt Rejection to Enthusiastic Embracement: Changing State Discourses on Israeli Emigration," *GeoJournal* 68, no. 2–3 (2007): 271. *Yoredim* literally means "those who descend, physically and morally."

118. Uriel Abulof, *'Al pi tehom: umah, eimah u-musar ba-siah ha-tsiyoni* (Haifa, 2016).

119. Jakob Klatzkin, "A Nation Must Have Its Own Land and Language," in *The Zionist Idea*, ed. Arthur Hertzberg (New York, 1966), 318.

120. See, for instance, Don-Yehiya, "Galut"; Zambrowsky, *American Jewish Literature*; and Olga Zambrowsky and Malka Or-Chen, "American Jewry as Reflected in the Secondary School Curriculum in Israel," in *Beyond Survival and Philanthropy: American Jewry and Israel*, ed. Allon Gal and Alfred Gottschalk (Cincinnati, 2000), 131–49.

Chapter 5

1. Saul Bellow, "A Jewish Writer in America," *New York Review of Books*, October 27, 2011 (excerpted from a talk given in 1988). https://www.nybooks.com/articles/2011/10/27/jewish-writer-america/.

2. Anita Shapira, "Le-an halekhah 'shelilat ha-galut'?" *Alpayim* 25 (2003): 13–23.

3. Ron Kuzar, *Hebrew and Zionism* (Berlin, 2001), 137–85.

4. Tzvi Adar, *Ha-hinuch ha-yehudi be-Yisrael uve-Arszot Ha-brit* (Tel Aviv, 1969), 56–59.

5. Gideon Nevo, "Eternal Jews and Dead Dogs: The Diasporic Other in Natan Alterman's *The Seventh Column*," in *Modern Jewish Literatures: Intersections and Boundaries*, ed. Sheila E. Jelen, Michael P. Kramer, and L. Scott Lerner (Philadelphia, 2010), 252–59.

6. Nathan Alterman, *Ha-tur ha-shevi'i: 1948–1952* (Tel Aviv, 2012), 161–62. For a full English translation of the poem by Lisa Katz, see Gur Alroey, "Two Historiographies: The Israeli Historiography and the Mass Jewish Migration to the United States, 1881–1914," *Jewish Quarterly Review* 105, no. 1 (2015): 99–100.

7. Alterman, 358.

8. Yochai Oppenheimer, *Sham me-ahorai li kor'a yabeshet: zichron ha-galut ba-sifrut ha-'ivrit* (Jerusalem, 2105), 218–40.

9. Shimon Halkin, *Yehudim ve-yahadut be-Amerika* (Jerusalem, 1947), 23.

10. Halkin, 24.

11. Halkin, 50–51.

12. Halkin, 47.

13. Halkin, 48.

14. See Shapira, "Le-an halekhah," 27.

15. Adar, *Ha-hinuch ha-yehudi*, 144–45, 149–53.

16. Adar, 65. See also Olga Zambrowsky and Malka Or-Chen, "American Jewry as Reflected in the Secondary School Curriculum in Israel," in *Beyond Survival and Philanthropy: American Jewry and Israel*, ed. Allon Gal and Alfred Gottschalk (Cincinnati, 2000), 131–49.

17. See Gideon Katz, "Shivato shel Pinchas Sadeh el ha-yahadut," *Israel* 17 (2010): 191–209; Gershon Shaked, *Ha-siporet ha-'ivrit 1880–1980*, vol. 5 (Tel Aviv, 1998), 97–102.

18. Shaked, 99–100; Ruth Yardeni, *She'arim le-gan na'ul: Binyamin Tammuz—temurot be-yetsirato* (Tel Aviv, 2012), 23–57.

19. Yardeni, 57.

20. Similarly revealing is Amos Oz's assertion in a *New York Times* interview from 1975 that "with the exception of Saul Bellow, I'm not terribly happy with the Jewish American novelists. The others are too wise, their characters exchange punchlines instead of talking to each other, their books are just clever sociology. They don't have the echo of the universe, you don't see the stars in their writings" (Herbert Mitgang, "A Talk with Amos Oz," *New York Times*, October 26, 1975, 276). As American journalist David Remnick summed it up harshly in an interview thirty years later: "[Oz] seems not merely indifferent to [Jewish American novelists of his generation, such as Bellow, Malamud and Roth], but even haughtily dismissive of their work and their subjects" (David Remnick, "The Spirit Level: Amos Oz Writes the Story of Israel," *New Yorker*, November 8, 2004, 90).

21. Yosef Gorny, *The State of Israel in Jewish Public Thought: The Quest for Collective Identity* (New York, 1994), 82.

22. Baruch Karu, "Hakdamah," in *Sofrim yehudim be-sifrut ha-olam*, ed. Emil Feuerstein (Tel Aviv, 1959), 6. For a discussion of the rhetoric of "restoration from captivity" prevalent in the Zionist discourse on the Hebrew translation of Heinrich Heine, see Na'ama Rokem, *Prosaic Conditions: Heinrich Heine and the Space of Zionist Literature* (Evanston, Ill., 2014), 47–72.

23. Ahad Ha'am, "Riv leshonot," in *Kol kitvei Ahad Ha'am* (Tel Aviv, 1947), 405.

24. Hayim Nahman Bialik, "Od al kinus ha-ruah," *Devarim she-be'al peh*, vol. 1 (Tel Aviv, 1935), 70.

25. Karu, "Hakdamah," 6.

26. Yisrael Cohen, "Yafyuto shel shem be-'oholey yefet," in *Sha'ar ha-havhanot* (Tel Aviv, 1962 [1957]), 136.

27. Cohen, 6.

28. Joel Blocker, "Literary Export," *Commentary* 26 (July 1, 1958), 92.

29. Gorny, *State of Israel*, 88.

30. Gorny, 83.

31. Gershon Zack, "'Ayin doma'at ve-'ayin smeha," *Davar*, August 27, 1970, 11.

32. See M. Moshe, "Hollywood shel shnot ha-shloshim," *Ma'ariv*, January 16, 1981, 36.

33. "Kol yom daf gemara," *Ma'ariv*, October 27, 1978, 89.

34. Shulamith Hareven, "Hevrat behira: ha-yehudim shel Hayim Potok," *Ma'ariv*, July 5, 1974, 38.

35. Hanoch Bartov, "Ehad midrash ve-ehad Elie Wiesel," *Ma'ariv*, August 27, 1976, 35.

36. Nathan Rotenstreich, *Al hakiyum ha-yehudi ba-zman ha-ze* (Tel Aviv, 1972), 106.

37. Yaakov Rabi, "Le-harhiv et nahalat ha-'Ivrit," *Moznayim* 38, no. 1–2 (December 1973): 92.

38. Rabi, 93.

39. Rabi, 93.Original emphasis.

40. Yaakov Rabi, "Leshonot yehudiyot—ve-'Ivrit," *'Al ha-mishmar*, January 10, 1983.

41. Ehud Ben-Ezer, "Shakran be-hesed 'elyon," *Davar*, January 4, 1980, 18.

42. Ben-Ezer, 18.

43. Ehud Ben-Ezer, "Al ge'onim, hagavim ve-raglei hagavim," *Davar*, January 25, 1983, 10.

44. Hayim Nahman Bialik, "Ha-sefer ha-'ivri," in *Kol kitvei Hayim Nahman Bialik* (Tel Aviv, 1950), 217.

45. Hillel Halkin, *Letters to an American Jewish Friend: A Zionist Polemic* (Philadelphia, 1977), 182.

46. Halkin, 167.

47. Halkin, 168.

48. Halkin, 103–4.

49. Hillel Halkin, "The Translator's Paradox," *Commentary* 125, no. 6 (June 1, 2008): 40–41.

50. Halkin, "Translator's Paradox," 41.

51. Halkin, 42.

52. Saul Bellow, "I Said That I Was an American, a Jew, a Writer by Trade," in *American Jewish History: A Primary Source Reader*, ed. Gary Phillip Zola and Marc Dollinger (Waltham, Mass., 2014), 380.

53. Bellow, 380.

54. Pinhas Elad-Lender, "'Al meshorer 'ivri ve-sofer yehudi," *Temurot* 1–2 (1977): 53.

55. Zachary Leader, *The Life of Saul Bellow: To Fame and Fortune 1915–1964* (New York, 2015), 575.

56. Leader, 575.

57. A. B. Yehoshua, *Between Right and Right* (New York, 1981), 138.

58. Yehoshua, 138

59. Yehoshua, 130.

60. Hayim Nahman Bialik, "'Al uma ve-lashon," in *Devarim she-be'al peh*, vol. 1 (Tel Aviv, 1935), 16.

61. A. B. Yehoshua, *Ahizat moledet* (Tel Aviv, 2008), 78–79.

62. Yehoshua, 78–79.

63. Revital Blumenfeld, "A. B. Yehoshua: Americans, Unlike Israelis, Are Only Partial Jews," *Haaretz*, March 18, 2012, https://www.haaretz.com/1.5206064.

64. Amos Oz, "Imagining the Other," in *The Writer in the Jewish Community: An Israeli–North American Dialogue*, ed. Richard Siegel and Tamar Sofer (Rutherford, 1993), 116.

65. Oz, "Imagining the Other," 119.

66. Oz, 121–22.

67. Oz, 122.

68. Oz, 120.

69. Oz, 123.

70. Gershon Shaked, "Alexandria," in *Ein makom aher: 'al sifrut ve-hevra* (Tel Aviv, 1988). The revised English version, "Judaism in Translation: Thoughts on the Alexandria Hypothesis," appeared in Alan Mintz, ed., *Hebrew in America: Perspectives and Prospects* (Detroit, 1993), 277–95. In what follows, I quote from the English version, unless words or passages were omitted from the English translation, in which case I rely on Shaked's original Hebrew essay, and note the interference in translation.

71. Shaked, "Alexandria," 159.

72. Shaked, 160–61.

73. Shaked, 153. When this passage appeared in English translation, its critical tone was much subdued: "Indeed these two cultures differ: one is a secular culture which is entirely Hebraic, constantly developing in its old-new language, while the other is an ethnic-religious culture developing in the local vernacular and contributing both to itself and its locality" (Shaked, "Judaism in Translation," 281). This ideological shift in translation corresponds with the patterns of protective mediation of Hebrew literature that we have seen in chapter 3.

74. See Shaked, "Alexandria," 139, 143, 145, 151, 153, 154–59, 160–61, 168–72.

75. Bialik, "'Al uma ve-lashon," 16.

76. Shaked, "Judaism in Translation," 283.

77. Shaked, "Alexandria," 161. Once again, these critical observations on American Jewish culture were omitted in full from the English translation.

78. Shaked, "Judaism in Translation," 287.

79. Shaked, "Judaism in Translation," 287.

80. Shaked, "Alexandria," 143, 156.

81. Shaked, "Judaism in Translation," 289.

82. Shaked, "Judaism in Translation," 285. Yet again, Shaked's notion of translation as a bridge is largely unilateral; his major source for Jewish identity is markedly Israeli, reconfirming the hierarchy of Hebrew and other languages, and of the competing Jewish cultures of Israel and the diaspora.

83. Shaked, 291.

84. Shaked, 293.

85. This was most notable in the literary production of thinkers of earlier generations. It is evident in the portrayal of American Jewry by Nathan Alterman and Shimon Halkin, in the Israeli reception of American best-sellers such as *Exodus*, and in the unfavorable depictions of American Jewish life in Nathan Shaham's *Hutsot Ashkelon* (1985) and Moshe Shamir's *Yaldei ha-sha'ashu'im* (1986).

86. Joseph Agassi, *Bein dat ve-le'om: likrat zehut le'umit yisraelit* (Tel Aviv, 1983), 203.

87. Eliezer Ben-Rafael, "Israel–Diaspora Relations: 'Transmission Driving-Belts of Transnationalism,'" in *Reconsidering Israel–Diaspora Relations*, ed. Eliezer Ben-Rafael, Judit Bokser Liwerant, and Yosef Gorny (Boston, 2014), 458.

88. Oz, "Imagining the Other," 119.

89. Shaked, "Alexandria," 160.

90. Bialik, "'Al uma ve-lashon," 15.
91. Gorny, *State of Israel*, 243.
92. Yehoshua, *Ahizat moledet*, 178–79.

Conclusion

1. Some devoted American Zionists, such as Marie Syrkin and Meyer Levin, criticized works by authors such as Bellow and Roth as indications of the cultural dearth of Jewishness in America, borne out of a shrinking Jewish spiritual life in a non-Jewish environment. Some Israeli reviewers criticized Oz and Yehoshua vehemently for their harsh portrayal of the Zionist metanarrative.

2. Paul Ricœur, *Sur la traduction* (Paris, 2004); Anthony Pym, "On Empiricism and Bad Philosophy in Translation Studies," in *The Sustainability of the Translation Field*, ed. Hasuria Che Omar, Haslina Haroon, and Aniswal Abd. Ghani (Kuala Lumpur, 2009): 28–39, esp. 29–30.

3. Arnold Eisen, "Breaking the Language Barrier: Literary Dialogues between Israel and the Diaspora," in *The Writer in the Jewish Community: An Israeli–North American Dialogue*, ed. Richard Siegel and Tamar Sofer (Rutherford, 1993), 114.

4. Michael Walzer, "Israel70; Diaspora70: Reflections of an Old Zionist," *Fathom*, April 2018, http://fathomjournal.org/israel70-diaspora70-reflections-of-an-old-zionist/.

5. Simon Rawidowicz, "Jerusalem-and-Babylon," in *Jews and Diaspora Nationalism*, ed. Simon Rabinovitch (Waltham, Mass., 2012), 229.

Index

STANFORD STUDIES IN JEWISH HISTORY AND CULTURE
David Biale and Sarah Abrevaya Stein, Editors

This series features novel approaches to examining the Jewish past in the form of innovative work that brings the field into productive dialogue with the newest scholarly concepts and methods. Open to a range of disciplinary and interdisciplinary approaches, from history to cultural studies, this series publishes exceptional scholarship, balanced by an accessible tone that illustrates histories of difference and addresses issues of current urgency. Books in this list push the boundaries of Jewish Studies and speak compellingly to a wide audience of scholars and students.

Yael Zerubavel, *Desert in the Promised Land*
2018

Sunny S. Yudkoff, *Tubercular Capital: Illness and the Conditions of Modern Jewish Writing*
2018

Sarah Wobick-Segev, *Homes Away from Home: Jewish Belonging in Twentieth-Century Paris, Berlin, and St. Petersburg*
2018

Eddy Portnoy, *Bad Rabbi: And Other Strange but True Stories from the Yiddish Press*
2017

Jeffrey Shandler, *Holocaust Memory in the Digital Age: Survivors' Stories and New Media Practices*
2017

Joshua Schreier, *The Merchants of Oran: A Jewish Port at the Dawn of Empire*
2017

Alan Mintz, *Ancestral Tales: Reading the Buczacz Stories of S.Y. Agnon*
2017

Ellie R. Schainker, *Confessions of the Shtetl: Converts from Judaism in Imperial Russia, 1817–1906*
2016

Devin E. Naar, *Jewish Salonica: Between the Ottoman Empire and Modern Greece*
2016

Naomi Seidman, *The Marriage Plot: Or, How Jews Fell in Love with Love, and with Literature*
2016

Ivan Jablonka, *A History of the Grandparents I Never Had*
2016

For a complete listing of titles in this series, visit the Stanford University Press website, www.sup.org.